W9-AUW-830

This is a great book. No superficial answers but well-thought-out responses to puzzling and controversial Bible questions. Read it and then keep it nearby for ready reference. You will need it, if not today then tomorrow when you are asked a difficult Bible question that needs an answer!

DR. ERWIN W. LUTZER
Pastor Emeritus, The Moody Church, Chicago

It has been said that once you start asking questions, ignorance is gone. What Dr. Rydelnik does so beautifully with this book is not only list 50 of the most important questions about Scripture, but he provides clear, concise, thoughtful, well-researched, and thoroughly biblical answers with the hope that you and I will better "contend" for the faith and grow up in Him. This book will be a part of your legacy library and a constant companion as you study the Word.

JANET PARSHALL
Nationally syndicated talk show host

I could not think of a better person to write this book than Dr. Michael Rydelnik. Michael has spent years answering questions related to the Bible asked by everyone from atheistic skeptics to seminary students. His grasp of biblical literature, Jewish history, and the original languages, combined with his simple love for Jesus, make Michael an extraordinary communicator of biblical truth. He has a compelling way of taking complex Bible questions and breaking them down into clear and understandable answers. I highly recommend Michael's latest book, *50 Most Important Bible Questions*.

DR. MARK JOBE
President of the Moody Bible Institute

Such a valuable resource for anyone who wants to know more about the Bible. Dr. Rydelnik tackles key questions concisely but thoroughly. You'll want at least two copies—one for yourself and one to give others with questions.

CHRIS FABRY
Author and host of Moody Radio's *Chris Fabry Live*

The Bible consistently stimulates our curiosity. But when that curiosity is left unsatisfied, the doubts can be debilitating. So thanks to my "rabbi" friend Michael, some of the most important questions have been surfaced and answered in concise and helpful ways. In fact, the way that he has dealt with the questions will give you a deeper appreciation of the beauty of Scripture and the glory of God, its author!

DR. JOE STOWELL
President Emeritus, Cornerstone University, Grand Rapids, MI

50 MOST IMPORTANT

BIBLE

QUESTIONS

MICHAEL RYDELNIK

MOODY PUBLISHERS

CHICAGO

© 2021 by
Michael Rydelnik

All rights reserved. No part of this book may be reproduced in any form without permission in writing from the publisher, except in the case of brief quotations embodied in critical articles or reviews.

Question 29 ("What Does the Old Testament Reveal About the Messiah?") is adapted with permission from Michael Rydelnik, "What Does the Hebrew Bible Say about the Coming Messiah?," *The Apologetics Study Bible*, ed. Ted Cabal (Nashville, TN: Holman Bible Publishers, 2007), 1351–53.

Some content has been adapted from content previously published on michaelrydelnik.org and todayin theword.org.

All Scripture quotations, unless otherwise indicated, are taken from the New American Standard Bible®, Copyright © 1960, 1962, 1963, 1968, 1971, 1972, 1973, 1975, 1977, 1995 by The Lockman Foundation. Used by permission. www.Lockman.org

Scripture quotations marked HCSB are taken from the Holman Christian Standard Bible®, Copyright © 1999, 2000, 2002, 2003, 2009 by Holman Bible Publishers. Used by permission. Holman Christian Standard Bible®, Holman CSB®, and HCSB® are federally registered trademarks of Holman Bible Publishers.

Scripture quotations marked CSB have been taken from the Christian Standard Bible®, Copyright © 2017 by Holman Bible Publishers. Used by permission. Christian Standard Bible® and CSB® are federally registered trademarks of Holman Bible Publishers.

Scripture quotations marked (ESV) are from the ESV® Bible (The Holy Bible, English Standard Version®), copyright © 2001 by Crossway, a publishing ministry of Good News Publishers. Used by permission. All rights reserved.

Scripture quotations marked KJV are from the King James Version.

Scripture quotations marked (NIV) are taken from the Holy Bible, New International Version®, NIV®. Copyright © 1973, 1978, 1984, 2011 by Biblica, Inc.™ Used by permission of Zondervan. All rights reserved worldwide. www.zondervan.com The "NIV" and "New International Version" are trademarks registered in the United States Patent and Trademark Office by Biblica, Inc.™

Scriptures marked NET are from the NET Bible® http://netbible.com copyright ©1996, 2019 used with permission from Biblical Studies Press, L.L.C. All rights reserved.

Scripture quotations marked (CEV) are from the Contemporary English Version Copyright © 1991, 1992, 1995 by American Bible Society, Used by Permission.

Scripture quotations marked (NLT) are taken from the Holy Bible, New Living Translation, copyright ©1996, 2004, 2015 by Tyndale House Foundation. Used by permission of Tyndale House Publishers, Carol Stream, Illinois 60188. All rights reserved.

Scripture quotations marked (GNT) are from the Good News Translation in Today's English Version- Second Edition Copyright © 1992 by American Bible Society. Used by Permission.

Names and details of some stories have been changed to protect the privacy of individuals.

Edited by Jamie Janosz
Interior Design: Ragont Design
Cover Design: Kaylee Lockenour
Cover image of Bible by Sincerely Media on Unsplash

Library of Congress Cataloging-in-Publication Data

Names: Rydelnik, Michael, 1957- author.
Title: 50 most important Bible questions / Michael Rydelnik.
Other titles: Fifty most important Bible questions
Description: Chicago : Moody Publishers, [2021] | Includes bibliographical
  references. | Summary: "The Bible is full of great truths for our lives
  . . . and a lot of mysteries that we don't understand. But there are
  good answers to them all. Don't stay in the dark any longer. Get the
  answers from an expert and let your confusion turn to understanding"--
  Provided by publisher.
Identifiers: LCCN 2021021157 | ISBN 9780802420312 (paperback) | ISBN
  9780802498939 (ebook)
Subjects: LCSH: Bible--Introductions. | BISAC: RELIGION / Biblical
  Reference / General | RELIGION / Christian Living / General
Classification: LCC BS475.3 .R935 2021 | DDC 220.6/1--dc23
LC record available at https://lccn.loc.gov/2021021157

Originally delivered by fleets of horse-drawn wagons, the affordable paperbacks from D. L. Moody's publishing house resourced the church and served everyday people. Now, after more than 125 years of publishing and ministry, Moody Publishers' mission remains the same—even if our delivery systems have changed a bit. For more information on other books (and resources) created from a biblical perspective, go to www.moodypublishers.com or write to:

Moody Publishers
820 N. LaSalle Boulevard
Chicago, IL 60610

3 5 7 9 10 8 6 4

Printed in the United States of America

Dedication

To Larry Feldman,
who has read the Bible *every day* since 1972,
knows the answers to all these and probably every
other Bible question, and is the most faithful friend
a person could have.

"A friend loves at all times,
and a brother is born for a difficult time."
Proverbs 17:17 HCSB

CONTENTS

QUESTIONS ABOUT BIBLICAL CONCERNS AND PRACTICES

ACKNOWLEDGMENTS

I t is impossible to write one's best if nobody else ever has a look at the result,"[1] C. S. Lewis wrote in a letter to his friend Arthur Greeves. Obviously, Lewis's point is that effective writing requires others to engage, criticize, correct, challenge, and generally improve the work. This book answering Bible questions is no different—a number of people have enhanced it through their kind efforts, and I must express my gratitude.

To begin, thanks must go to the many listeners who have called Moody Radio's *Open Line* program with their Bible questions. Their courage to call and their teachable spirits to listen and learn are an encouragement to me. I'm so grateful we can meet each week around the radio kitchen table for our "Bible study across America."

Additional thanks go to my friend and colleague, Dr. Bryan Litfin, who not only served as acquisitions editor for this book, but was also my cheerleader, sounding board, and encourager throughout. Also, I'm grateful for the producer of *Open Line*, Tricia McMillan. As just a small part of her work, she keeps track of every question answered on the program. She gave me tremendous help in identifying the most common questions so I could be sure to include them in this book.

I'm especially thankful for Jamie Janosz, my colleague for many years on the Moody faculty and now the editor of *Today in the Word*, Moody Bible Institute's daily devotional publication. She graciously agreed to serve as the editor of this book. The fingerprints of her editorial wisdom and skill are evident throughout.

Words can't express how grateful I am to my wife Eva, who read every word of this manuscript, repeatedly, and offered invaluable suggestions. And she always did so with unending grace, kindness, humor, and encouragement.

All of these people as well as others at Moody Publishers certainly made this book better. Nevertheless, any faults or weaknesses in it remain my own.

Above all, thanks be to God for His indescribable gift—the Messiah Jesus (2 Cor. 9:15). He has strengthened and sustained me throughout the writing process. *Blessed are You, O Lord our God, King of the Universe, who has granted us life, sustained us, and allowed us to reach this day. Amen.*

INTRODUCTION

(PLEASE READ THIS FIRST!)

Everyone has questions about the Bible. Age doesn't matter, nor does gender, nor does the state of your spiritual condition. Regardless of where we might be on our spiritual journeys, when we encounter the Scriptures, we all have questions. Once, my neighbor, who had decided to read the New Testament for the very first time, read the first verse ("The record of the genealogy of Jesus the Messiah, the son of David, the son of Abraham," Matt. 1:1), and burst out with questions: "Wait a minute! Who's this David and who's this Abraham?" Another friend, a woman from our congregation, became a follower of Jesus some 75 years ago and has written numerous Bible study guides. Still, she'll call me from time to time with some technical question about the laws of the Levites and Priests or the meaning of an obscure prophetic text. From seekers to new followers of Jesus, from growing believers to mature teachers of the Word, we all have questions about the Bible.

BECOMING THE "BIBLE-ANSWER GUY"

I was leading a congregation when I first realized that many people had many questions about the Bible. As a result, for the next 10 to 12 years during worship services, I would periodically take time, not to give a sermon, but to answer questions. During that service, people could ask me any Bible question they had, and I'd do my best to answer. Now I didn't always know the answer, but I did know how to do biblical research. And if I couldn't answer immediately, I would give an answer the next time we gathered together.

When I became a professor at Moody Bible Institute, one of my favorite parts of teaching became answering the many Bible questions my students had—and they have tons of questions. When Moody Radio's Donald Cole retired from *Open Line*, the program in which he answered questions as radio pastor, people were still calling in with Bible questions. So I had the privilege of stepping in to answer Bible questions once a week for several years on the Moody Radio Chicago's morning program. When Moody Radio realized that listeners still needed their Bible questions answered on a regular basis, they decided to revive *Open Line* as a Saturday morning program. Since 2012, I have spent two hours every Saturday morning answering listener questions about the Bible, God, and the spiritual life.

There are some questions that people ask over and over again. But many of the questions are new to me. I am amazed at the depth of the questions our listeners ask. These are the times when I not only do not know the answer, but I would never have thought of the question! Those are some of my favorite questions because they drive me back to do further biblical research. These difficult questions keep me learning more and more. One of the most important lessons I've learned is that while most questions can be answered now, there are some things we won't know until the Lord tells us in glory. It is this background as a radio Bible-answer guy that formed this book about the 50 most important questions people have about the Bible.

CHOOSING THE QUESTIONS

It's safe to say that I've answered thousands of Bible questions on the radio. So how did I choose these 50 as most important? I'd like to say that there was some scientific survey done, but that's not the case at all. Some were chosen because they're asked so frequently. If many people ask the same questions, it must be important to answer them.

Other questions were chosen because they deal with foundational truths of Scripture. Understanding the Bible often requires that we go back to the basics. Still others were chosen because they deal with the dilemmas and difficulties that have been raised against the Scriptures. In this day, with atheist websites and social media criticism of Scripture and God, it is essential to deal with some of these challenges to the truth and veracity of the Bible. Finally, some questions were chosen because, in my judgment, they teach important truths about the Bible, God and the spiritual life. I guess it could be said that these are, *in my opinion*, 50 of the most important Bible questions.

ANSWERING THE QUESTIONS

Frequently people call *Open Line* and ask, "What do you think about (fill in the blank)?" Regardless of the topic, my automatic response is that it doesn't matter what I think, "Let's look at what the Bible has to say about that." Of course, I have opinions, but I will always try my best to anchor my answers on biblical revelation. That is the underlying premise of every answer in this book. Whatever the subject, I will do my best to answer these questions biblically.

I believe that the Bible is God's inerrant Word; it is inspired, harmonious, understandable, and relevant to our lives. It not only addresses lofty theological issues but also the daily issues of our lives. Most importantly, I want to answer these questions in a way that brings honor to the Lord Jesus the Messiah. Since He is the central subject of the Scriptures, answering questions with an emphasis on what the Bible reveals is the best way I know to honor our King, the Messiah Jesus.

CLARIFYING SOME ISSUES

Answering Bible questions actually takes some audacity. I often ask myself, "Who do you think you are, Rydelnik, answering Bible questions as if you're some big authority?" I have to keep reminding myself, and I'll remind you as well, that I'm doing my best with my fallible and limited knowledge. I certainly don't think I have the final word on what the Bible means. In light of that, here are just a few issues I need to clarify.

First, there will be disagreements with the answers I give to some of these questions. Although I'm trying to reflect all that the Scriptures have to say, I recognize that there are Bible teachers, both responsible and respectable, who would differ with me about a number of these answers. That's okay. As long as we're coming at these questions in a way that honors our Lord Jesus and respects the divine inspiration and authority of Scripture, we can agree to disagree. If you find that you disagree with an answer, that's also okay. Just be sure to check the biblical support I've laid out and then determine what is the better biblical answer *in your opinion.*

Second, please remember there are some mysteries about God that we'll never fully understand. For some, there are hints given to us in Scripture. For others, the Bible just does not comment. God warned Israel about this: "The secret things belong to the LORD our God, but the things revealed belong to us and to our sons forever" (Deut. 29:29). My goal in answering these questions is to only go as far as Scripture reveals and no further. This approach follows Paul's exhortation that we are "not to exceed what is written" (1 Cor. 4:6). We need to learn the limitations of our knowledge. Just as the Lord said, "For as the heavens are higher than the earth, so are My ways higher than your ways and My thoughts than your thoughts" (Isa. 55:9). We can't fully understand the omniscient God with our finite minds. But the good news is that although we can't have all our curiosity satisfied, God has revealed more than enough in His Word to grant us everything we need for "life and godliness" (2 Peter 1:3).

Third, you may notice some of my idiosyncrasies as you read. One in particular that I want to point out is my use of one specific word. Throughout this book, you'll see that I tend to use the word "Messiah" where you expect to see "Christ." You may not be aware that both words mean exactly the same thing. Messiah is derived from the Hebrew word *mashiach* meaning "Anointed One" and Christ comes from the Greek word *christos* which also means "Anointed One." I prefer to use "Messiah" for a couple of reasons. First, most people really don't understand the word "Christ" and too often treat it as a last name rather than a royal title for God's Son. Second, as a Jewish person, I was raised to look for the coming of the Messiah who would deliver Israel and bring peace to the world. Only when I heard that Christ means "Messiah" did I understand who Jesus was claiming to be. Since virtually the whole New Testament was written by Jewish authors within a Jewish context, it seems best to me to use the word "Messiah" when writing about Jesus of Nazareth.

FINAL THOUGHTS

Every week, I end *Open Line* by saying, "Keep reading the Bible, and we'll talk about it next week." That's exactly what I hope for you as you read this book. As you realize that there are solid biblical answers to these biblical questions, I hope you'll be motivated to keep reading the Bible, God's Word. And, as you read, you will find more and more questions, certainly more than this book will answer. But hopefully, this book will give you the encouragement to keep studying and find the answers for yourself, straight from Scripture. Now get out your Bible, grab a cup of coffee, and let's start studying God's Word.

QUESTIONS

about

THE GOSPEL AND SALVATION

What is the gospel?

Imagine you see a terrible car accident. You're the first to reach the driver who is clearly in bad shape—seemingly on the point of death. At the last moment, he turns to you and says, "I'm afraid to face God—how can I know that my sins are forgiven?" Would you be able to explain the good news of Jesus to this desperate person, in 25 words or less?

Why start this book with this question and this scenario? It's because this situation demonstrates that the good news of the gospel, found in Jesus the Messiah, is our most important message. In 1 Corinthians 15:1–8, Paul explains the meaning of the gospel and declares that this message is "of first importance." Since the gospel is our most essential message, it is crucial that we understand what it is and be able to explain it.

But, unfortunately, while the message of the gospel is clearly a priority for the follower of Jesus, I've found that many committed, educated, biblically astute, mature Jesus followers are unable to present this most basic issue. So, at the very outset of this book, I want to ask and answer this most important question: What is the gospel? What is the good news that we proclaim? What must a person believe in order to experience God's forgiveness and new life in Jesus?

THE MEANING OF GOSPEL

In 1 Corinthians 15:1, Paul uses the word "gospel," two Greek words put together into one, to mean "good news." In verses 1–2 Paul says that he proclaimed this message of good news and the Corinthians have "received" it; they were able to "stand" in it, and most vitally, they were "saved" by it. This is the essential message of the faith, and he delivered it to them as of first importance. Just as Paul and his listeners understood this core message, we too must understand and believe the gospel message in order to experience God's redemption and forgiveness in Jesus. So, what exactly is the gospel?

The Substitutionary Death of Jesus

The first part of this good news is found in 1 Corinthians 15:3–4: the *Messiah Jesus died*. Paul gives the reason for the death of God's Son, Jesus Christ—it was "for our sins." Jesus died as a sin substitute, taking the punishment we deserved. Paul then gives evidence that Jesus really died as our sin substitute. The first part of the evidence is biblical—it was "according to the Scriptures," meaning Old Testament passages like Isaiah 53 which foretold Messiah's substitutionary death on our behalf. In His death, Jesus received the punishment we deserved. The second part of Paul's gospel-proving evidence is historical: "He was buried." Paul is asserting that Jesus really died; it wasn't a sham. Our Savior didn't merely swoon or appear to be dead. He really, truly, honestly died. If He had not died, He would not have been buried. So, the first part of the good news is that the Messiah Jesus died for us. What's the second part?

The Resurrection of Jesus

The second aspect of the good news, found in 1 Corinthians 15:4-8, is that the Messiah Jesus was raised from the dead ("He was raised on the third day," 1 Cor. 15:4). This crucial element is frequently overlooked when explaining the good news by preachers, theologians, even evangelists. Too often, they mistakenly assume that everyone knows that Jesus not only died, but was raised from the dead as well. I would remind us that, in our current culture, we can't assume that all our listeners know or agree that Jesus was resurrected from the dead and is now alive.

One reason the resurrection is so important is that it validated Jesus' deity; it proved He is really God. You see, anyone can claim to be God but how do we know that Jesus, who claimed to be God in the flesh, really *was* God? The proof is found in the resurrection. God the Father validated Jesus' claim by raising Him from the dead. That's why Romans 10:9 says, "If you confess with your mouth Jesus as Lord, and believe in your heart that God raised Him from the dead, you will be saved." The word "Lord" here is a reference to Jesus being Lord God, not the master of our lives. Additionally, this verse links His deity to His resurrection from the dead. The Lord Jesus claimed to be deity and the Father confirmed that He is, by raising Him from the dead.

A second reason the resurrection of Jesus is so crucial is that it gives us new life in Him. The Bible says, ". . . as Christ was raised from the dead through the glory of the Father, so we too might walk in newness of life" (Rom. 6:4). It is because Jesus is alive that we have His resurrection power to live new lives in Him.

Just as he did for the death of the Messiah, Paul gives two lines of evidence for His resurrection. First, the biblical evidence is that it was "according to the Scriptures" (1 Cor. 15:4). Likely Paul has in mind passages like Psalm 16:10 and Isaiah 53:10–11, which predicted the Messiah's resurrection. Second, there's historical evidence that He was seen alive after the crucifixion. "He appeared to Cephas, then to the twelve. After that He appeared to more than five hundred brethren at one time . . . then He appeared to James, then to all the apostles; and last of all, as to one untimely born, He appeared to me also" (1 Cor. 15:5–8). This evidence proves that Jesus really is alive.

So often, when I hear people presenting the good news, they say that "Jesus died for our sins." That's true but that's not all of it. We must include that second part: Jesus is alive, that He was raised from the dead! The Romans crucified some 20,000 Jewish men in the first century. But only One, our Redeemer, was raised from the dead. So, when presenting the good news, we should never presume that those who hear the message will know that Jesus was raised.

Friends, let me give you a challenge—listen carefully to

the various presentations you hear about the good news—it might be a commercial on Christian radio, or a pamphlet you might read, or a website, or a message at your congregation, or anywhere. Note how frequently people leave out the resurrection. It's not that people don't believe in the resurrection—they just don't realize how essential it is to the gospel.

FINAL THOUGHTS

So, here's the good news in a nutshell: Messiah Jesus died for our sins and rose again, proving He is God. That's it! The gospel is not about going forward at an altar call, raising our hands, getting baptized, joining a church, or even feeling really, really bad for all the wrong we've done. The gospel doesn't require that we know everything in the Bible, repeat the Westminster Catechism, or anything else people have proposed. It's a simple, essential truth: Messiah Jesus died for our sins and rose again, proving He is God.

Now what would I say to the guy in the car accident, in 25 words or less? Here it is: *The wrong things we do separate us from God. Messiah Jesus died, taking our punishment, and rose again proving He is God. Trust in Him.* That's exactly 25 words!

What is the relationship between faith and repentance in salvation?

When the Philippian jailer asked Paul, "What must I do to be saved?" (Acts 16:30), Paul's response was clear: "Believe in the Lord Jesus, and you will be saved" (Acts 16:31). On the other hand, Peter's message after healing the lame man at the temple called for his hearers to "repent and return, so that your sins may be wiped away" (Acts 3:19). So, what is required for salvation: faith or repentance? Or are both required? Let's examine the relationship between faith and repentance.

THE MEANING OF SAVING FAITH

The Definition of Faith

The English word *"believe,"* used in Acts 16:31, is in the same Greek word group as *faith*. The noun *pistis* means "faith" or "belief" and the verb *pisteuō* means "to have faith," "to trust" or "to believe." So, when an English Bible reads "believe" it could also be translated as "have faith." In New Testament Greek, it is the same word.

Probably the most important verse about the role of faith in salvation is Ephesians 2:8, "For by grace you have been saved through faith." God's gracious gift of salvation is secured when we believe. But what must we believe? Paul makes the contents of faith clear in 1 Corinthians 15:1–8. We are saved by trusting in the message of the gospel, that the Messiah Jesus died for us and rose again (see Question 1).

The Components of Faith

The problem with this simple explanation arises when we see people who seem to believe and then abandon the faith. Did they really have saving faith and lose their salvation, or is there something else at work here? The answer is found in James 2, which distinguishes between faith as mere intellectual assent and the full and true faith that leads to behavioral change or good works. James asks, "What use is it, my brethren, if someone says he has faith but he has no works? Can that faith save him?" (James 2:14). The second question should be translated as "Can that kind of faith" or "such faith" save him? That kind of faith, James is saying, is mere intellectual assent and not genuine saving faith. This is evident when James goes on to point out that "The demons also believe, and shudder" (James 2:19). Demons don't have saving faith—they merely know about God but have not trusted in Him.

So, what exactly is saving faith? This faith encompasses the whole person: mind, heart, and will. The mind indicates an intellectual knowledge of the facts of the gospel, that Jesus died for our sins and was raised again, proving He is God. The heart experiences an emotional conviction of the truth of the gospel. The will refers to our volitional acceptance of the gospel. Based on these three components of faith, here's my personal definition of saving faith: Saving faith is to have an intellectual understanding of the Messiah Jesus' saving work, an emotional conviction of the truth of the gospel, and a willing reliance on Jesus as Savior.

THE ILLUSTRATION OF SAVING FAITH

I've heard these three components (mind, heart, will) compared to the way people responded to the life boats on the Titanic. Some people on the Titanic didn't even know that there were life boats—so they lacked the information (mind), and they perished. Others knew there were life boats, but lacked the emotional conviction (heart) that they were truly in mortal danger or if they were, that the boats could actually save them in the wild waters of the Atlantic. They didn't get in the boat and were lost at sea. Still others knew they were in danger of drowning and were convinced that the life boats could save them but didn't want to get in the boat and leave a spouse to drown on the ship. So, they made the choice (will) to stay on the ship and they were drowned. To be saved on the Titanic required all three components of faith: people knew of the life boats, had the conviction that they were in mortal danger and the boats could save them, and they chose to get into the life boats. Saving faith not only acknowledges the facts of the gospel, it means we are convinced of our sinfulness and the truth of the gospel, and then we decide to trust in Jesus alone. This makes sense, but where does repentance fit?

Many people maintain that we are living in an age of "easy believism" and have forgotten about the need to repent of our sins in order to be saved. They cite verses like Acts 2:38 and 3:19 that call on people to repent in order to be saved. They argue that faith in Jesus is not enough; we also need to repent of sin. Is this true? Have we lost our understanding of true biblical repentance?

THE MEANING OF REPENTANCE

A Change of Mind

The basic Greek New Testament word for repentance is *metanoia* which literally means "a change of mind." The command form of the verb directs the hearer to change his or her mind. Surprisingly, the word doesn't address turning from sin but having a change of thought about some issue. The issue to which it refers is determined by the context of the passage. So, let's look at some of these repentance passages in context to help determine their meaning.

The first is found in Acts 2:36–38, the culmination of Peter's sermon at Pentecost. In that message, Peter declared that the house of Israel had rejected Jesus as the Messiah, leading to His death at the hands of sinful people, including both Jews and Gentiles. The Lord reversed this tragic death through the resurrection of Jesus. "Therefore," Peter declared, "let all the house of Israel know for certain that God has made Him [Jesus] both Lord and Christ" (Acts 2:36)! Peter's listeners "came under deep conviction and said . . . 'Brothers, what must we do?' (Acts 2:37 HCSB). Peter's response is clear—"Repent" (Acts 2:38)! He did not want them merely to feel badly about their sins, but to change their minds about who Jesus really was. They were to leave their rejection of Him behind and turn to Him as both their Lord (God) and Messiah. This passage in context isn't about forsaking sin or even feeling bad about sin, but about changing one's mind, moving from rejecting Jesus to recognizing Him as both Lord and Messiah.

A second passage similar to this one is Acts 3:19. Here Peter tells his listeners to "repent and return, so that your sins may be wiped away." In context, Peter had proclaimed that Israel had rejected Jesus as the Messiah but that Jesus' suffering was in fulfillment of the messianic predictions of the Hebrew Prophets (some examples not specifically cited but certainly what Peter had in mind were Isaiah 52:13–53:12 and Psalm 22). Therefore, according to the context, the audience was called upon to change their minds about rejecting Jesus as the Messiah and instead, believe in Him.

In Acts 20:21, Paul tells the Ephesian elders that in his ministry he had taught them faithfully, "solemnly testifying to both Jews and Greeks of repentance toward God and faith in our Lord Jesus Christ." Paul's point was that his message always called upon people to change their minds about God and to place their trust in Jesus.

A Change in Direction

The second New Testament word related to repentance is *epistrepho* and it is often the translation for the Hebrew word *shuv*. They both mean "to turn" or "to return." A good definition of *epistrepho* is "to change one's belief or conduct; to change one's mind." In most repentance passages, *epistrepho* indicates turning away from something (repentance) and instead turning to God (faith). A good example is Acts 14:15, where Paul challenged some pagans in Lystra to repent. He called on them to repent of their idolatry ("turn from these vain things") and put their faith in the one, true God ("to a living God, who made the heaven and the earth"). Once again, this exhortation was not for these people to feel bad about paganism but a call to exchange their false gods for the One true God.

Sorrow vs. Repentance

Sometimes we feel as if we should restore the old revivalist's Sinner's Bench, so those who trust in Jesus can sit and weep and wail for their sins, promising to forsake every wrong behavior, in order to be saved. But even those passages that do teach about experiencing sorrow for our sins (James 4:8–9) don't teach that sorrow is a part of repentance. Rather, Paul says that "godly grief produces a repentance not to be regretted and leading to salvation, but worldly grief produces death" (2 Cor. 7:10 HCSB). Ungodly grief and sorrow for sin lead to remorse, not to repentance. Consider Judas Iscariot, who regretted his betrayal of the Lord Jesus but never turned in faith to Him for forgiveness. Instead, Judas sought to pay for his own sin by returning the money he had earned by betraying Jesus and then hanging himself (Matt. 27:3–5).

THE RELATIONSHIP OF REPENTANCE AND FAITH

The relationship of repentance and faith are best understood as two sides of the same coin. Repentance occurs when we change our minds and forsake that which we trusted in before. Faith is when we trust in Jesus to forgive our sins. The strongest example of repentance and faith is found in 1 Thessalonians 1:8–10, even though Paul only uses the word "turn" (*epistrepho*) there. In verse 8, Paul tells the Thessalonians that "in every place your *faith* toward God has gone forth." Then He celebrates that they "turned to God from idols" (v. 9), a phrase that includes both concepts. First, they had exercised *faith* by turning to God through trusting in Jesus. Second, they had repented by forsaking the idols in which they had previously trusted. As a result of their trust and repentance, they now "wait for [God's] Son from heaven" (v. 10).

FINAL THOUGHTS

Once we understand the relationship of faith and repentance, we need to ask, "Now what?" One step we can take is to follow Paul's admonition to the Corinthians when he told them, "Test yourselves to see if you are in the faith; examine yourselves!" (2 Cor. 13:5). Every person should ask: Have I turned from any false dependency for salvation (my good deeds, my religiosity, my good character) and instead trusted in the Lord Jesus alone with my entire being, mind, heart, and will? If the answer is *no*, now is the time to turn in faith to the Lord Jesus.

A second action we can take is always to be clear when we present the good news of Jesus and invite someone to respond. We need to call people to turn from whatever they are trusting and put their trust in Jesus alone. Part of this includes explaining what we mean by the word *faith* or *trust*. We must be clear that it involves all of our being, not just intellectual agreement, not just an emotional experience, and not just a desire to follow Jesus. Faith has to include all three components of a person: mind, heart, and will.

A number of years ago, a contractor, Victor, was building a back deck for our house. Every evening, when he was done with his work and before going home, he would join me at my kitchen table for a glass of iced tea. He was intrigued by my faith in Jesus and my weird job (in his mind) as a pastor and Bible teacher. He came from a Christian tradition and was part of a religious family. Yet he kept saying "there's something different about what you and Eva are about." One evening, I asked Victor, "When you stand before God at the judgment and He says, 'Why should I forgive your sins?,' what will you say?" He immediately jumped to his religion, good works, and church attendance. Then, we read Ephesians 2:8–9 together. The moment Victor saw the words, "For by grace you have been saved through faith," he exclaimed, "That's what I believe!" In that instance, he turned from his reliance on his religion and good works (repentance) and trusted that Jesus had died for him and had been raised from the dead (faith). It was the most immediate and clear example of someone who instantly and truly understood the meaning of faith and repentance. Vic's response is the prototype for anyone who wants to grasp the two-sided coin of faith and repentance.

Is it possible for true followers of Jesus, people who have genuinely put their trust in Jesus, to lose their salvation?

Mark has been my friend for about 35 years. Although he loves and follows Jesus, it seems every year or two, he calls me with a crisis—he fears he has lost his salvation. I've seen this concern expressed by many followers of Jesus. Some people fear they've committed "the unpardonable sin" or they want to know the meaning of an admittedly confusing passage like Hebrews 6 (see Question 5 on Heb. 6:1–8 and 10:26). The main issue always revolves around the possibility that genuine believers can lose their salvation.

If this is your concern, rest assured. I am convinced that the Bible teaches that we are absolutely secure in our salvation, and we need never be worried or concerned about losing our redeemed relationship with God through Jesus the Messiah. The simple reason you can know that your salvation is secure is that it is based solidly on the unified work of the God-head—Father, Son and Holy Spirit. The saving work of each Person of the one true God allows us to be assured of our security in the Lord.

GOD THE FATHER

God Is Holy

We know that our salvation is protected through God the Father's work of gracious forgiveness. This is based on three simple truths. First, we need to remember that *God is completely holy* (see Lev. 11:44 and Isa. 6:3). In 1 John 1:5 it says, "God is Light, and in Him there is no darkness at all." This means God is completely righteous and there is no evil in Him whatsoever. It shows the high standard we have to meet in order to have a relationship with God. Imagine what it would be like to stand before a judge who never has and never will sin. In fact, our God is One who only does what is good and righteous.

We Are Sinful

This leads to a second biblical truth: *Humanity is utterly sinful.* For example, Ecclesiastes 7:20 says, "Indeed, there is not a righteous man on earth who continually does good and who never sins." The Hebrew prophet Isaiah says "For all of us have become like one who is unclean, and all our righteous deeds are like a filthy garment; and all of us wither like a leaf, and our iniquities, like the wind, take us away" (Isa. 64:6). He is saying that even the good that we do is not good enough for God. This is why Paul says that we all sin and fall short of God's glory (Rom. 3:23). As a result, we are spiritually "dead in . . . trespasses and sins" (Eph. 2:1). How could any of us fallen and broken people ever expect to enter into a relationship with a holy God?

Salvation Is by Grace Alone

The good news is that there is a third simple truth: *Salvation is entirely by God's grace.* One of the clearest teachings of Scripture is that God's forgiveness is a gift from Him. Ephesians 2:8–9 says, "For by grace you have been saved through faith; and that not of yourselves, it is the gift of God; not as a result of works, so that no one may boast." God the Father forgives because of His undeserved kindness. His gift of salvation does not come from anything we do, but comes entirely from Him. How can a holy God give such a gift?

The Bible reminds us that God's forgiveness is based entirely on His work and not ours. An important passage that discusses this is Romans 3:24–28. It teaches that we are declared righteous before God only by God's grace through the redemption that is available through the death and resurrection of the Lord Jesus. God demonstrated that He is a just judge, a Holy God, who wouldn't overlook sin but required a satisfying punishment for sin, a punishment paid for by God the Son, the Lord Jesus. By forgiving us in this way, God would both be "righteous and declare righteous the one who has faith in Jesus" (Rom. 3:26 HCSB). Our forgiveness and deliverance from the penalty of sin is entirely God's gracious gift and God's gracious work. Again, it is not from our effort or our individual level of goodness.

So how does all of this result in our security in the Lord? It's simple. We did nothing to achieve our salvation. In ourselves, we have no good works, no righteous deeds, no balancing act of trying to do good more than bad. Our righteousness is all from God. Here is the encouraging part: if we can do nothing good enough to obtain salvation, then we can do nothing bad enough to lose it. Did you get that? It means that if we can't earn our salvation by doing good, we cannot lose it by sinning. Our salvation is entirely a work of God and therefore no human action can undo it.

GOD THE SON

Besides the work of the Father, we are also spiritually protected because of God the Son's work in securing our salvation. These biblical passages teach that the Lord Jesus keeps us safe in God's family in four ways.

The Messiah's Obedience

First, the obedience of the Messiah Jesus keeps us secure. In John 6:37–40, the Lord Jesus said He will receive us, keep us, and ultimately raise us in the last day. But let's focus on what He said of doing the Father's will. "For I have come down from heaven, not to do My will, but the will of Him who sent Me. This is the will of Him who sent Me: that I should lose none of those He has given Me" (John 6:38–39 HCSB). The Son of God became a man in order to do the will of His

Father. If just one time the Lord Jesus failed to do His Father's will, then He would not be who He claimed to be. The Lord Jesus staked His entire identity on always doing the Father's will. And what is one specific desire of His Father? Jesus tells us: "that I should lose none of those He has given Me." Our confidence in the Messiah Jesus' obedience to the Father should give us absolute certainty that if we have come to Him, He will keep us absolutely safe.

The Messiah's Grip

Second, the strong grip of the Messiah Jesus keeps us secure. The Good Shepherd made this promise to those who truly trust in Him: "No one will snatch them out of My hand. My Father, who has given them to Me, is greater than all; and no one is able to snatch them out of the Father's hand" (John 10:28–29). The image the Lord uses is clear: He is holding us in His hand, and we are safe in that. In fact, we are even more secure because the Father guarantees His protection as well.

When my son was a toddler, we lived in New York City near Queens Boulevard, a massive eight-lane street. When we crossed that street with our little boy, my wife Eva and I would grasp each of his little hands in ours so there was no way he could get away from us. Some have objected that while no one can snatch us from our Savior's hand, maybe we can escape ourselves. Well, we can't snatch ourselves out of the Messiah's hand any more than my toddler could have gotten away from his parents. If we have come to know Jesus, we are held tightly in His grip.

The Messiah's Love

A third way we're safe with the Lord is the love of Messiah Jesus. Paul makes this abundantly clear in Romans 8:38–39: "For I am convinced that neither death, nor life, nor angels, nor principalities, nor things present, nor things to come, nor powers, nor height, nor depth, nor any other created thing, will be able to separate us from the love of God, which is in Christ Jesus our Lord." Nothing can separate us from the Lord Jesus! Some may object saying, "Although nothing outside can separate me from the Lord, I can separate myself from Him!" Just remember, we too are created beings, and even we don't have the power to separate ourselves from the love of God found in the Messiah Jesus.

The Messiah's Intercession

Fourth, we are secure in the intercession of our Messiah Jesus. If you're like me, you might think, I'm so sinful and mess up so frequently, I certainly should be able to lose my salvation. But no, Hebrews 7:25 says Jesus "always lives to make intercession for" us to the Father. And in 1 John 2:1–2, we are told that even when we sin, "we have an Advocate with the Father, Jesus Christ the righteous; and He Himself is the propitiation [or satisfaction] for our sins." Yes, we fail, but we have a living Messiah Jesus, who is our intercessor and advocate with the Father, who assures us we are forgiven. God the Son secures our salvation through His obedience, grip, love, and intercession.

GOD THE HOLY SPIRIT

Yet a third reason for our security is found in God the Holy Spirit's supernatural protection. The Holy Spirit's work begins at the moment of salvation when the Holy Spirit baptizes every individual believer into the body of Christ. Paul writes, "For by one Spirit we were all baptized into one body . . ." (1 Cor. 12:13). The word "baptize" here means to "immerse" and this is saying that all believers are immersed or placed into the universal body of all believers. Since this refers to all believers, we know it must happen at the moment someone receives the Lord Jesus.

The Holy Spirit also indwells every believer at the moment of salvation. In Romans 8:9, Paul says "the Spirit of God dwells in you" and that "if anyone does not have the Spirit of Christ, he does not belong to Him." Additionally, Paul reminds believers that each believer is "a temple of the Holy Spirit who is in you" (1 Cor. 6:19).

In addition, the Holy Spirit seals every believer. Paul writes, "Having also believed, you were sealed in Him with the Holy Spirit of promise" (Eph. 1:13). Furthermore, this sealing is "for the day of redemption" (Eph. 4:30). The idea of a seal is two-fold: identification and security. First, a seal was used as an identifying mark on a letter or a package. Second, a seal was put in place to provide security until the letter or package arrived, only to be opened by the recipient. These verses in Ephesians say that the Holy Spirit *seals* all believers to identify them as belonging to the Messiah Jesus and to keep them safe and secure until their day of redemption, when they stand in the presence of their Lord. For anyone to lose his or her salvation, it would be necessary to remove them from the universal body of believers, to expel the Holy Spirit from His indwelling presence, and to break the unbreakable seal of God on the believer.

FINAL THOUGHTS

The work of the Father, Son, and Holy Spirit, the triune God, assures us that we are secure in our salvation. How should that affect our lives? First, we can relax! That's the great news for anyone who feels like a spiritual failure or unworthy of salvation. We are right in our assessment of ourselves but mistaken in our view of God. We don't become God's children by being good; we become His children by entering into a forgiven relationship with God because of what the Lord has done for us. He's redeemed us by grace that is greater than all our sin.

Second, we can draw great comfort from knowing we are safe in the hands of the Lord Jesus. As a dad, I always assured my boys that I would always love them, always care for them, and they would always be mine. Even if they abandoned everything I ever taught them and did something terrible, I would still love them. Now as adults, they tell me what a tremendous encouragement it was to know they were unconditionally loved. How much more reassuring is it to know that the Lord Jesus will always keep us secure in His love?

Third, we need to respond to God's gift of gracious security by living holy lives, reflecting that we are sons and daughters of the King. We won't choose to sin more and more to get more and more of His grace (Rom. 6:1–4). Rather, we recognize what He has done for us in redeeming us and so we'll live for the Lord Jesus, to bring honor to His name.

Why do believers worry that they can lose their salvation? If the Scriptures are so clear that we can't, why are so many concerned about it?

The simple answer is that too often we let our faulty human perspectives cloud our clear understanding of Scripture. There are a few ways we let smoke get in our eyes and blur our understanding and assurance of salvation.

REASONS WE DOUBT OUR ETERNAL SECURITY

We sometimes doubt the security of salvation because of our experiences with others. I'm sure everyone knows a person who seemed to have a vital walk with the Lord Jesus, and then abandoned the faith. We wonder, *What about them? They have gone so far from God*, we think, *that person must be absolutely, positively lost.*

Some of us doubt the security of our salvation because we struggle with sin. Our persistent sin may be an addictive behavior, like drugs or alcohol, or persistent sexual sins. We may wonder why we continue to strive and strain without seeing transformation in our lives. Without the kind of growing obedience we believe should come with salvation, we may begin to wonder if we're actually lost.

Still others struggle with difficult passages like Hebrews 6:4–6 or 10:26–27. (For an explanation of these verses, see the next question.) Despite so many verses (like the ones pointed out in the previous question and answer) that seem to assure us of our salvation, these difficult ones are sticky and can strain our confidence in our security.

FINDING ASSURANCE OF SALVATION

Scripture, not Experience

Here are some suggestions that have helped me clear my confusion about this issue and have given me assurance of salvation. First, we need to interpret our experiences through the lens of Scripture and not the other way around. Although we recognize that the Lord Jesus will never leave us or forsake us, that He holds us securely in His hands, and that nothing will ever separate us from His love, too often we say, "But what about Fred and Gina? They seem to have lost their salvation." Rather than look to others as our source of proof, let's always start with what the Bible teaches. We must look to God's Word for explanations of our experiences instead of prioritizing our personal experiences and using them to interpret the Word of God.

Unclear in Light of the Clear

Second, we need to interpret unclear passages in light of the clear teaching of Scripture. When I was a freshman student at Moody Bible Institute, I believed in the security of the believer, but I was tortured by Hebrews 6. I remember badgering one of my professors for an explanation and nothing he said would satisfy me. Finally, he taught me this crucial interpretive principle: we need to interpret the unclear verses of the Bible in light of the clear ones. That resolved the issue for me. I know the Bible is harmonious and clearly teaches the perseverance of our Savior. From then on I would always pursue the meaning of Hebrews 6 and other difficult passages in light of what the Bible plainly taught.

Loss of Rewards, Not Loss of Salvation

Third, we must remember that oftentimes passages that seem to refer to the loss of salvation actually refer to the loss of rewards. For example, when Paul says he disciplines himself so that, after preaching to others, "I myself will not be disqualified" (1 Cor. 9:27), he actually refers to being disqualified from receiving a crown (or rewards). Paul is not saying that he could lose his salvation.

Not Genuine Believers

Finally, we need to remember that people who seem to abandon the faith may have never known the Lord at all. That's why 1 John 2:19 says, "They went out from us, but they were not really of us; for if they had been of us, they would have remained with us; but they went out, so that it would be shown that they all are not of us." It's why the Lord Jesus will tell some at the final judgment, "I **never** knew you; depart from Me" (Matt. 7:23, emphasis added) not "depart from Me, you lost it." As for those who really do know the Lord but have wandered, one day, before it's all over, they will actually repent and be restored.

FINAL THOUGHTS

Too often we struggle because of our own human inconsistency. We have good days and bad days. On good days, we feel God's love in a tangible way. But on a bad day, we wonder how anyone could love us, let alone God Himself. But God will never love us more or less than He does right now (Rom. 8:37–39). Claire Cloninger, a six-time Dove Award–winning Christian songwriter, expressed this beautifully, "On a scale of one to ten, God loves me ten on my best day and a ten on my worst day. There's no way I can lose God's love by what I do or don't do. There's nothing I can do to make Him love me less or more. Amazing!" She goes on to say it's the best kept secret of the spiritual life, "The little understood mystery, we call 'amazing grace.'"[2]

It seems that Hebrews 6:1–8 and 10:26–27 both teach that believers can lose their salvation. How do you explain these passages?

Probably the toughest passage for those who struggle to believe in eternal security is Hebrews 6:1–8, and Hebrews 10:26–27 is also difficult. Let's look at these two troubling passages in that order.

HEBREWS 6:1–8

Hebrews 6:1–8 seems to say that believers can fall away, and in doing so, they re-crucify and shame the Lord Jesus. Therefore, it is impossible for them to be renewed to repentance (Heb. 6:4–6). The answer begins by recognizing that the book of Hebrews was written to Jewish believers in Jesus who had begun to experience persecution for their faith. Therefore, some of them were considering abandoning their new messianic Jewish faith and returning to Judaism without Jesus.

Genuine Believers Persevere in the Faith

The five warning passages in Hebrews (2:1–4; 3:7–4:13; 5:11–6:20; 10:26–31; 12:25–29) are addressed to these potential deniers of the faith. The writer is letting them know that the mark of genuine followers of Jesus is endurance in their faith. That's what is meant by saying that we are part of the Messiah's household "if we hold fast our confidence and the boast of our hope firm until the end" (Heb. 3:6). Note that the opposite is true as well—if we don't hold fast our confidence and hope, it demonstrates that we are not presently part of Messiah's household. Similarly, Hebrews 3:14 says we have become partakers of the Messiah only "if we hold fast the beginning of our assurance firm until the end." If we have not become partakers of Messiah, we won't hold fast to our faith. Both of these verses show that genuine believers do hang on to their faith in Messiah Jesus while those who abandon it never really knew Him at all.

Moving from Old Testament Hope to Faith in Messiah

In light of their potential status as people who had not yet fully trusted in Jesus, Hebrews 6 was actually calling on these people to move from an Old Testament faith, anticipating the coming of the Messiah, to a full-fledged complete faith in Jesus the Messiah (6:1–2). They are told to "press on to maturity" (6:1), a word better translated "completion," referring to a complete faith in Jesus. The elementary teaching they are to leave (Heb. 6:1) does not refer to the foundational principles of faith in the Messiah Jesus but to the Old Testament preparation for faith in the Messiah. If the elementary teaching about the Messiah referred to the foundational teachings of their faith in Jesus, the writer of Hebrews would not tell them to leave it behind but to build on it.

This warning calls on them to advance beyond six aspects of elementary teaching about the Messiah: 1) repentance; 2) faith; 3) teachings about washings; 4) laying on of hands; 5) resurrection of the dead; and 6) eternal judgment (Heb. 6:1–2). Each of these ideas were taught in the Old Testament preparation for the Messiah although it seems that they could refer to New Covenant ideas as well. The evidence that this list refers to Old Testament faith is in the word "washings" (6:2). It refers exclusively to Old Testament ritual washings, (although some English versions sometimes mistranslate it as "baptisms"). It makes more sense that the author is telling them to leave their Old Testament faith and move on to a New Testament faith in the Messiah Jesus. We can conclude that this warning is to Jewish people whom the writer fears have not yet genuinely put their complete trust in Jesus.

In Hebrews 6:4–6, the writer fears that their faith was close but not genuine. Perhaps they were "enlightened," meaning they understood Jesus as the fulfillment of prophecy, but they did not necessarily comprehend His spiritual provision. This is similar to lost false teachers in 2 Peter 2:20–22. Maybe they had "tasted the heavenly gift," meaning they had experienced the Holy Spirit's conviction, but they had not yet experienced His indwelling (similar to the way the word "tasted" is used in Matthew 27:34 csb). This is a significant difference. They were "partakers of the Holy Spirit" (Heb. 6:4) in the sense that they saw His miracles and power (Heb. 2:4) but were not indwelt by Him. They had possibly also tasted God's Word and God's power because of their presence in the community of believers but had not yet experienced their own personal faith.

The Danger of Falling Away

The danger that some of these readers faced was that after coming so close, if they fell away, humanly speaking it would be "impossible to renew them again to repentance" (Heb. 6:6). Having experienced so much of the Lord's power in the community of true believers, denying Jesus would be like agreeing with those who crucified Him and putting Him to open shame. The word "crucify" (an adverbial participle) is usually translated with a causal sense—"because they crucify again." However, it seems that a temporal sense is just as valid and would make the translation, "while they crucify again." This would mean that should they deny and reject Jesus, agreeing with those who crucified Him, it would be impossible for them to repent. However, we also know that nothing is impossible for God, and He could surely, by His Spirit, bring anyone He so chooses to repentance.

Hebrews 6:4–6 is calling on these doubters to consider whether they were genuine in their faith in Jesus to begin with, and if not, to put their trust in Him fully. Moreover, the author is convinced that, once they consider these things, they will recognize their own genuineness of faith, saying, "Beloved, we are convinced of better things concerning you, and things that accompany salvation" (Heb. 6:9).

HEBREWS 10:26–27

As for Hebrews 10:26–27, the writer is concerned that if these doubters "go on sinning willfully after receiving the knowledge of the truth," the sacrificial death of Messiah would not be beneficial for them and they would only face "a terrifying expectation of judgment." Some people think that "to go on sinning willfully" refers to believers caught in habitual sin or those who commit especially serious sins such as stealing, extramarital sex, or even murder. If this is so, Messiah Jesus' sacrifice would no longer be of help to them. They would lose their salvation and face eternal judgment.

In context, however, Hebrews 10:26–27 is referring to those who have forsaken "assembling together" (Heb. 10:25). They are the same doubters described in Hebrews 3:6, 14, and 6:1–8. They had been close to the faith but had separated themselves from the messianic community and were now considering returning to traditional Judaism without Jesus. The specific sin they are warned about, in context, is forsaking the community of Messiah (10:25). If they were to persist in this act of abandonment, they would reveal that they had not yet trusted in the Messiah Jesus and were refusing to put their faith in Him still. If they maintained this attitude, the Messiah Jesus' sacrificial death would be of no benefit to them and they would face judgment.

FINAL THOUGHTS

People frequently make faith decisions, trusting in Jesus as long as life is easy and smooth. But Jesus promised, "In the world you have tribulation, but take courage; I have overcome the world" (John 16:33). When they encounter the difficulties, troubles, and persecution He promised, some may choose not to take courage but to abandon their faith. When anyone departs from the faith, it reveals a person who has not really come to know Him. When difficulties come, we need to "hold fast our confession" of faith in Jesus (Heb. 4:14). If we decide to jump ship and abandon our faith, it's essential to reassess and make the decision to trust in the Messiah Jesus genuinely and completely and experience His perfect and eternal forgiveness.

How were people saved in the Old Testament?

When the Philippian jailer asked Paul and Silas, "What must I do to be saved?," their answer was simple: "Believe in the Lord Jesus, and you will be saved" (Acts 16:30–31). That same uncomplicated answer holds true today.

However, there are several issues that arise when we consider the difference between salvation in the Old Testament and in the New Testament. First, some believe that people were saved in the Old Testament by keeping the Law of Moses but in the New Testament they are saved through God's grace in Jesus the Messiah. They base this idea on John's words: "For the Law was given through Moses; grace and truth were realized through Jesus Christ" (John 1:17).

Second, others believe that since the Lord Jesus had not yet come in the Old Testament, people alive during that time could not yet consciously believe in Him, as they do now. So, they ask, how was it possible to be saved in Old Testament times? How can someone be saved without explicit knowledge of and faith in the Lord Jesus?

Third, in the Old Testament there was a required system of sacrifice for atonement, particularly on the Day of Atonement (Lev. 16). Hebrews 10:4 says "it is impossible for the blood of bulls and goats to take away sins." Since this was done away with in the New Testament, what was the point of all those sacrifices? Let's examine these three issues one at a time.

BY GRACE THROUGH FAITH

Salvation was, and has always been, by God's grace through faith. This means that the forgiveness of our sin (i.e., salvation) was given by God's undeserved kindness (grace) through trust (faith). No one could ever be justified (declared righteous by God) by works of the Law (Rom. 3:20, 28; Gal. 2:16; 3:5). In fact, the Law served to demonstrate the inability of people to keep it, "for through the Law comes the knowledge of sin" (Rom. 3:20). Paul taught that justification by faith isn't contrary to the Law; in fact, it is precisely what *is* taught in the Law. He asked, "Do we then nullify the Law through faith? May it never be! On the contrary, we establish the Law" (Rom. 3:31), meaning Paul is establishing what the Law also teaches. How so? In the following paragraph of Romans (after an unfortunate chapter division), Paul, in Romans 4:1–5, quotes Genesis 15:6, "Abraham believed God, and it was credited to him as righteousness." Here he demonstrates that the Law of Moses taught justification by faith just as the New Testament does.

So, what does John 1:17 mean? It should be understood from the perspective of emphasis. On the one hand, Moses, as the Lawgiver, accentuated God's law. On the other hand, the arrival of Jesus the Messiah stressed God's grace. Clearly, there was both grace and truth in the Mosaic covenant (cf.

Ex. 34:6–7); in the same way there is the law, as well as grace, in the New Covenant (cf. 1 Cor. 9:20–22). In both situations, people are saved by God's grace through faith.

THE CONTENT OF FAITH

If salvation was always by grace through faith, what did people have to believe before the coming of Jesus the Messiah? A good way to understand the content of faith is that it was, and always will be, the revealed will of God. So, what was revealed in Old Testament times? First, a person needed the object of his or her faith to be the one true, merciful God, trusting in His undeserved kindness as the basis of forgiveness: "The LORD, the LORD God, compassionate and gracious, slow to anger, and abounding in lovingkindness and truth; who keeps lovingkindness for thousands, who forgives iniquity, transgression and sin . . ." (Ex. 34:6–7).

Second, a person had to offer a blood sacrifice, believing that it would serve as a substitution for personal sin. The Law of Moses says, "For the life of the flesh is in the blood, and I have given it to you on the altar to make atonement for your souls; for it is the blood by reason of the life that makes atonement" (Lev. 17:11). From the time that God provided the skins of animals for Adam and Eve (Gen. 3:21) and then commanded blood offerings as an obligation of the Law of Moses, animal sacrifice was God's requirement as a substitution for sin.

Third, Old Testament believers had to trust that God would send the Messiah. The messianic idea began with Genesis 3:15, which promised that the offspring of the woman would one day crush the head of the serpent. It included the prediction about the Servant of the Lord, who would "render Himself as a guilt offering" (Isa. 53:10) for sin. The hope of the Messiah also contained the expectation that a descendant of David would come to establish an eternal house, kingdom, and throne (1 Chron. 17:14; 2 Sam. 7:16). The messianic idea was so central to the Old Testament that believers living under its authority needed to trust that the Messiah would come one day.

This was different than conscious faith in Jesus of Nazareth. It was clear to the Old Testament prophets that the Messiah would come in the distant future. However, they did not know the "person or time," meaning they did not know who He would be or when He would come (1 Peter 1:10–12). They understood that their prophecies were about the Messiah, but they did not know the specific person who would be the actual referent. As a result, people were to have faith in the future Messiah but they could not have explicit faith in Jesus of Nazareth, who had not yet come.

It's clear that people in every generation were saved by grace through faith in the revealed will of God. What God revealed in Old Testament times was that people were to trust in the merciful one true God, the efficacy of the sacrifices offered in faith, and the hope of a future Messiah. But since animal sacrifices could not take away sin, what was the role of sacrifice until the substitutionary death and resurrection of Jesus?

THE ROLE OF SACRIFICE

The Law of Moses established the principle of substitutionary atonement when it made provision for sacrifices to be offered for unintentional sin. The sin offering entailed a four-step process, beginning with *substitution*. An animal was selected to die as a substitute (Lev. 4:3, 14, 23, 28, 32; 5:7, 11).[3] The next step was *identification,* when the person who offered the sacrifice placed a hand on the animal (Lev. 4:4, 15, 24, 29, 33) as a symbolic transfer of guilt from the person to the animal. What followed was the *death* of the animal, with its blood poured on the altar. In this way, the animal's life paid for the transferred sin. The final aspect was *the exchange of life* (Lev. 4:4, 24, 29, 33), meaning that because the animal had given its life in payment of sin, the person could now live. After the full disposal of the animal (Lev. 4:8–12, 19, 31, 35), indicating the complete removal of sin, the person was genuinely forgiven (Lev. 4:20, 26, 31, 35; 5:6, 10). The exchange of life principle was established to prepare Israel to understand the significance of the Messiah's substitutionary atonement.

But how were intentional sins forgiven? Although some have contended they couldn't be, it's more likely that the sacrifices of the Day of Atonement (Lev. 16) were given for all sin, both intentional and unintentional. The blood remained on the altar for the entire year, making provision for the sins of the people. But since sin offerings and Day of Atonement offerings did not actually take away sin, how did they work? Sacrifices were temporary payments, holding off the debt of sin. My experience with college students provides a way to understand this.

Suppose you are a college student and you have just received your first credit card. Anxious to use it, you go to the bookstore and purchase your books for the upcoming semester, paying with the credit card. That was so easy that when you grew tired of the student dining room food, you would go to your favorite burger joint for dinner and pay with your credit card. Then you would go on a date and use the credit card to pay for everything. This continued until the monthly bill came. You looked at it and said, "I don't have the money to pay for this!" So, you paid just the minimum amount, merely covering part of the interest on the card. This pattern continued, month after month, with more and more credit taken, and only a small part of the accrued interest paid. In this way, the debt was paid monthly, but the principal and interest kept building.

This is similar to the way the animal sacrifices worked, particularly the Day of Atonement offerings. They never completely took away the actual debt of sin, but they held off the divine bill collector until the next payment was due. It covered what was owed but the debt was not really resolved. That's why the author of Hebrews could say "it is impossible for the blood of bulls and goats to take away sins" (Heb. 10:4).

Animal sacrifices were the minimum payment, but they never covered the growing principal and interest of the debt of sin. But when the Messiah Jesus came, He "offered one sacrifice for sins for all time" (Heb. 10:12), paying both the entire principle and all the interest for all sins, past, present and future. In this way, the death and resurrection of the Lord Jesus offers the only actual payment for the sins of all people, for all time.

One issue that remains is that some contend that since people in the Old Testament could be saved by believing in the coming of the future Messiah and that His atonement was applied to them after His substitutionary death and resurrection, perhaps this is so today. Would it be possible for someone today, who is hoping in a future Messiah without explicit faith in Jesus, to still have a forgiven relationship with God? The answer is no, that's no longer possible because it misses the point of the phrase "the revealed will of God." Hebrews begins by saying that indeed God has spoken by the prophets in many parts and ways in the past, but "in these last days [He] has spoken to us in His Son" (Heb. 1:1–2). Today, we are saved by grace through faith in God's revealed will, which is trusting that Jesus the Messiah died for us and rose again. At present, we must have explicit faith in the Lord Jesus. Just as Jesus said, "For unless you believe that I am He [His messianic Deity], you will die in your sins" (John 8:24). Now that the Messiah Jesus has come, all people are called to have explicit faith in Him.

FINAL THOUGHTS

To sum up, all people, for all time, are saved by God's grace through faith in the revealed will of God. It is impossible for us to go back to Old Testament times because we now live in the time of the New Covenant. God has made full provision for us to experience total forgiveness for all our sins—past, present, and future. We must believe that Jesus died as our substitute sacrifice for sin and was raised again, proving He is God, and then we will enter a forgiven and eternal relationship with the God of the universe.

Is baptism required for the forgiveness of our sins? How does Acts 2:38 fit in with what is taught elsewhere in Scripture about salvation by faith alone?

It's possible to make the Bible teach anything, no matter how wrong it might be. It is easy to take verses out of context or misunderstand them by ignoring the rest of Scripture. One verse that is frequently misunderstood and misused is Acts 2:38. Located at the climax of Peter's sermon at Pentecost, Peter calls on his listeners to respond to the message he had just given, declaring, "Repent, and each of you be baptized in the name of Jesus Christ for the forgiveness of your sins; and you will receive the gift of the Holy Spirit" (Acts 2:38). Bible readers are frequently confused by this verse. In fact, this verse raises three specific questions. First, are people required to repent of all their sins to be saved or is faith alone in Jesus the only necessity? Second, in addition to faith, is baptism necessary for salvation? And third, are people to be baptized "in the name of Jesus" or "in the name of the Father and the Son and the Holy Spirit" (Matt. 28:19)? Let's look at each of these questions in order.

THE QUESTION OF REPENTANCE

The issue of the need for repentance is so crucial that this book devotes a whole question to the relationship of repentance to faith (see Question 2). Still, since it's clearly mentioned in Acts 2:38, I'll address it here briefly. One of the clearest teachings of Scripture (Eph. 2:8–9) is that people are saved by God's grace (undeserved kindness) by faith in Jesus (trust in His death and resurrection for us). Yet, here it seems that Peter's exhortation calls for his listeners to repent, not just to believe. As a result, it is commonly expected that if someone wants to come to know the Lord Jesus, they must turn away from all their sin, or at least feel badly for their sins. I would maintain that, although turning from sin and sadness for sin are both good and proper, they are not essential for salvation.

Resolving the difficulty with this verse is in recognizing that the word "repent" used in Acts 2:38 does not mean to feel remorseful. As used here, the word "repent" means to "change your mind." In this context, Peter is calling on his Jewish audience to move from their previous rejection of the Lord Jesus to trust in Him as their Messiah. He is saying, "Change your mind about Jesus—move from rejecting Him to trusting Him." In reality, repentance and faith are two sides of the same coin. The repentance side demands that we stop trusting what we previously thought and the faith side demands that we trust in Jesus. Repentance as found here doesn't mean we must feel bad about our sins but rather we need to change from rejecting Jesus to believing He is both Lord (God) and Messiah (cf. Acts 2:36).

THE ROLE OF BAPTISM

The second issue in this verse is that Peter seems to be saying that baptism is a required part of the repentance and faith process. When he said, "Repent, and each of you be baptized . . . for the forgiveness of your sins" (Acts 2:38), it seems that, according to Peter, baptism is an added requirement. Of course, the Bible consistently teaches that salvation is by grace alone, through faith alone, "not as a result of works" (Eph. 2:9; cf. John 3:16, 36; Rom. 4:1–17; Gal. 3:8–9). Requiring baptism for salvation would add a work on our part to God's grace. Moreover, when the Lord Jesus promised the thief on the cross that they would be together in Paradise, He didn't demand that the thief get off his cross and be baptized first. The thief's faith alone in Jesus alone was enough. By faith, he would join the Lord Jesus in eternity ("Paradise"; Luke 23:42–43).

So how should we understand this call to baptism? One possible explanation is to translate the word "for" in the phrase "for the forgiveness of your sins" as "on account of." That would make Peter's message, "Repent and be baptized *on account of* forgiveness of your sins." This ties forgiveness of sin to turning to Jesus and then makes baptism a consequence, not a cause, of that forgiveness. This translation is possible because the Greek word (*eis* used with a noun in the accusative case) is used that way elsewhere in Scripture (Matt. 3:11; 12:41; Mark 1:4). The problem with this explanation is that this grammatical usage is quite rare and only found in the Gospels, never in Acts.

A second, and better option, is to understand the call to be baptized as a parenthetical thought. This idea is also consistent with the Greek grammar. The command to repent is a plural verb in Greek. Similarly, the pronoun "your" in "forgiveness of your sins" is also plural, linking these two concepts together. But the command to be baptized is singular, as evident in the phrase "*each of you* be baptized." So here is a paraphrase of Peter's point: "Repent all of you (and if an individual does so, let each one be baptized) for the forgiveness *all y'all's* sins" (a little Southern slang clarifies this verse). The main thought of the verse is "All of you repent for the forgiveness of all y'all's sins." The parenthetical idea expressed here is that "if someone does repent, that individual should be baptized."

This interpretation fits well with the rest of Luke's writings. For example, Luke writes, "everyone who believes in Him receives forgiveness of sins" (Acts 10:43) and there is no mention of a need to be baptized. Also, Luke declares that repentance (the other side of faith) brings forgiveness of sins to Israel (Acts 5:31) with no mention of baptism. The same idea is found in Luke 24:47, saying that "repentance for forgiveness of sins would be proclaimed" to the nations (without including baptism). Taking the command for individuals to be baptized as a parenthetical statement in Acts 2:38 makes the most sense because it's in harmony with the Greek grammar and with the other statements in Acts, mentioned above.[4] So Peter is calling people to believe in Jesus as their Messiah, and then, in recognition of this commitment, to be baptized.

THE BAPTISMAL FORMULA

The third issue has to do with the formula for baptism. In the Great Commission, the Lord Jesus called on His disciples to "make disciples of all the nations, baptizing them in the name of the Father and the Son and the Holy Spirit" (Matt. 28:19). This is the clearest baptismal formula. When we baptize new followers of Jesus, we declare this Trinitarian statement. Yet, in Acts 2:38 (cf. Acts 8:16; 22:16), Peter says that individuals who repent should be "baptized in the name of Jesus."

Calling for people to be baptized in the name of Jesus is not to be considered a formula but rather an explanation of baptism. We need to remember that the apostles were Jewish men raised in first-century Jewish culture. In Judaism, whenever a person took an action or gave a teaching, they didn't do so on their own. Rather, they acted or taught "in the name of" their rabbi or teacher. So, in rabbinic writings, it might say, "Rabbi Gamaliel taught in the name of Rabbi Hillel" or "Rabbi Shimon took this action in the name of Rabbi Jochanon." In this way, they identified their own teacher and master.

The call to be baptized in the name of Jesus was a way of saying that a person was identifying with the Lord Jesus as his or her master. It was a public declaration that "I have become a follower of Jesus!" The formula used in baptism was the Trinitarian one but the actual act of baptism was a symbol of public identification with the Lord Jesus as their Messiah and Lord.

FINAL THOUGHTS

There are differences of opinion about baptism. Some sprinkle water while others practice full immersion. Some baptize infants while others only baptize believers. I happen to fall on the "immersion in water for believers, not babies" side of this debate. But here's what we all can agree on: That turning to Jesus in faith is what saves us, and baptism isn't required for remission of sins. Also, we can know that baptism is an outward symbol of salvation, not a requirement for it. Further, we can all recognize that when we are baptized in the name of the Father, Son, and Holy Spirit, we are publicly identifying the Lord Jesus as our eternal Redeemer and the Master of our lives.

How do God's sovereignty and human responsibility work together in salvation?

In Homer's *The Odyssey*, the sea monster Charybdis lived inside a rock on one side of the Strait of Messina while the sea monster Scylla lived inside a much larger rock on the opposite side. Sailors would need to navigate the narrow strait to escape each deadly monster. Unfortunately, avoiding one monster often led directly to the other one. Similarly, when we consider divine sovereignty and human responsibility, theologians have tended to veer towards one of the two biblical teachings to the exclusion of the other. Not only does this lead to conflicts between fellow believers but an imbalance in our understanding the truth of God.

It's far better not to choose one over the other but to accept both equally true principles as an antinomy—an apparent contradiction that is supra-rational, beyond our human capacity to understand. God is sovereign in our salvation, and we human beings are responsible before God to respond to the good news. That both those ideas can be true is certainly beyond human comprehension, yet they are resolved in the mind of God. Both are clearly taught in Scripture and have practical implications for our lives.

THE BIBLICAL TEACHING

God's Sovereignty

The sovereignty of God is taught throughout Scripture, from Old Testament to the New. Many Old Testament verses declare God's dominion over all creation. For example, "Whatever the Lord pleases, He does, in heaven and in earth, in the seas and in all deeps" (Ps. 135:6). God's sovereignty is uniquely His, so He declares, "'Remember the former things long past, for I am God, and there is no other; I am God, and there is no one like Me, declaring the end from the beginning, and from ancient times things which have not been done,' saying, 'My purpose will be established, and I will accomplish all My good pleasure'" (Isa. 46:9–10).

The New Testament is even more specific, emphasizing God's sovereignty over salvation. This is seen in Ephesians 1:3–7, which emphasizes God's election (God the Father "chose us in Him before the foundation of the world") and predestination ("He predestined us to adoption as sons through Jesus Christ to Himself, according to the kind intention of His will") of believers. Paul also adds that the believer's inheritance is obtained, "having been predestined according to His purpose who works all things after the counsel of His will" (Eph.1:11). The word "chose" refers to God's pre-temporal (before time) election of believers for salvation. The word "predestined" means "to fix or determine beforehand." These words are only used of those who have put their trust in Jesus.

Besides *election* and *predestination*, another key term in understanding God's sovereignty is *foreknowledge*. Paul linked *foreknowledge* to *predestination* when he wrote, "For those whom He foreknew, He also predestined to become conformed to the image of His Son" (Rom. 8:29; cf. 1 Peter 1:2). Some want to minimize election and predestination by saying that God, who is omniscient, knew in advance who would respond to the gospel, and only chose them. But the word "know" in Scripture is generally a relational term, even used of physical relationships (e.g., Gen. 4:1). For God to foreknow a person means the Lord entered into a saving relationship with that person in advance. This asserts that both election and predestination happened before time began.

Another crucial passage for understanding God's sovereignty in salvation is Romans 9:10–24. Paul's point in explaining election is that "there is no injustice with God, is there? May it never be!" (Rom. 9:14). Although it is hard for us to grasp, Paul maintains that God "has mercy on whom He desires, and He hardens whom He desires" (Rom. 9:18). God has the authority to do this even as a potter has authority over clay (Rom. 9:21). Therefore, God was fully just in making "known the riches of His glory upon vessels of mercy, which He prepared beforehand for glory" (Rom. 9:23).

Although it would be sufficient to point to these two passages, other verses also emphasize God's sovereignty in salvation. Another is "as many as had been appointed to eternal life believed" (Acts 13:48), indicating that God's unconditional election is the source of individual faith. Acts also shows that salvation begins with divine initiative, exemplified in Lydia's decision to believe as "the Lord opened her heart to respond to the things spoken by Paul" (Acts 16:14). Similarly, the Lord Jesus Himself declared that "all that the Father gives Me will come to Me" (John 6:37), demonstrating that salvation begins with God's initiative. The sovereignty of God is not a random or occasional idea found in Scripture but permeates the entire Bible. Nevertheless, human responsibility is also clearly taught in God's Word.

Human Responsibility

In every command in the Bible, whether in the Old or New Testament, God holds humanity responsible for obeying Him. At the end of the Mosaic Law, God calls Israel to obedience, saying "For this commandment which I command you today is not too difficult for you, nor is it out of reach. It is not in heaven, that you should say, 'Who will go up to heaven for us to get it for us and make us hear it, that we may observe it?' Nor is it beyond the sea, that you should say, 'Who will cross the sea for us to get it for us and make us hear it, that we may observe it?' But the word is very near you, in your mouth and in your heart, that you may observe it" (Deut. 30:11–14). It is evident that God held the Jewish people responsible for believing and keeping the message of the Torah.

In the New Testament, just as Romans 9 emphasized God's sovereignty in salvation, Romans 10 demonstrates God's expectation of human responsibility to respond to the message of the gospel. Paul declares, "Whoever will call on the name of the Lord will be saved" (Rom. 10:13). The need to respond to the gospel with faith is emphasized in the next verse, asking "How then will they call on Him in whom they have not believed? How will they believe in Him whom they have not heard? And how will they hear without a preacher?" (Rom. 10:14).

When Paul was asked, "What must I do to be saved?," his answer wasn't "Determine if you are elect" but "Believe in the Lord Jesus, and you will be saved" (Acts 16:30–31). Jesus said, "He who believes in the Son has eternal life; but he who does not obey the Son will not see life, but the wrath of God abides on him" (John 3:36). We can be absolutely certain that God expects people to respond to Him with the obedience of faith.

Divine Sovereignty vs. Human Responsibility

Someone might object that these two ideas are found in different parts of the Bible and that, therefore, they are just examples of biblical contradictions. However, surprisingly, we frequently find both concepts presented in the same passage. It's not as if two separate authors disagree about the subject. Rather, the authors of Scripture actually affirmed both ideas at the same time! In Romans 9, Paul emphasizes divine sovereignty immediately followed in Romans 10 by an emphasis on human responsibility! How can this be?

Another example is found in Luke 22:22, when Jesus said, "the Son of Man is going as it has been determined [divine sovereignty]; but woe to that man by whom He is betrayed [human responsibility]!" God's sovereign plan included the betrayal and crucifixion of Jesus, but Judas was held responsible for his actions. Similarly, in Acts 4:27–28, an unnamed disciple, in a prayer, refers to the conspiracy of human guilt for the death of Jesus, including Herod, Pontius Pilate, some Jewish people and some Gentiles, thereby indicating their human responsibility. Nevertheless, he points to God's role by saying that they did "whatever Your hand and Your purpose predestined to occur" (v. 28; cf. Acts 2:23). These combinations of both ideas in the same passage demonstrate that biblical authors accepted *both divine sovereignty and human responsibility as consistent and not contradictory thoughts.*

OUR PERSONAL RESPONSE

Accepting the Antinomy

In light of the truth that election and human responsibility are both taught in the Bible, how should we respond? First, we must accept this truth from God. Too often we want to argue the issue because, humanly speaking, we feel election is unfair. That's Paul's point when, having just explained God's sovereign election, he frames the words of an objector, "You will say to me then, 'Why does He still find fault? For who resists His will?'" (Rom. 9:19).

Some 48 years ago, when I first read those words, my heart jumped. I had been struggling with the doctrine of election because of my dad's great hostility to the gospel. If God was sovereign over this, I wondered, why does He still hold people accountable? I was thrilled because I thought, "Here comes the answer to my question!" Yet, Paul's response was not at all what I expected. He says, "On the contrary, who are you, O man, who answers back to God?" (Rom. 9:20). Paul didn't try to harmonize both truths and neither should we. Instead, he reminded believers that we are to submit to the sovereign God and accept both the truth of divine election and human responsibility. We may not be able to explain this seeming contradiction, but we are called to believe it is completely resolved in the mind of God.

Those whose minds are ruled by science and logic will often object to believing antinomies because they insist that both thoughts can't be true. Yet scientists recognize that light is both a wave and a particle at the same time, a seeming contradiction that is accepted as a mystery.[5] In the same way, we can accept this mystery that God, as both the Sovereign of the universe and Supreme Judge, holds humanity responsible for their decisions and actions.

Trusting in God's Will

People are frequently anxious about whether they are elect. They say, "I want to believe but I don't know if I'm elect." My advice is simple: relax and trust God. Jesus said, "All that the Father gives Me will come to Me, and the one who comes to Me I will certainly not cast out" (John 6:37). That you are searching and asking these questions demonstrates that God is at work in your heart and mind. You would not want to believe without the Father drawing you. We can put complete trust in God's will. The fact is that people believe because they are elect, and they are elect because they believe.

Renowned preacher Donald Grey Barnhouse asked people to imagine a door with a sign above it saying, "Whosoever will may come." Having entered through the door, the sign on the other side over the door says, "Elect before the foundation of the world." Friend, we can relax in the Lord. We are called to trust in Jesus alone and can safely leave our concerns about election in God's hands.

Preach the Gospel

Finally, we should continue to reach out to others with the good news. We need to adopt the apostle Paul's attitude: "Woe is me if I do not preach the gospel" (1 Cor. 9:16). Followers of Jesus are called upon to present the good news without concern as to whether or not those who receive the message are elect. After all, even if we did know, it would not do us any good! Instead, let's be obedient to the Great Commission and tell everyone we can about Jesus (Matt. 28:16–19). As the great preacher Charles Spurgeon is alleged to have said, "If God would have painted a yellow stripe on the backs of the elect, I would go around lifting shirts. But since He didn't, I must preach 'whosoever will' and when 'whosoever' believes I know he is one of the elect."[6]

FINAL THOUGHTS

When Spurgeon was asked how he reconciled God's sovereign election and humanity's responsibility to believe, he responded, "I wouldn't try. I never reconcile friends."[7] How right he was! These truths may seem to be opposed to each other, but they are united in the mind and heart of God. The truth of God's sovereignty and our personal responsibility are both used to bring people to Him. It's time we become friends with these truths as well.

QUESTIONS

about

THE BIBLE
IN GENERAL

With so many versions of the Bible available, how do I know which one to choose? Which is the right or best one?

As you might imagine, through the years, I've answered thousands of Bible questions on my radio program, *Open Line*. But the first question I was ever asked (and one that people have asked me repeatedly ever since) is this: *Which version of the Bible is the best?*

UNDERSTANDING THE METHODS OF TRANSLATION

Formal Equivalence

In order to choose a version of the Bible, it helps to understand that there are three basic approaches to translating the Bible. The first is called *formal equivalence*. This translation is done "word for word" or is literal in its approach. A good example of formal equivalence is the New American Standard Bible (which I think is a great, literal translation). However, since the Bible was written in ancient Hebrew, Aramaic, and Koine Greek, this approach sometimes produces a clunky, less readable translation that doesn't always fully capture the meaning of ancient idioms or translate ancient syntax into modern sentences. Galatians 2:4 is an example of this: "But it was because of the false brethren secretly brought in, who had sneaked in to spy out our liberty which we have in Christ Jesus, in order to bring us into bondage." We almost need a roadmap to follow the thought of the apostle Paul here in the NASB.

Dynamic Equivalence

The second approach to Bible translation is called *dynamic equivalence*. This method translates "thought for thought" and some popular examples of this would be the *New Living Translation* and the *New International Version*; both are very helpful translations. This method tries to bring the idioms and figures of speech into modern language, with an emphasis on making the text of Scripture clear and readable. The weakness is that sometimes these kinds of translations can take liberties with thoughts. This method of translating the text can become so interpretive that it may not always completely reflect the biblical author's true intention or become so interpretive that it leaves out other options for possible interpretation. An example of this is in Romans 1:5, a verse that uses the phrase "the obedience of faith." But the NIV translates it "the obedience that comes from faith"—a valid interpretation but not the only possibility. Alternatively, the phrase can mean "the obedience that is faith," meaning obedience to God's command requires trust in Him. The problem is that many readers of Scripture would prefer the literal translation so they can determine the meaning for themselves.

Optimal Equivalence

There is a third method of translation that tries to strike a middle road between formal and dynamic equivalence. Some have called this method *optimal equivalence*. Some examples of this method include the original Holman Christian Standard Bible, the Messianic Bible version called the Tree of Life Bible, and the English Standard Version. These translations tend to be more readable than a formal equivalence version, using English style and adapting idioms. Nevertheless, this method still allows some room for readers to interpret the meaning of the text since they're reading a more literal translation of a passage than the dynamic equivalent version. Here's how Galatians 2:4, the verse that was so wooden in the NASB, reads in the CSB: "This matter arose because some false brothers had infiltrated our ranks to spy on the freedom we have in Christ Jesus in order to enslave us." It's a much smoother read and therefore, easier to understand.

CHOOSING THE BEST TRANSLATION

So, which version should you read? I believe all of these methods of translation are valuable, and we should definitely read them all. For deep study, I suggest using a formal equivalence translation like the New American Standard Bible. Many read this all the time, but I find it most helpful when I am doing an in-depth study because it gives me the most literal rendering of the text. For times when I want to read quickly, covering a huge portion of Scripture, I will turn to a dynamic equivalence version like the *New Living Translation* or the *New International Version*. But for my regular daily reading of Scripture, I love the middle choice. I find the combined approach (optimal equivalence) to be most helpful most of the time. That's why I choose the original Holman Christian Standard Bible for my regular reading of Scripture. (Note that when the original Holman Christian Standard Bible version was revised into the Christian Standard Bible, it only changed 10 percent of the text, but it changed some of my minor preferences, like using the word "languages" (HCSB) for "tongues" (CSB) or "Messiah" (HCSB) for "Christ" (CSB). The new version is good but I still prefer the original.)

CAUTIONS FOR CHOOSING
A BIBLE TRANSLATION

The King James Version

Here are three cautions for choosing the best Bible translation. *First, be careful not to consider the King James Version as the only legitimate Bible translation.* The KJV was a great English translation into the common English spoken in seventeenth-century England. It also used the best biblical manuscripts available at the time. We should all be grateful for this beautiful and accurate translation. But, in the last 400 years, the English language has changed dramatically, making it hard to understand the archaic usages found in the KJV. For example, the KJV uses a word like "conversation" when it actually means "conduct" or the word "suffer" when it really means "permit."

A more serious problem with the KJV is that we know so much more today about the original manuscripts of Scripture than was known in 1611. Many of the manuscripts available today were not even known when King James sat on the throne of England. In fact, the New Testament of the KJV is based on the Greek text of the New Testament produced by Desiderius Erasmus (1469–1536). He used several Greek manuscripts, none of which contained the entire New Testament or were earlier than the twelfth century. Moreover, they were all from one family of manuscripts from the same geographical area. Since then, many more Greek manuscripts have been found going back to a much earlier date, including some papyri dating from as early as the second century, from a variety of geographical locations. Although none of the textual differences found in the KJV affect any doctrinal or ethical teaching of Scripture, it is best to use a Greek text of the New Testament that makes use of the earliest and best Greek text types.

The KJV Old Testament is based on the Masoretic Text (a Hebrew text preserved by Rabbinic Judaism which is based on the earliest extant complete Hebrew manuscripts of the Old Testament) which was certainly the best available. However, in 1896 many Hebrew texts were found in the Cairo Genizah (a burial or storage place for Scripture in an ancient synagogue). Also, in 1947, the discovery of the Dead Sea Scrolls, biblical texts and fragments found at a place called Qumran in the Judean wilderness, provided a deeper understanding of the original Hebrew text. These Hebrew fragments and texts date from 150 BC to AD 70 and contain at least parts of every Old Testament book but Esther. One scroll of the complete book of Isaiah is from the first century BC and is virtually identical to the Masoretic text that is dated one thousand years later. Although modern Bible translations still rely on the Masoretic Text, the more recent discoveries of these ancient scrolls and fragments in Egypt and Israel refine our understanding of the original Hebrew Bible. Unfortunately, when the KJV was produced, the translators did not have access to these early manuscripts.

While the KJV is a beautiful and good translation, we must not assume it is the best or only true version. Modern translations are more accurate because they are based on the earliest and best manuscripts of the Bible.

Translations with a Theological Agenda

A second warning is that we should be careful not to use a translation with a theological agenda. An example would be the New World Translation, which tries to justify the theological errors of the Jehovah's Witnesses. While these specialized versions may translate some parts of Scripture accurately, in many passages their translation is flat out wrong. The *New World Translation* seeks to justify Jehovah's Witness false doctrine and so the translation corrupts the truth found in Scripture. One example from the Old Testament is Exodus

3:14: "God said to Moses, 'I AM WHO I AM'; and He said, 'Thus you shall say to the sons of Israel, 'I AM has sent me to you.'" But the New World Translation takes the phrase as "I Will Become What I Choose to Become." And added, "This is what you are to say to the Israelites, 'I Will Become has sent me to you.'" This incorrect translation leads to a wrong understanding of Jesus' words in John 8:58: "Before Abraham was born, I am."

Another example is from the New Testament. In John 1:1, we read, "In the beginning was the Word, and the Word was with God, and the Word was God." Since Jesus is the Living Word made flesh (cf. John 1:14), the first verse in John's gospel is declaring that Jesus is God. To avoid affirming the full deity of the Lord Jesus, the New World Translation instead translates the passage as, "In the beginning was the Word, and the Word was with God, and the Word was a god." Since Jehovah's Witnesses do not believe that the Lord Jesus is fully God, they mistranslate these and many other verses that teach the Trinity or the deity of the Lord Jesus.

Idiosyncratic Translations

Finally, we should be wary of idiosyncratic translations—versions that reflect the views of just one person rather than a translation team. Examples of these would be Eugene Peterson's *The Message*, or J. B. Phillips' *The New Testament in Modern English* or David Stern's *Complete Jewish Bible*. These may be helpful in our devotional readings, but we should be mindful that they really only reflect one person's perspective. They don't have the safeguard of multiple translators checking each other's work. In a sense, they're just one person's interpretation of the text of Scripture and not really a thorough translation. So although they may be helpful for personal reading or study, we should view these idiosyncratic translations as personal interpretations of Scripture.

FINAL THOUGHTS

Finally, I would give you one last piece of advice. The most important issue in choosing the best translation for you is to find one that you can understand and that you will actually read. That's why, when my wife Eva is asked what she thinks is the best translation of the Bible, she will always reply, "The one that you'll actually read, study, and apply."

Is the Bible really God's Word?

People frequently want to know what I believe about the Bible. But even more important than knowing what I believe is understanding what the Bible says about itself. So, more than any one person's opinion, it's vital that we examine what the Scriptures say about their own inspiration.

UNDERSTANDING INSPIRATION

A key verse about inspiration is found in 2 Timothy 3:16: "All Scripture is inspired by God and profitable for teaching, for reproof, for correction, for training in righteousness." The phrase: "All Scripture is inspired by God" highlights three important principles.

The Bible, Not the Authors

First, the Scriptures themselves are inspired, not the authors of the Bible. Although the authors of the Scriptures were said to be moved by God's Spirit (2 Peter 1:21), Paul writes to Timothy that it is the Bible itself that is *inspired*, which means literally, *God-breathed*. This single word indicates that the Bible comes from God, that God exhaled the Scriptures into being. When you read the word *inspired*, you may think it means breathing *into* something. Rather, this verse is saying that God breathed *out* the Scriptures. The very words we read in the biblical text are "breathed out" by God. They don't become inspired when we read them and find something of value for our lives. The text of Scripture stands as God's Word even if we don't read it (but of course we should).

The Whole Bible

Second, the entire Bible is inspired. The Scriptures are God's Word in their entirety. Some people say that when Paul wrote 2 Timothy 3:16, he was only referring to the Old Testament and not the New Testament. But in his previous letter to Timothy, Paul said, "For the Scripture says, 'You shall not muzzle the ox while he is threshing,' and 'The laborer is worthy of his wages'" (1 Tim. 5:18). Paul is quoting two verses of Scripture here, one from Deuteronomy 25:4 in the Old Testament and the other from Luke 10:7 in the New Testament. Notice that he calls them both "Scripture." It's likely that the Gospel of Luke was only written about five years earlier than Paul's quotation of it as Scripture. At about the same time, Peter, the acknowledged leader of the apostles, wrote in 2 Peter 3:16 that Paul wrote about salvation "in all his letters, in which there are some matters that are hard to understand. The untaught and unstable twist them to their own destruction, as they also do *with the rest of the Scriptures*" (HCSB). This shows Peter considered Paul's letters to be Scripture. Here's the point: By the time Paul wrote 2 Timothy 3:16 and said,

"All Scripture is inspired," he meant that the whole Bible was inspired, including both Testaments.

Divine Human Authorship

Third, God's Holy Spirit moved human beings to produce the Bible. The Bible verse describing how God used human authors to write the books of the Bible is 2 Peter 1:21: "For no prophecy was ever made by an act of human will, but men *moved* by the Holy Spirit spoke from God." The Holy Spirit empowered people to write Scripture by "moving" or "bearing along" human authors to speak, and by inference, to write their words down. The word translated *moved* (*phero* in the Greek) is used in Acts 27:15 about a ship being driven by the wind. In the same way the wind bears a sailboat along, so the Holy Spirit moved the human authors to write the Bible. This explains the varying writing styles and perspectives of biblical authors. Just as the same wind can bear differing ships with different kinds of sails along in different ways, so the Holy Spirit can move writers with unique personalities and different styles to write down God's words.

UNDERSTANDING INERRANCY

Since the whole Bible is inspired, it is completely true or inerrant. In the Torah (also known as the Pentateuch, or the first five books of the Bible), Moses wrote, "God is not a man who lies, or a son of man who changes His mind. Does He speak and not act, or promise and not fulfill?" (Num 23:19 HCSB). Paul made a similar statement in Romans 3:4: "God must be true, even if everyone is a liar" (HCSB). Furthermore, the Lord Jesus, God incarnate, said of Himself, "I am the way, and the truth, and the life" (John 14:6). Jesus calls Himself the truth, and He is the divine author of Scripture. Since God is true and He breathed out the Scriptures, the Lord Jesus said in His High Priestly prayer for His followers, "Your Word is truth" (John 17:17). This line of reasoning is where we get the teaching that the Scriptures are inerrant. The point is that the Bible is as true as God Himself and completely trustworthy.

Original Autographs

To help you better understand the concept of inerrancy, here are some specific points to remember. *First, the inerrancy of Scripture is limited to the original autographs.* This means that the original scroll of Isaiah or the actual letter Paul wrote to the Romans are inerrant. It doesn't mean that every copy we have today will be a perfect replica of the original. The good news is that textual criticism, the study of comparing the surviving ancient manuscripts with one another, is highly accurate. That's why we can be confident that what we have today reflects more than 99 percent of the original documents. And for those parts that remain in question, none of them affect biblical doctrine or prescribed behavior. That's why I can hold my Bible with the unwavering certainty that it is inerrant. I know it is based on texts copied years after the original manuscripts and then translated into English, and I can still claim it is completely true.

What the Bible Affirms

Second, inerrancy only refers to what the Bible affirms. Some statements in the Scriptures are accurately recorded but not actually what the Bible teaches. For example, when the serpent tempted Eve, he misquoted God, claiming that God prohibited eating from *any* tree (Gen. 3:1). The Bible records what the serpent truly said but his words remain untrue.

Ordinary Language

Third, inerrancy assumes that the Bible uses ordinary, normal language. The Bible mentions the four corners of the earth (Isa. 11:12) and the sunrise (Ps. 113:3). This doesn't mean that the Bible teaches the earth is a square or that God's Word denies a heliocentric view of the universe. The Scriptures are not using scientific precision any more than a meteorologist on local news is when he tells what the times are for sunrise and sundown.

FINAL THOUGHTS

When my kids were little, I enjoyed playing a game called Jenga with them. We'd build a tower, adding wooden piece upon piece, until it fell down. My younger boy was a little mischievous and sometimes he would deliberately pull out the bottom piece in order to make the whole tower collapse. This example reminds me of the inspiration of Scripture. It is foundational to every other teaching. If we pull that one teaching out, then all the others will fall apart. It's why our affirmation of the inspiration and truth of God's Word is so vital. If we take it away, it puts our entire faith in jeopardy.

Why should we even read the Bible?

A few years ago, I read a magazine article titled, "21 Overrated Books You Don't Have to Read Before You Die."[8] The author, novelist Jesse Ball, included the Bible as number 12 on that list. Even though many more billions of people have read the Bible than have even heard of GQ, the author wrote: "The Holy Bible is rated very highly by all the people who supposedly live by it but who in actuality have not read it. Those who *have* read it know there are some good parts, but overall it is certainly not the finest thing that man has ever produced. It is repetitive, self-contradictory, sententious, foolish, and even at times ill-intentioned."

I'd never heard of Jesse Ball before reading his assessment of the Bible nor have I ever read any of his novels. He may be a great writer—I wouldn't know. But he certainly fails as a literary critic. My simple response to him would be that people often criticize what they don't understand, and he doesn't seem to understand the Scriptures. Here's why I believe we need to read the Bible.

THE BIBLE IS GREAT LITERATURE

I would assert that the Bible is a great literary masterpiece. Too often we think of the Bible as a mixture of commandments, genealogies, obscure poems, and strange stories of talking donkeys and snakes, along with other incomprehensible material. But the Bible is actually a library of 66 books that each have a clear and consistent literary structure. When we read these books and understand the author's strategies, we'll be awed by the grandeur and beauty of the Bible. But that would require people to sit down and actually read the Bible on its own terms without imposing their world view on it. To truly appreciate the Bible, we have to give up our preconceived notion and let the Scriptures speak to us.

THE BIBLE IS DIVINE TRUTH

The Bible is important for us to read because it tells the truth. Jesus said to God the Father, "Your Word is truth" (John 17:17). A Muslim critic of the Bible once asked me how I could believe the Bible since it presents godly people in such a negative light. For example, Abraham lied about his wife and called her his sister (a half-truth); Moses is seen to have an explosive temper by killing the Egyptian taskmaster and breaking the tablets of the Ten Commandments; David's adultery with Bathsheba and his murder of Uriah is in the Bible for all to see. I replied that was *why* I believe the Bible is absolutely truthful. The Bible is not a cover-up or religious propaganda. Instead, it shows the heroes of the faith as they really were, with all their faults exposed. We are told both the good with the bad.

THE BIBLE IS A SUPERNATURAL MIRROR

Another reason to read the Bible is that it reveals who we really are. That is why James compares the Scriptures to a mirror (James 1:23)—it shows what we are really like. According to James, the problem with our inability to see ourselves isn't the fault of the mirror, it is a problem with our memory. If we don't act on what we see in Scripture, we become like a person "who looks at his natural face in a mirror; for once he has looked at himself and gone away, he has immediately forgotten what kind of person he was" (vv. 23–24). The best way to understand ourselves—our selfishness, pride, bad habits, and greed—is by looking at the mirror of Scripture, what James calls "the perfect law, the law of liberty" (v. 25–26). It will show us our great need for God and transform our lives so we can become effectual "doers" of God's Word (v. 22).

THE BIBLE IS THE ULTIMATE LOVE STORY

One of the most important reasons to read the Bible is that it is the greatest love story of all time. It reveals the Creator's love for us and His desire to have a relationship with us. The most foundational verse of the Bible is John 3:16: "For God so loved the world that he gave his One and only Son, that whoever believes in him shall not perish but have eternal life" (NIV). The apostle Paul put it this way: "But God demonstrates His own love toward us, in that while we were yet sinners,

Christ [the Messiah] died for us" (Rom. 5:8). This is the story of the Bible from start to finish. The Hebrew Scriptures point forward to the Messiah and the forgiveness He would provide. The New Covenant Scriptures reveal that Messiah Jesus has come and that we must believe in Him. The whole Bible put together is the story of the Messiah Jesus who died for us and rose again. It is all about God's sacrificial love for us.

Are there things in Scripture that are uncomfortable or hard to understand or challenging to my life? Absolutely. But as the Psalmist said of the Bible, it's "more desirable than gold, yes, than much fine gold; sweeter also than honey and the drippings of the honeycomb" (Ps. 19:10). That's not only why we should read God's Word, but why we should re-read it, again and again.

I'm always being encouraged to read the Bible *daily*. What good will that do? Isn't reading it at church enough?

Someone once said that every person seems to be listening to the same radio station: WIIFM. That's right, WIIFM. Those call letters represent five words: What's In It For Me? When we are called upon to act differently, to give generously, or to risk dangerously, we may find ourselves asking, "What's the benefit to me?"

The same attitude may creep in when we think about reading Scripture daily. One woman told me that she didn't like reading the Bible. She said she loved the Lord but didn't like to read at all. She said, "Why should I read the Bible every day? I go to a weekly Bible study and I go to worship every week and hear a sermon. I'm so busy that I don't even have 15 minutes a day for myself, let alone to read the Bible." In other words, she was asking, *What's in it for me?*

Seeking to answer her question, I read through the longest psalm in the Bible, Psalm 119. It's a song written about the Scriptures. And as I read it, I noted seven benefits of reading the Bible. Here are those seven reasons, and hopefully they will convince all of us of the importance of spending daily time reading God's Word.

MORAL PROTECTION

First, reading the Bible provides moral protection. Psalm 119:9–11 says," How can a young man keep his way pure? By keeping it according to Your word. With all my heart I have sought You; do not let me wander from Your commandments. Your word I have treasured in my heart, that I may not sin against You." Reading the Bible helps us distinguish between right and wrong, especially in this relativistic age. It changes the way we think and reminds us to follow God's standards, not our own.

GENUINE FREEDOM

Second, reading the Bible gives us genuine freedom. Psalm 119:45 says, "I will walk at liberty, for I seek Your precepts." This verse literally says, "I will walk in a wide-open place." How different this is than what we usually think! Many people think that the Bible restricts and limits us. Instead, this verse says that the Scriptures guide us to what is best for us, and we have liberty to go there. Real freedom isn't doing anything I want but rather doing what is best. For example, I don't want a fire to have the liberty to rage across my living room. I much prefer the blaze to be free to burn in the fireplace.

NEW LIFE

Third, reading the Bible offers us new life. Psalm 119:93 declares, "I will never forget Your precepts, for by them You have revived me." The Word of God has the power to invigorate and sustain us. Without it, we shrivel up. The Bible is our spiritual nutrition. A healthy serving of the Scriptures on a daily basis transforms us so we can walk in newness of life.

SUPERNATURAL WISDOM

Fourth, reading the Bible bestows supernatural wisdom. This is what Psalm 119:98–100 says: "Your commandments make me wiser than my enemies, for they are ever mine. I have more insight than all my teachers, for Your testimonies are my meditation. I understand more than the aged, because I have observed Your precepts." The first part of this verse could be translated, "Your commandments give me skill for living." The message of the Bible is not about a bunch of "begats" and "thou shalt nots." God's Word is about practical, everyday, successful living based on God's perspective, not ours. It's amazing how skillful we can become in marriage, parenting, business, friendship, work, you name it, when we live according to God's wisdom.

DIVINE DIRECTION

Fifth, reading the Bible provides divine direction. A great reminder from Psalm 119:105 is, "Your word is a lamp to my feet and a light to my path." I'm convinced that much of the will of God is found in the Word of God. As we wonder what our steps should be in a dark world, the Word of God guides us. We don't need this spiritual flashlight only on special occasions; we need the light of God's Word for every step we take.

ABSOLUTE TRUTH

Sixth, reading the Bible presents absolute truth. We live in an age when people actually believe that truth is relative and that there is no objective reality. Some believe that truth can be individualized, so that your truth is different from my truth. But the Bible disagrees: "The sum of Your word is truth, and every one of Your righteous ordinances is everlasting" (Ps. 119:160). In this relativistic, equivocating world, we can rely on the absolute truth of God's Word.

EMOTIONAL SECURITY

Seventh, reading the Bible gives us emotional security. Psalm 119:165 says, "Those who love Your law have great peace, and nothing causes them to stumble." Jesus taught that in this world we'll have tribulation (John 16:33), and doubtless we have all experienced troubles. Nevertheless, I've also found that the way to find peace in any crisis, whether it's health problems, family difficulties, financial stress, challenges at work, or anything, comes from reading and gaining comfort from the words of Scripture.

FINAL THOUGHTS

These are just seven reasons that demonstrate the great benefit in daily Bible reading. I believe that it should be a life essential for us all. It is helpful to have a contemporary, easy-to-understand translation of the Bible. By spending just 10 to 15 minutes a day reading God's Word, we will grow as believers. If you are new to Bible reading, there are many good reading plans available. Find one and use it. And remember what the evangelist D. L. Moody is widely attributed to have said: "The Bible was not given for our information but our transformation." We can begin to experience God's transformation of our lives as we read the Scriptures every day.

The Bible seems like such a hard book. How can I read it with any understanding?

Many people feel guilty for not reading the Bible but when they try it seems like a closed book. This makes sense. Although the Bible has one consistent story leading to Jesus the Messiah, it really is a library of books written between 3,500 and 2,000 years ago. Also, most people think the Bible uses archaic and technical language that is beyond the ability of ordinary people to understand. But the Bible can be understood, and reading it can enrich and change our lives. So here are some ways you can read the Bible and understand it!

CHOOSE A MODERN TRANSLATION

When we consider reading the Bible, we often think of the King James Version with its old-fashioned English. Today, we never address people as "thee" or "thou," and we would never say "*suffer* the little children" to come to Jesus (Matt. 19:14 KJV). That's why it's so important to read a Bible translated into modern English. You can choose from a number of reputable versions and translations (see Question 9), but for now, make sure you find a version that's easy to understand. If you're committed to the King James Version, you may want to try the New King James. Many people find the New Living

Translation especially easy to understand. My wife likes the New American Standard Version, I like the Holman CSB, and many of my friends read the English Standard Version or New International Version. The version you select is a matter of personal choice. Go to a bookstore, look through several versions, read a chapter or two in the Gospel of Mark and decide which one you like and understand. That's the one to read.

READ SYSTEMATICALLY, NOT RANDOMLY

Too often people read a verse or chapter here or there, instead of reading complete books of the Bible. It's much better to read whole books with a plan and purpose. If you're just starting, take the book of Ephesians in the New Testament. Read one chapter a day for six days. Then start again, rereading the same book. At the end of the month, you will have read Ephesians five times. If you're still having a tough time understanding, try paraphrasing it, paragraph by paragraph. Also, it's a good idea to get a Bible reading plan or use a daily Bible study devotional, so you can read systematically through books.

READ WITH PRAYER AND EXPECTATION

The psalmist gives us a great example of how to begin reading when he prayed, "Open my eyes so that I may contemplate wondrous things from your instruction" (Ps. 119:18 CSB). We need God's Spirit to help us grasp what we are reading. Yet, sometimes people expect a spiritual jolt when reading the

Scriptures, sort of like Popeye eating a can of spinach. It's true, sometimes we'll read and find a verse that will jump out and give us great encouragement. But reading the Bible is much more like taking a daily vitamin pill or eating a basic nutritious meal. We should not expect to have a spiritual liver quiver every time we read, but instead a gradual strengthening. By reading prayerfully and with an appropriate expectation, we'll get more out of reading God's Word.

VARY YOUR APPROACH

People think that reading the Bible always requires slow, careful analysis. But it's also important to get a holistic overview of Bible books. So, for example, let's say we wanted to study the book of Hebrews. It would be helpful to start by reading the whole book in one sitting. That should take about 45 minutes (less time than most procedural crime dramas we watch on Netflix or than we spend checking social media). Then, you can slow down. For the next 13 days, read a chapter a day of Hebrews so you can take a more careful in-depth approach. After that, read the whole book once again and see how much better it's understood.

KEEP VERSES IN CONTEXT

When we read verses in isolation, we can't possibly understand what they mean. Rather than reading one verse at a time, we should read the verses that come before and after it.

That way we can ensure we have the correct understanding of that verse. I once received a Christmas card with Revelation 11:10 on it: "Those who dwell on the earth will rejoice over them and celebrate; and they will send gifts to one another." Sounds good until we realize that the context reveals that this is about people of the earth celebrating the murder of two of God's future witnesses whose message of repentance tormented them. Remember, context is king.

IDENTIFY THE ORIGINAL AUDIENCE

Many books of the Old Testament were written to God's people, the nation of Israel. The New Testament letters were written to specific churches. Knowing the original audience will help you better understand the message. For example, God promised Israel great prosperity if they obeyed the Law of Moses (Deut. 28:11–12), their national constitution in the land of Israel. But the New Testament doesn't promise material prosperity for obedience but a harvest of righteousness (Rom. 6:16). Certainly, all Scripture is applicable to us today, but identifying the audience helps us to know how to apply it.

KEEP THE PLAIN SENSE OF THE WORDS

One of the first interpretive principles I ever heard has held up all these years: "If the plain sense makes sense, then seek no other sense, lest it result in nonsense." That means that we need to read the Bible looking for the plain meaning. If the author uses the word "Israel," it means Israel. If a miracle occurs, like the parting of the Red Sea, it's a real miracle, not merely low tide. However, that doesn't mean there are no metaphors or other figures of speech in the Bible. When Jesus said He was the door (John 10:9), that doesn't mean He had hinges on His side or a door-knob in His midsection. It is plainly a metaphor for faith in Jesus, who is our entryway to knowing God.

RECOGNIZE THE GENRE
AND READ ACCORDINGLY

There are several *genres* or *literary forms* in Scripture. The three most basic are narrative, poetry, and prose. When we read a narrative or a story, we look for the general principle being taught in that story. For example, the familiar story of David and Goliath reveals that Saul had been rejected as king (1 Sam. 15) and David, the shepherd boy, had been anointed as future king (1 Sam. 16). So the reader wonders why was David chosen and not one of his brothers? The story of David and Goliath (1 Sam. 17) reveals that David was so desirous of preserving God's honor that he was willing to sacrifice his own safety and security. That's the kind of person God chooses to use.

But poetry, as found in the Psalms, is written and understood in a different way. The psalms express passionate feelings using figures of speech. For example, the psalmist writes, "As the deer pants for the water brooks [a simile], so my soul pants for You, O God" (Ps. 42:1). The psalm writers use emotional word pictures to help convey their emotions toward God.

Prose is a much more straightforward style of writing—it reveals directly and explicitly what is being said. So, when Paul writes, "preserve the unity of the Spirit in the bond of peace" (Eph. 4:3), it's clear that we're to make every effort to stay unified with fellow followers of the Lord Jesus. While many people think the biblical prophets are hard to understand, remember their books are filled with both prose and poetry. Understanding what genre the author is using can help open our eyes to the meaning of the Bible.

USE HELPFUL AND TRUSTWORTHY
BIBLE RESOURCES

There are some terrific tools that help us understand Scripture. Of these, every Bible reader should have two resources. The first is a good one- or two-volume commentary on the whole Bible. A commentary will have an introduction to orient you to each Bible book and it will help clear up the meaning of verses or words that are hard to grasp. A good commentary also helps a reader understand the flow of thought in the Bible book or address theological issues present in the text. My suggested commentary is *The Moody Bible Commentary*, written by the Moody faculty. I had the privilege of contributing to this work and co-editing it.[9] There are other good one- or two-volume commentaries and everyone should be sure to own one.

A second helpful Bible tool is a Bible dictionary. This doesn't just explain words or concepts like Webster's. Instead, it also has brief articles on just about everything found in the Bible. If we're reading Paul's epistles to the Corinthians, then look up the article on Corinth and learn about that city. Maybe we see the term "Messiah" or "propitiation" and wonder about its meaning—we should look that up in a Bible dictionary. There are a number of excellent dictionaries but I suggest *The New Unger's Bible Dictionary*, a work authored by Merrill Unger and edited by R. K. Harrison, two acclaimed Bible scholars.[10] It will be a great resource for studying the Bible.

READ WITH A VIEW TO ACTION

Howard Hendricks, my former professor of blessed memory, always said, "We haven't studied until we've applied." He gave his classes an acronym, as a little memory device, to keep in mind as we read Scripture. He would tell us we need to put on our **SPECS** when we read the Bible. Ask these questions:

Is there a **Sin** to avoid?
Is there a **Promise** to claim?
Is there an **Example** to follow?
Is there a **Command** to obey?
Is there a **Statement** of truth (to believe)?

If we keep these questions in mind as we read, we won't be merely filling our minds with facts but transforming our lives with Scripture.

FINAL THOUGHTS

Too often we're afraid of the Bible. We think it's too deep or too challenging or just too hard to grasp. But I'm convinced that the best way to understand the Bible is by reading it. And if we don't understand it the first time, we need to read it again. Moreover, it's okay if we don't understand everything all at once. There are mysteries in Scripture that we'll never understand. The Bible says, "The secret things belong to the LORD our God, but the things revealed belong to us and to our sons forever, that we may observe all the words of this law" (Deut. 29:29). The book of ancient Jewish wisdom, the Talmud, says, "By all means a person should study (the Bible), even though he is liable to forget, yea, even if he does not understand all that he studies" (Avodah Zerah 19a). This reminds me of Mark Twain's alleged comment: "It ain't those parts of the Bible that I can't understand that bother me, it is the parts that I do understand." This is so true for us—the parts we understand will speak right into our lives and transform us to be more and more like Jesus.

QUESTIONS

about

THE PRIMEVAL

WORLD OF

GENESIS

Is the story of creation in Genesis to be taken literally? How can a modern person believe that God created the world in six days?

It seems every time a follower of Jesus runs for public office, someone in the press will ask, "Do you believe in the creation story as found in the Bible or do you believe in evolution?" If candidates say they believe the Bible, the press will ridicule them for being unscientific and unfit for public service. And this is not just a hot-button issue for hostile reporters. Sometimes, friendly seekers will ask followers of Jesus the same question. There are genuine and thoughtful people who are considering faith in Jesus as their forgiver of sin and their leader in life, but stumble over the issue of creation as revealed in the book of Genesis. That's why it's essential for believers to understand the answer to this most basic question: Can a sane and thinking person believe the literal story of creation as found in Genesis 1–2?

I believe the answer to this question is an emphatic "Yes!" While many Bible-believing Christians hold to other views, I believe God created the world in six literal days. The following explains why I believe what I do about the creation narrative.

THE MEANING OF THE CREATION STORY

To begin, I believe in a young earth. By that I mean that the world is not billions and billions of years old, as Carl Sagan put it. Rather, the Scriptures point to a world made much more recently. That doesn't mean Bishop Ussher's creation date of 4004 BC is correct. The sixteenth-century biblical scholar came up with that date by counting up the years in the genealogies in the early parts of Genesis. What he seemed to overlook is that these ancient genealogical records didn't have to include every name in a family—a genealogy might just record every fourth or fifth generation or maybe even skip more than that. So, for the earth to be young, it need not be a mere 6,000 years old. Creation might have begun in 20,000 BC or even 50,000 BC. None of us really knows the actual date of creation.

Second, I believe that the word "day" as used in Genesis 1 of the six days of creation refers to a normal 24-hour day. That's not to say that the word can't mean a period of time. In fact, that's exactly how it is used in Genesis 2:4—it calls the six days of creation "the day" or the period of time in which God made the world. Of course, we know the Bible also talks about the day of the Lord, and that's not a 24-hour day but an extended period of time (e.g., Joel 2:31; 3:14). As a result, there are some respectable and responsible Bible interpreters who view the six days of creation as figurative for six ages in which God oversaw the evolutionary development of the world. Even though I don't agree with them, I believe that they are still fellow followers of Jesus. On this we can certainly agree to disagree without being disagreeable.

The reason the word "day" in the first chapter of Genesis should best be understood as referring to an actual 24-hour day lies in the text's emphasis on "morning and evening." This phrase indicates a normal 24-hour rotation of the earth. Moreover, if these days were actually ages and not 24-hour days, that would require animals to have died to create the fossil record. If that were so, it would mean death entered the world before Adam sinned and that contradicts Genesis 2:17: "From the tree of the knowledge of good and evil you shall not eat, for in the day that you eat from it you will surely die." It seems clear that death, for humans and animals alike, could only come into the world after Adam sinned.

THE SUPPORT FOR THE LITERAL
CREATION STORY

If we're to take the story of creation in the Bible literally, what answers can be given about the seemingly old age of the earth and the fossil record? Should those issues be ignored? Absolutely not! Here are three ideas which help address these issues.

Apparent Age

First, it seems that God created the world with apparent age. Consider the creation of the first man, Adam. When God made him from the dust of the ground (Gen. 2:7), when he was just a few minutes old, he didn't appear as an infant. Rather, God made him a fully grown man with apparent age. In the same way, when God made the world, He built age into everything that was made. That would even include the light shining from the stars. Some people assert that since those stars are many light years away, it would have taken much longer for their light to reach the earth, requiring each day to be an age. But if God made them with apparent age, He could also have created their light to shine and reach the earth immediately. So much of the record that points to an old earth can be resolved by recognizing that God has the unique ability to create fully grown trees, fully developed valleys and mountains, and in fact, to present everything with apparent age.

Cataclysm

Second, it also seems that much of the fossil record can be explained by cataclysm. This means that earthly catastrophes can leave remnants that appear to have happened much earlier than they actually did. The eruption of Mount St. Helens in 1980 is an example of this. That volcanic eruption deposited over 1 million trees from the top of the mountain into Spirit Lake below. When those trees became water logged, they submerged to the bottom of the lake. And since the roots took on even more weight than the trunks of the trees, they seemingly planted themselves in the bottom of the lake in vertical fashion. So now, if we were to scuba dive there, we'd see a fossilized forest underwater. Significantly, if we didn't know that this event happened after 1980, we'd think that this forest existed long ages ago and that a lake developed over it over many thousands of years. The same is true with the canyons surrounding Mount St. Helens. In fact, there is a mini-grand canyon with a river in it. It was formed in one day of eruptions in 1980 but if we didn't know better, we'd believe it took millions of years to form.

Of course, the Bible depicts a major catastrophic event, the flood in Noah's day (Gen. 6–8), that could explain much of the alleged evidence for a seemingly much older earth. At that time, it didn't just rain, but the Bible says "all the fountains of the great deep burst open, and the floodgates of the sky were opened" (Gen. 7:11). This indicates there were earthquakes and likely volcanic eruptions in addition to tremendous rain. When people look at the effects of that cataclysm today, they believe it took millions of years to develop, not just the 40 days described in Genesis. Like the eruption of Mount St. Helens, the Noahic Cataclysm could have caused fossilization and canyons of epic proportions much more recently than the superficial examination of them would indicate.

Question Uniformitarianism

A third essential to accepting the creation story is not to assume that uniformitarianism is true. This is a scientific theory that presumes that the earth has always changed in the same exact way. Of course, everything really isn't uniform. For example, in the primeval period, according to the biblical record, people lived much longer than they do today (cf. Gen. 5:3–32). Why can't we believe that of animals as well? Moreover, even scientists recognize that changes of the earth's temperature and climate have caused changes on the earth in a non-uniform fashion. That's yet another reason it's not necessary to believe that creation evolved over millions and millions of years.

FINAL THOUGHTS

Finally, here's what's most important: The Bible teaches that there is a Creator who made the world. Moreover, He made humanity, you and I, and He cares for us so much that He wants to have a relationship with us. That's why the Creator became a man, the God-Man, Jesus of Nazareth, who died for us and rose again. If we trust in Him, we can have an eternal personal relationship with the Creator of the universe.

Why does it seem like there are two separate and contradictory creation stories in Genesis?

There is probably no part of the Bible that receives more criticism than the Genesis creation story. The major critique comes from the theory of evolution which challenges God as the Creator of the world. However, a literary attack alleges that the Genesis narrative contains two separate and contradictory creation stories. This critique asserts that the first creation story (Gen. 1:1–2:3) describes God's creation of the world in six days and His resting on the seventh. It also alleges that a second story occurs in Genesis 2:4–25, depicting God's creation of humanity and the animals.

UNDERSTANDING THE LITERARY STRUCTURE

This allegation misunderstands the literary structure of the creation story in Genesis. The author laid out the narrative in a progressively more detailed way. The narrative begins in Genesis 1:1 with a summary statement: "In the beginning God created the heavens and the earth." This synopsis declares that God is the Creator of everything. The phrase, "the heavens and the earth" is called a *merism*, a figure of speech that uses two contrasting or opposite parts to describe the whole. So, if you say that you've searched your house from "top to bottom," you are using a merism, meaning you searched your entire house. In the same way, God's creation of "the heavens and the earth" means that God made everything, the whole world.

In Genesis 1:2–2:3, the author provides a more detailed description of how God made the world in six days, and then how He ceased His creative activity on the seventh day. God begins His creative work by identifying what He made initially—a world described as "a wilderness and a wasteland" (a more descriptive translation than the more common "formless and void"). God made the world and set the raw materials of creation entirely under water. Then "the Spirit of God was moving over the surface of the waters" as the agent who would carry out the formation of the world into a habitable place for humanity (Gen. 1:2). The rest of the chapter describes God's creative work over the six days of creation: Day One—Light (1:3–5); Day Two—Separation of Sky and Water (1:6–8); Day Three—Land/Vegetation (1:9–13); Day Four—Luminaries (1:14–19); Day Five—Birds/Sea Creatures (1:20–23); Day Six—Animals and Humanity (1:24–31). Then, on the seventh day, God rested or ceased from His creative activity (2:1–3).

After detailing the events of the six days of creation, the narrative continues with even greater specificity in Genesis 2:4–25. This section focuses entirely on the sixth day of creation and provides the particulars of the forming of the first man and first woman, concluding with the establishment of marriage.

It is helpful to look at the creation story as happening in three movements. The first movement begins with a summary statement, declaring that during "the beginning" God made everything (Gen. 1:1). The second movement gives the details of creation by showing how God formed everything in six days and ceased His creative activity on the seventh (Gen. 1:2–2:3). The third movement focuses on the events of the sixth day, particularly how God made the first man and first woman and established marriage. The creation narrative is one story, explained with more and more specificity, not two separate and competing creation accounts.

THE ANSWER TO THE TWO-CREATION ALLEGATION

So what prompted the idea of two competing stories? Three pieces of evidence are cited to maintain that 1:1–2:3 is separate and distinct from 2:4–25. First, the alleged use of two different names for God. Second, the allegation of conflicting times for the creation of vegetation. And third, the contention that the two stories invert the sequence of the creation of animals and humanity. There are some simple answers to these arguments, and you will see that we don't need to abandon the unity of the creation story in the face of these "problems." Let's consider each of these in turn.

Two Differing Names for God

First, there is the alleged use of two differing names for God. Critics maintain that in version one, the author uses *Elohim* (Gen. 1) but in version two God is called *Yahweh Elohim* or Lord *God* (Gen. 2). Although two different names for God are used in the creation account, this does not indicate two different stories. It's not uncommon for the Scriptures to use different names and/or titles for God within the same book or passage (see Ex. 3:4, 4:5; Lev. 21:6; Deut. 6:4; Ps. 14:5–6). It is also common for Ancient Near Eastern literature to use different names and/or titles for their deities without critics contending that these non-biblical stories have different sources and authors. In the Bible, different names for God are used for different purposes. *Elohim* (God) refers to God's power. Therefore, it's used in Genesis 1 when describing God's power to create the world in six days. Alternatively, *Yahweh Elohim* (Lord God) is God's relational name. That's the reason it's used in the story about creating humanity. *Yahweh* is the preferred name when describing God's covenantal relationship with people (Gen. 12:1–9; 15:1–21).

An illustration of these two uses of God's names is in Psalm 19. In the first six verses, the psalmist uses the name *Elohim* (God) because it describes God's powerful creation as a way He disclosed Himself to the world. In verses 7–14, the psalmist repeatedly uses *Yahweh* (the Lord), God's relational name, because it describes the Lord's relationship with those who know Him as their Rock and Redeemer (v. 14). Clearly,

Psalm 19 is a unified poem about God, but it uses two different names of God to reveal Him.

Differing Order of Creating Vegetation

The second supposed proof of competing stories has to do with the creation of vegetation. It is argued that in version one, God makes vegetation on the third day (Gen. 1:11–12) but in version two, there is no vegetation yet, even on the day God made humanity, what would be the sixth day (2:5). It is true that Genesis 1:11–12 says that on the third day God brought forth "vegetation, plants yielding seed, and fruit trees on the earth bearing fruit . . . with seed in them." Yet, in the next chapter, describing the sixth day, it states that "no shrub of the field was yet in the earth, and no plant of the field had yet sprouted" (2:5). On the surface, this appears to be a contradiction, but a closer look will reveal that they harmonize easily if the words are understood correctly.

Describing the sixth day, in Genesis 2:5, the word "shrub" is a general Hebrew term for thorns and thistles and the words "plant of the field" speak of cultivated grains. Only after Adam sinned would God tell him that, as part of the consequences for sinning, he would now have to work the fields, eating the plants he cultivated by battling thorns and thistles (3:18). Therefore, in Genesis 2:5, the lack of thorns and thistles (weeds) and cultivated grain was merely because no rain had yet fallen. By the sixth day, humanity had not yet been created to work the fields, and most importantly, there had not yet been any sin, so there were no thorns or thistles. On the third day, God had indeed made wild seed-bearing vegetation and fruit trees (1:11–12) but as of yet, on the sixth there were no weeds or cultivated grains (2:5).

Differing Order of Creating Animals and Humans

The third allegation of two separate stories has to do with the order of the creation of animals and humans. It is claimed that in version one God made the animals first and then humans (Gen. 1:20–26) but in version two, God made Adam first (2:18–20) and then the animals. This alleged contradiction about the chronological order of creation can again be harmonized with a simple understanding of the Hebrew language.

According to Genesis 1:24–31, on the sixth day God made the animals first (vv. 24–25) and then He made humans (vv. 26–27). In the more detailed description of the creation of humanity (Gen. 2:4–25), there was no mention of the animals initially, but God formed man out of the dust of the earth (2:7). Then, to demonstrate that the man needed a female partner, the Lord brought a parade of animals to him and Adam gave them names (not Rover or Fido, but species names). Since this chapter had not yet mentioned the creation of animals, the verb in Genesis 2:19 should be translated as a pluperfect: "Out of the ground the Lord God *had* (previously) formed every beast of the field and every bird of the sky, and (now) brought them to the man . . ." The second chapter of Genesis details God's creation of humanity as male and female. The animals were only mentioned here to demonstrate that it was not good for the man to be alone and the previously created animals (Gen. 1:24–31) were not sufficient to fill the need for human partnership.

ONE UNIFIED CREATION STORY

By better understanding the literary context and Hebrew language, it is clear that there is one harmonious and consistent creation story in Genesis told in three movements, with each movement giving a more detailed look at God's creative activity. It's not two separate stories put together in a contradictory patchwork but a unified and consistent whole.

FINAL THOUGHTS

Most importantly, this unified creation story reveals that the Creator of the universe is the very same God who chose Abraham, Isaac, and Jacob, delivered the twelve tribes of Israel from Egypt, gave them the Sinai Covenant, and guided them through the wilderness to the Promised Land. Ultimately, the Creator, the God of Israel, became a man, Jesus of Nazareth, who died as a sacrifice to pay for sin and was raised from the dead, granting forgiveness and an eternal relationship to any person who trusts in Him.

The early chapters of Genesis are so confusing. How could God create light on the first day if He didn't create the sun, moon, and stars until the fourth day? And, after killing Abel, who did Cain fear would kill him and where did he find his wife? How did Noah fit all the animals on the ark?

S ome people struggle with believing the Bible because of the types of questions that are raised by the first eleven chapters of Genesis. There is a presumption that the biblical narrative doesn't make sense or that it's meant to be understood as a series of mythical stories. Probably the biggest issue I've heard people pose is how they can square God's creation of the world in six days with modern science (see Question 14). While some of these questions need longer explanations and the understanding that we will never know completely, I do believe there are some simple answers that will help. Let's look at some of the most common concerns in order.

LIGHT ON THE FIRST DAY

At first read, it doesn't seem possible that God would create light on the first day (Gen. 1:3–5) and then create the luminaries on the fourth day (Gen. 1:14–19). In fact, there couldn't be three days before the creation of the sun, since the earth rotates once in 24 hours in relation to the sun. The answer is relatively simple. God did create the luminaries on the first day, but He only declared their purpose on the fourth day.

The way the fourth day of the creation narrative is written is distinct from the other days, emphasizing the purposes of the luminaries, not their formation. A literal translation of Genesis 1:14–15 shows this: "'Let the lights in the expanse of the heavens be to separate the day from the night, and let them be for signs and seasons and for days and years; and let the lights be in the expanse of the heavens to give light on the earth'; and it was so." This passage includes three purpose clauses revealing why they were made on the first day: to separate day and night; to indicate signs, seasons, days, and years; and to give light to the earth. The middle purpose, related to signs and seasons, days and years is a significant preamble to the Law, since their purpose was to create a worship calendar for the people of Israel. The word "seasons" is the same Hebrew word used for "the Lord's appointed *times*," referring to the festivals of Israel (Lev. 23:2).

But why did God create them on day one and wait to declare their purpose on day four? This delay was part of the literary design of the six days of creation. According to the narrative, for the first three days God formed the world, and then, parallel to that creation, on the next three days, God filled the world. The following chart reveals this parallel structure.

FORMED	FILLED
Day	**Day**
1. Light/Darkness 1:3–5	4. Sun, Moon, Stars 1:14–19
2. Sky/Water Separated 1:6–8	5. Birds/Sea Creatures 1:20–23
3. Land/Vegetation 1:9–13	6. Animals/Man 1:24–31
RESTED	
Day 7 2:1–3	

Following this structure, the light and darkness were filled with the luminaries, the sky and water with birds and sea creatures, and the land and vegetation with animals and humanity. Waiting until the fourth day to declare the purpose of the luminaries was a literary device that followed the "formed and filled" pattern.

Having declared the purpose of the luminaries (Gen. 1:14–15), the story returns to their creation. So, the next verses (Gen. 1:16–17) should be understood to mean, "So God (and no other) had (previously) made the two great lights . . . and God had (previously) placed them in the expanse of the heaven . . ." This literary reading of the narrative explains how there could be light and even actual days for the first three days. The sun, moon, and stars were made on day one and their purposes were not declared until day four.

THE ENEMIES AND WIFE OF CAIN

After Cain killed his brother Abel, the Lord punished him by forcing him to "be a vagrant and a wanderer on the earth" (Gen. 4:12). Cain complained that "whoever finds me will kill me" (Gen. 4:14). Therefore, God gave Cain a special mark to keep anyone from attacking him (Gen. 4:15). Cain then traveled eastward, away from Eden, and settled in the land of Nod where he found a wife and had children (Gen. 4:16–17). The natural question arises, if Cain and Abel were the only two children of Adam and Eve, where did these other people come from? Who did Cain fear would attack him and where did he find his wife?

The simple answer is that Adam and Eve had other children who are not mentioned in the Genesis account. God told Adam and Eve to "be fruitful and multiply" (Gen. 1:28), and He gave the pre-flood people long lives (Adam lived 930 years; cf. Gen. 5:5). So it is logical that they could have had many more children. These other children may have had life stories not as significant as those of Cain, Abel, and Seth, so they were not included in the Genesis narrative. It also makes logical sense that Cain would have been fearful of his own siblings, nephews, nieces, and other relatives who desired vengeance for his murder of their relative.

Cain's wife was also one of his relatives—she might have been a sister, niece, or even a grandniece. Clearly, the Bible forbids incest, but if you are from the very first family, it would seem that there would have been no other choice for a mate. Furthermore, Adam and Eve had no mutant genes and therefore Cain's marriage to a relative would not have produced harmful traits in their children. Also, because of the long lives and childbearing years of Adam and Eve, Cain would likely have married someone whom he had not grown up alongside. The issue of Cain's enemies and wife is not difficult to resolve if we accept that biblical narratives are selective rather than comprehensive. The Bible does not include all the facts, just those pertinent for the reader.

THE ANIMALS ON THE ARK

Skeptics today love to mock the story of Noah and the flood, particularly the animals being brought onto the Ark. How could Noah have possibly fit all of those creatures on one small boat? How was he able to feed them? What about all that waste? Although the Bible treats the story as true (Isa. 54:9; Ezek. 14:14, 20; Matt. 24:37–38; Luke 17:26–27; Heb. 11:7;

2 Peter 2:5; 3:6), skeptics view it as a fairy tale. Yet, I assert that this story is true, and here's how it could have happened.

The Kinds of Animals

Three kinds of animals are mentioned in the biblical record: birds, land vertebrates (Hebrew *behemah*), and creeping things (Hebrew, *remes*, which can mean a number of things, but likely here it refers to reptiles). These would not have included sea creatures, fish, or water animals, which could survive a flood without an ark. Moreover, this would not include every species of animal, only their genera. With these limitations, Noah would only need to have brought some 16,000 animals on board.[11]

The Space on the Ark

People presume, incorrectly, that every animal was an adult and determine they would not have fit on the ark. But, more likely, Noah would have brought baby animals aboard. If that is so, then some have conjectured only 11 percent of the baby animals would have been larger than a sheep. And the average size of a baby animal would have been about that of a miniature Yorkshire Terrier. Still, would the ark have been large enough for even these small animals?

The ark measured 300 x 50 x 30 cubits (Gen. 6:15). If we estimate a cubit to be 18 inches, the size of the ark would have been 450 x 75 x 45 feet. The corresponding volume of the ark would be 1,518,750 cubic feet. A typical semitrailer of 48 x 13.5 x 8.5

feet has a volume of 5,508 cubic feet. Therefore, the ark would have been equivalent to 275 semi-truck trailers. According to the *Livestock Trucking Guide*, a triple-decker semitrailer can comfortably hold 302 wooly sheep. Therefore the ark could have carried 83,050 sheep, much more than the 16,000 estimated sheep sized animals that survived the flood on Noah's ark.[12]

The Practicalities of All Those Animals

Still people wonder about the practicalities of caring for those animals for 374 days (Gen. 8:14). There are some simple and reasonable ways that they could have been cared for. As for food, likely Noah brought compressed food and grains. It's also possible that many animals entered a state of hibernation, limiting the amount of food needed. Sufficient water was likely collected from all that rain. The floor of the ark would have been built on a slope to make for easy washing away of the refuse. These are just some simple possibilities to show that the story of Noah and the ark was not a fairy tale but indeed can be understood as an actual and true event.

FINAL THOUGHTS

There's no question that it takes faith for us to believe all of the accounts in the early parts of Genesis. But we have faith based on reasonable evidence. In addition, the main point of all these stories in Genesis is that there is a Creator, who loves us and to whom we are all accountable.

Many skeptics believe something much more incredulous: that all life, including humanity, evolved from a sudden bolt of lightning in the primordial soup. Further, they believe that life sprang from non-life, and then life randomly developed from one living cell to the complexity of our world. It takes far more faith to believe that humanity developed by mere chance than to believe that God made the sun, moon, and stars, that Cain married his sister, and that Noah saved the animal kingdom on the ark.

Who are the "sons of God" in Genesis 6:1-4? Did fallen angels really cohabit with earthly women? Who were the Nephilim?

M any people wonder about the statement that "the sons of God saw that the daughters of men were beautiful; and they took wives for themselves, whomever they chose" (Gen. 6:2). It is thought that out of these unions came the "Nephilim," a supposed race of giants that corrupted the earth (Gen. 6:4).

VIEW ONE: FALLEN ANGELS

One view of Genesis 6:1–4 does indeed understand the passage as referring to the unions of fallen angels ("sons of God") with humanity ("daughters of men"), resulting in a race of giants on the earth. In fact, "sons of God" is used elsewhere as a title for angels (Job 1:6). Moreover, some maintain that the New Testament affirms this interpretation when it speaks of "angels when they sinned" (2 Peter 2:4) and "did not keep their own domain, but abandoned their proper abode" (Jude 6).

But there are some problems with this interpretation. First, the phrase "sons of God" may mean angels but more frequently refers to humanity (Deut. 14:1; 32:5; Ps. 73:15; Isa. 43:6; Hos. 1:10; 11:1; Luke 3:38; 1 John 3:1–2, 10). Second, the New Testament passages in 2 Peter and Jude more likely only refer to angels following Satan in his rebellion against God and not sexual relations with women. Third, and most important, the Lord Jesus taught that angels were not capable of marriage and sexual reproduction (Matt. 22:30).

VIEW TWO: DYNASTIC RULERS

A second interpretation identifies the "sons of God" as dynastic rulers, primordial kings or despots who corrupted the earth by forming harems. Thus, their sin was polygamy. The support for this interpretation is that a king in the ancient Near East was frequently called a "son of god." However, this view also has some problems. First, while an individual king might have been called a "son of god" in the ancient Near East, there were never groups of dynastic kings called "the sons of God" as found in Genesis 6:2. Moreover, even though monogamy was the ideal for marriage in the Bible, it does not seem that polygamy was treated as a sin that was so great that it should lead to God's destruction of the world by flood. Considering the problems that Abraham caused by taking Sarah's advice about Hagar and the tensions between Jacob's wives, Leah and Rachel, it's surprising that God didn't cancel the Abrahamic covenant. If God didn't take the covenant away for polygamy, it's certain He wouldn't destroy the world over it.

VIEW THREE: THE RIGHT OF THE FIRST NIGHT

A third view, derived from the dynastic rulers' view, is called *the right of the first night*. This interpretation maintains that the "sons of god" were local dynastic rulers who demanded sexual relations with each new bride in their kingdoms on the night before the bride married her husband. In essence, local rulers raped each young woman before marriage. The support for this view comes from an ancient Babylonian work called *The Gilgamesh Epic* (2150–1400 BC), which asserts that Gilgamesh would have sexual relations with each bride before she was joined to her husband. Certainly, if there was a general right of such behavior in the ancient Near East, it was abominable and wicked.

The problem is that *the right of the first night* view does not seem to fit with what is happening in Genesis 6 for five key reasons: 1) The "sons of God took wives," a phrase used for marriage; 2) The Hebrew Bible would certainly use an expression like "he took her and lay with her by force" (Gen. 34:2) to describe this behavior, not words for marriage ("they took wives for themselves," Gen. 6:2); 3) The sinful behavior of these vile kings would not explain the corruption of the earth leading to God judging the earth with a flood; 4) This view presumes Moses, raised in Egypt, and the people of Israel, former slaves from Egypt and raised in the wilderness, were aware of a Babylonian epic without the benefit of the internet or cable news; and 5) The most compelling reason to reject the right of the first night view is that no such action is found anywhere in Scripture whatsoever.

THE INTERMARRIAGE OF THE GODLY
AND UNGODLY LINES

So what is the best interpretation? Genesis 6:1–4 is best understood as referring to *the intermarriage of the godly line of Seth and the ungodly line of Cain.* The genealogies in the context support this interpretation. The text recounts the genealogy of Cain, the first murderer (Gen. 4:17–24), immediately followed by the genealogy of Seth (Gen. 4:25–5:32), a godly line from which "men began to call upon the name of the LORD" (Gen. 4:26). After the listing of the two genealogies, Genesis 6:1–4 describes the uniting of these two groups (the Sethite sons of God and the Cainite daughters of men). The merging of these two lines produced offspring called the *Nephilim*, a Hebrew word that means "fallen ones," indicating that both lines were now corrupted. Although some consider these "fallen ones" to be superhuman giants, the more appropriate translation is "powerful," indicating that they became infamous as "the powerful men of old" (Gen. 6:4 HCSB). Regardless, their corrupting influence on the earth caused God's judgment of the world by flood in Noah's day (Gen. 6:8–8:22).

Although Canaanites are called *Nephilim* later in Numbers 13:31–33, they were not the physical descendants of those in Genesis 6 because all humanity was destroyed in the flood that followed the corruption of the earth. Rather, the use of *Nephilim* in Numbers more likely is identifying the Canaanites as a people who were both powerful and corrupt, like the *Nephilim* of Genesis 6.

FINAL THOUGHTS

There is a lesson in all this. Followers of the Lord Jesus should be careful to preserve their godly heritage. It is spiritually dangerous for a believer to marry someone who has not also become a committed follower of the Lord Jesus. As difficult as it is for two Jesus followers to raise a godly family, it is even harder for a spiritually divided couple to raise children that will love and fear the Lord.

QUESTIONS

about

THE OLD

TESTAMENT

Should followers of Jesus "unhitch from the Old Testament" or do we still need that part of God's Word?

18

Recently, a well-known and highly regarded Bible teacher declared that modern-day followers of Jesus need to "unhitch from the Old Testament." His words flew through social media, leading many to think that this teacher was somehow ready to cut the Old Testament out of our Bibles. But, let's be clear, he was in no way denying the full inspiration of the Old Testament. And, I believe the motive for his message was good. He was trying to help certain people who, having grown up with faith in Jesus and then having learned about the Old Testament, find the Old Testament laws troubling to their faith. He was saying that their faith was in Jesus, and their practice should be guided by the New Testament, not the Old Testament laws. Nevertheless, despite these good intentions, I think there is a better way to look at this issue. So, here are some reasons we still need the Old Testament (or as I like to call it, the Hebrew Bible).

TO BETTER UNDERSTAND
THE NEW TESTAMENT

We need the Hebrew Bible (the Old Testament) to better understand and appreciate the New Testament. Everything we read in the New Testament is based on the Old. Do you know that the New Testament quotes the Old Testament over 900 times? The New Testament bases many life principles on the Old Testament.

For example, Paul points out in Romans 4 that we get the principle of justification by faith from Genesis 15:6, where it says that Abraham believed God and it was reckoned to him for righteousness. Should we pay our pastors for teaching and shepherding us? Yes, in 1 Timothy 5:18, Paul quotes Deuteronomy 25:4, about not muzzling an ox, to make the case for paying your pastor. Try studying Jesus' words in the Sermon on the Mount without grasping the meaning of the Law of Moses. The Lord intensifies each of the commands to relate to our motives and intentions, not merely our actions. One last example: The New Testament prohibits immorality (1 Thess. 4:3) but doesn't specify what constitutes immorality. So, for example, there is no specific New Testament prohibition of incest. Does that mean that the New Testament approves of incest? Of course not. Anyone who has read Leviticus 18 and 20 would know that incest is considered highly immoral and so the New Testament prohibition of immorality would include incest. Without the Old Testament, the New Testament would become meaningless.

TO FULLY APPRECIATE
THE HOLINESS OF GOD

We also need the Hebrew Bible to fully appreciate the holiness of God. Too often we dismiss Leviticus, which details how Israel was to approach their holy God, with a "that was then, but this is now" attitude. But by revealing how the God of Israel was separate from sin, we can begin to appreciate what the Lord Jesus has done for us as our Great High Priest. Our holy God has not changed; rather, the Lord Jesus pioneered a new way for us to approach God with His holiness as Messiah representing us, just as the Old Testament prophets foretold. That's why, with Jesus as our High Priest, we can "draw near with confidence to the throne of grace" (Heb. 4:14–16).

TO RECOGNIZE THE MESSIANIC
CLAIMS OF JESUS

We also need the Hebrew Bible to recognize that Jesus is indeed the promised Messiah. It was through someone sharing the many predictions of the Messiah in the Hebrew Bible that I, and countless others, came to faith in Him. Some examples are Micah 5:2 about Jesus' birth in Bethlehem; and Isaiah 9:6 about Messiah being the unique God-Man; and Isaiah 52:13–53:12 about Messiah being our sacrificial substitute for sin.

Take a look at the book of Acts. There are two great truths that are used to proclaim Jesus. One of them is the resurrection of Jesus from the dead, a truth that is the essential basis of our faith. But the second great argument used in the book of Acts is that Jesus is the Messiah because He fulfilled the predictions of the Hebrew Bible. That's why Peter bases his first sermon in Acts on Jesus as the fulfillment of Old Testament prophecy (see Acts 2:22–36). In the middle of Acts, he says of Jesus the Messiah, "of Him all the prophets bear witness" (Acts 10:43). And the book of Acts ends with Paul persuading people "concerning Jesus, from both the Law of Moses and from the Prophets" (Acts 28:23). The apostles proclaimed faith in Jesus on the basis of the Old Testament (other passages in Acts that point to Jesus as the fulfillment of Old Testament prophecy are 3:21–26; 8:26–40; 13:26–41; 17:2–3, 11; 18:28; 26:22–23, 27).

TO LIVE ACCORDING TO GOD'S WISDOM

Another reason we need the Hebrew Bible is so we can live according to the wisdom of God. In Deuteronomy 4:6, Moses tells Israel, "Carefully follow them [the commandments], for this will show your wisdom and understanding in the eyes of the peoples. When they hear about all these statutes, they will say, 'This great nation is indeed a wise and understanding people" (HCSB). It is true that there are laws that have been adjusted by the New Covenant law of Christ (1 Cor. 9:21; Gal. 6:2). When we sin, we don't bring a sheep or a goat to the altar for forgiveness. But God gave the commandments as His divine wisdom. Therefore, there's an underlying wisdom principle in each commandment. If we understand what each commandment is saying, discern its wisdom principle, and live by that principle, we'll be wise in our walk with God. Here's an example: the command to keep the Sabbath is not repeated in the New Testament. But, if we're wise, we'll take a day (and according to Romans 14:5–6 we can choose whichever day we wish) and use it for both physical rest and spiritual renewal. That's not a New Testament command but an Old Testament wisdom principle.

FINAL THOUGHTS

Not too long ago I was at a conference and encountered Walter Kaiser, the great Old Testament scholar. I told him I was looking forward to his session but I was surprised that he was speaking on the New Testament. He replied, "I love the New Testament—it reminds me so much of the Old." His words capture the reason that New Testament followers of Jesus need to remain fervently hitched to both testaments, Old and New, because "all Scripture is inspired by God" (2 Tim. 3:16). We need all of it to "be complete, equipped for every good work" (2 Tim. 3:17 HCSB).

I wanted to read through the entire Bible this year but when I got into Leviticus, I got bogged down. I'm not sure I can finish. Why did God include Leviticus in the Bible?

'm sure you remember how exciting it was to start that Bible reading program; maybe it was on January 1st this past year. I'm guessing Genesis was fine for you, and Exodus seemed pretty good, at least more than half of it did, but then you came to Leviticus. Now you want to quit reading because your progress has come to a grinding halt.

Why do we find it so hard to read the book of Leviticus? One reason is that the Old Testament book is about sacrifices and rituals that no longer seem to matter to us. We no longer have a tabernacle or a temple. And, since there are no more sacrifices today, why should modern-day Christians bother reading Leviticus at all?

UNDERSTANDING THE HOLINESS OF GOD

The key to reading Leviticus is to remember that Leviticus is the Word of God. The book is not just filled with rules for ancient Israel, but it has transferable principles for our lives today. Leviticus contains truth that transcends time and culture. For example, one great aspect of Leviticus is that it reminds us of the holiness of God. Even though God desired a close fellowship with Israel, they couldn't enter His presence as if the Lord were their buddy or pal. God is the Creator of the universe, the king of the world, and His essence is glorious purity and total holiness. When we read the expansive list of rules about approaching God in Leviticus, we are reminded of just how holy He is. Most of us know that Peter's first New Testament letter reminds believers to be holy because God is holy. But do we realize that 1 Peter 1:16 is actually quoting from four separate verses from (you guessed it!) Leviticus (11:45; 19:2; 20:7, 26)?

UNDERSTANDING THE SIN OFFERING

Another example of a transferable truth from Leviticus is found in the entire sacrificial system. There are principles involved in all the different kinds of sacrifices, but the most foundational teaching is in the sin offering. Leviticus 4–5 shows how a sinner is to present an animal sacrifice (Lev. 4:28), by placing his or her hand on the sacrificial animal as a symbolic identification with the animal (v. 29). By this action, the sin was transferred from the person to the animal. The animal's death would follow (v. 29) and the sinning person would be forgiven and live (v. 31). This is a divine transaction—an exchange of life. The reason it is so important for us to understand the sacrifice is that without it we cannot fully understand the meaning of the Messiah Jesus' death for us. Jesus presented Himself to God as our sacrifice. Jesus identified with our sin while remaining sinless Himself (2 Cor. 5:21). Then the Lord Jesus died for us, paying the penalty for our sin (and rose again, proving He's God). If we have faith in His death and resurrection, then a great transaction takes place, His exchange of life. He died so that we might live.

The book of Hebrews reminds us that the Old Testament sacrifices never really took away sin but merely foreshadowed the coming sacrifice of the Messiah Jesus. Hebrews 10:4 declares: "For it is impossible for the blood of bulls and goats to take away sins." Those sacrifices pointed forward to the death of Messiah Jesus on our behalf. This whole idea of the Messiah Jesus' substitution is derived from the sin offering, as Paul states: "For what the law was powerless to do because it was weakened by the flesh, God did by sending his own Son in the likeness of sinful flesh to be a sin offering. And so he condemned sin in the flesh" (Rom. 8:3 NIV). This concept of Jesus' substitutionary sacrifice, that "God made Christ, who never sinned, to be the offering for our sin, so that we could be made right with God through Christ" (2 Cor. 5:21 NLT), wouldn't even be comprehensible without understanding the sin offering found in (surprise, surprise) the book of Leviticus.

WE ARE CONSECRATED PRIESTS

Here's one more example of the value of Leviticus for today: when the High Priest was consecrated to serve God, Moses took the ram of ordination, slaughtered it, and put some of its blood on Aaron's right earlobe, right hand, and the big toe of his right foot (Lev. 8:22–23). While this might seem weird, there was a purpose. The ear represents hearing; the thumb, doing; and the toe, walking. Basically, it was saying that the High Priest was to be consecrated to serve God every day in every way. He was separated for God's service, not just when he went into the tabernacle, but every minute of every day.

That's a great reminder to us because in Revelation 1:6, followers of Jesus are called "priests to [our] God and Father." We are mediating God's love to this world not just when we are at our congregations or serving in some ministry, but like Aaron, our whole lives—whether at work, school, or play—are to be consecrated to serving God (Col. 3:17). And this great principle is found in . . . wait for it, Leviticus.

FINAL THOUGHTS

There's so much more to Leviticus than can be addressed in this short space. But let's say this: Leviticus is God's Word and it can transform our lives. My own personal paraphrase of Proverbs 16:20, says, "He who gives attention to the Word, even the more challenging parts of it, will find good, and blessed is he who trusts in the Lord." So, I would encourage you to keep these key values in mind as you go back and read Leviticus.

As a follower of Jesus, can I claim the Old Testament promises made to Israel as my own?

Claiming biblical promises is one of God's great gifts to followers of Jesus. Peter says that through the Messiah Jesus' own glory and excellence, God "has granted to us His precious and magnificent promises, so that by them you may become partakers of the divine nature" (2 Peter 1:3–4). We do not want to claim promises that Scripture gave to someone else. However, we know the whole Bible is "breathed out by God" and designed to be "profitable for teaching, for reproof, for correction, and for training in righteousness, that the man [or woman] of God may be complete, equipped for every good work" (2 Tim. 3:16–17 ESV). How can we resolve the tension of knowing that some Scriptural promises were not given directly to us, while on the other hand, knowing that all Scripture should be relevant to our lives? The following are some interpretive principles for claiming promises of God in the Old Testament.

DETERMINE THE MEANING

Start by reading the biblical promise in its context to determine to whom it was given and what it meant for them. For example, one of the most beloved Old Testament promises is Jeremiah 29:11: "'For I know the plans I have for you,' declares the LORD, 'plans for welfare and not for calamity to give you a future and a hope.'" The context indicates that these words were found in a letter sent by Jeremiah to the leaders of the exiles of Israel in Babylon (Jer. 29:1). Additionally, the verse just previous to the promise states that the length of their captivity would only be 70 years (Jer. 29:10). The point of the promise in Jeremiah 29:11 is that although God had disciplined Israel with the exile, He had limited their captivity to 70 years, indicating that God's discipline was all part of His good plan for the nation. So, unless we are Israelites in the Babylonian exile, it's incorrect to claim this promise as directly belonging to us.

DISCOVER THE APPLICATION

A good rule of biblical interpretation is that although there is only one meaning to a given passage, there are many applications of that truth. That's why the whole Bible is profitable for us as members of the universal church, even if the direct meaning of a promise was designed for the people of Israel. So rather than claim the promise itself, we can apply the truth of that promise to our circumstances. Using Jeremiah 29:11, here's how to find the application.

IDENTIFY THE SIMILARITIES

Although a Gentile follower of Jesus is not part of ethnic Israel, there are a number of similarities, especially as they pertain to Jeremiah 29:11. The first resemblance is that just as Israel was chosen as a nation to represent God,[13] so we have been chosen as individuals for salvation (Eph. 1:4–5). So, just as God made promises to His elect nation, those promises must somehow apply to the chosen individuals who make up the church.

The second likeness is that just as God promised to discipline His chosen nation (Lev. 26:14–45), so the Lord promises to discipline individual believers as well (Heb. 12:7). The proof that God had adopted Israel was in His commitment to their correction. Likewise, discipline in the life of the believer is proof that we are His children.

The third similarity is that God designed Israel's national correction for their benefit, just as God's purpose for discipline in the lives of followers of Jesus is for our good (Heb. 12:10). The point of Jeremiah 29:11 is that God would use the devastation of the exile to restore Israel. Since the exile was intended for their well-being, it should give them hope for the future. In the same way, we can know that God uses the difficulties of our lives today, either to restore us to Him or to cause our spiritual growth. He does not allow us to suffer meaninglessly but with kind intentions for our good. That gives us hope for the future as well.

ARTICULATE THE PRINCIPLE

Having identified the similarities between Israel and us, we need to synthesize the truths of Jeremiah 29:11 into an enduring principle. The point of Jeremiah's promise to Israel was: Since God chose them for Him, He would use the difficulties they faced as means of correction and growth so they could have a hopeful future. In the same way, we can know that God chose you and me as His children and that He will use the difficulties and challenges of our lives for our correction and growth, giving us a hopeful future. As we walk with the Lord, when we struggle with difficulties, we can know that God has a good end in view, giving us a confident expectation as we anticipate the future (Phil. 1:6; 1 Thess. 5:24).

CONFIRM WITH THE NEW TESTAMENT

Having determined the simple meaning of a text and discovered the application, the third step in applying Old Testament promises is to confirm the application by comparing it to what is written in the New Testament. The promises should not be inconsistent. Jeremiah 29:11 indicates that God has a good purpose and plan for the difficulties we face, giving us a hopeful future. But does the New Testament also teach that? Absolutely! Specifically, in the most extensive New Testament passage about discipline, Hebrews 12:4–11, we are told that God uses difficulties in the life of a believer as a means of teaching and it is always done for our good. It even says that the outcome of persevering under difficulties will be good: "to those who have been trained by it, afterwards it yields the peaceful fruit of righteousness" (Heb. 12:11).

A second New Testament promise is that "God causes all things to work together for good to those who love God, to those who are called according to His purpose" (Rom. 8:28). A few years ago, a friend of mine, when he was in his early sixties, was laid off from a position he had held for many years. He was stressed because his circumstances were truly difficult and distressing. But when I asked how he was doing, he said this was just an opportunity for him to believe his life verse, Romans 8:28. He knew that God had a good plan in mind for him. In a sense, Romans 8:28 promises precisely the same thing as Jeremiah 29:11. All that to say, the New Testament confirms the principle given in Jeremiah's promise.

Just as an aside, here's an example of the reason New Testament confirmation is so crucial. In Deuteronomy 28:1–14, God promises Israel *material blessing* for obedience to the Law of Moses. The application could be that God promises us blessing for obedience to God's Word. However, the New Testament confirmation demonstrates that God promises *spiritual blessing* for obedience to the Scriptures, not material blessing (2 Peter 1:10–11). The New Testament clarifies the promise for us in the body of the Messiah, the church.

FINAL THOUGHTS

There's a popular and long-cherished praise song, *Every Promise in the Book is Mine:*[14]

> *Every promise in the book is mine,*
> *Every scripture, every verse, every line.*
> *All are blessings of His love divine,*
> *Every promise in the book is mine.*

Although the song contains a happy sentiment, it's not exactly true. We have to be careful to understand precisely to whom God gave each promise in His Word. Then, thoughtfully, we should develop a true and practical application of the promise, with confirmation from the New Testament. Although not every promise was written directly to us, the whole Bible is indeed profitable for us.

Will a spiritual revival heal our land of plagues, financial problems, and/or civil unrest?

It probably seems to all of us that 2020 will go down in history as the year of the plague. Many followers of Jesus were promoting the idea on social media that COVID-19 was a plague, a judgment of God, on our nation and world because we have abandoned the Lord and adopted all sorts of ungodly behavior.

Beyond the COVID-19 pandemic, that year included all sorts of other difficulties: economic stress, civil unrest, social isolation, and medical anxiety. In response to these challenges, many of God's people were advocating that if the United States would repent and experience a revival, God would relent and heal the land of the plague and all these other problems.

This isn't really a new idea. This same message was promoted during the economic downturn of the late 1970s and the great recession of 2008. Many turn to 2 Chronicles 7:14 to support the hope of revival as the key to the restoration of God's blessing on the United States. Here's how it reads in the most familiar way it is quoted: "If my people, which are called by my name, shall humble themselves, and pray, and seek my face, and turn from their wicked ways; then will I hear from heaven, and will forgive their sin, and will heal their land" (KJV).

The problem is, this verse isn't speaking about our nation or our difficult circumstances. Let's take a closer look.

THE ANCIENT TEMPLE IN JERUSALEM

First, we need to consider the biblical context. This passage is referring specifically to the ancient temple in Jerusalem, not Washington, DC or the United States. The verse falls in a chapter of Scripture detailing Solomon's dedication of the temple he built for the Lord. In 2 Chronicles 7:12–22, God gave His response to the temple dedication. God kept emphasizing the temple, saying He had "chosen this place for Myself as a house of sacrifice" (v. 12), that He would hear "prayer offered in this place" (v. 15), and that He had "consecrated this house [temple]" (v. 16). God also promised to destroy the temple in response to sin (v. 20). Of course, we have no holy temple in the United States and in fact, no temple exists anywhere today.

MY PEOPLE ISRAEL

Second, the phrase "My people, who are called by My name" refers to the people of Israel not to Americans, not even to American followers of Jesus. Throughout the whole Old Testament, the phrase "My people" refers to Israel. But, specifically, in 1 and 2 Chronicles, the phrase usually adds the word "My people Israel." In fact, in the books of Chronicles, God declared that David would be leader "over My people Israel"

(1 Chron. 17:7; cf. 1 Chron. 11:2), that He would "appoint a place [of worship] for My people Israel" (1 Chron. 17:9), and that He chose Jerusalem for His own namesake and for the Davidic dynasty to lead "My people Israel" (2 Chron. 6:5–6). So the phrase "My people" in 2 Chronicles 7:14 clearly refers to the people of Israel, not to Americans.

DISOBEDIENCE TO THE TORAH

Third, the sins described in 2 Chronicles 7:14 refer to disobeying the Torah (the Law of Moses). In verse 19, the sin of Israel is described as abandoning God's "statutes" and "commandments," words that describe the Law of Moses. Even the disciplines in the passage, "no rain" or "pestilence" (v. 13) are promised in Deuteronomy 28:21 and 24 as consequences of disobeying the Torah. In fact, ultimately, Israel would be dispersed from the land for their failure to obey the law of Moses. This isn't about the sins of the United States but the sins of the nation of Israel.

THE LAND OF ISRAEL

Fourth, the land to be healed was the land of Israel, not the United States. When God says He will heal their land, He is referring back to the promises in the Torah telling Israel that when they repent, God will restore them to their land (Deut. 30:1–6). This will yet take place "at the end of days" (Deut. 4:30), when the nation of Israel will turn to their Messiah Jesus in faith and God will circumcise their hearts (Deut. 30:6), so the whole nation will experience the New Covenant.

The evidence is clear: 2 Chronicles 7:14 doesn't really address any pandemic, economic downturn, civil unrest, natural disaster, or any other difficult circumstances in the United States. This is based on a crucial principle of biblical interpretation, that there is *only one meaning* to a given text of Scripture. This verse promises the restoration of the nation of Israel if they would repent.

APPLICATIONS FOR TODAY

There's another important principle to biblical interpretation. It is that although there can only be one meaning to a passage, there can be *many applications*. And we certainly can apply 2 Chronicles 7:14 today.

First, God desires revival in all places for all of His people. We are correct to think that God longs for the United States to have a mass return to Him by faith in Jesus. If God cared for Nineveh so much that He sent the prophet Jonah to preach to the pagan capitol of Assyria (Jonah 1:2; 3:2; 4:10–11), He certainly cares about our nation as well. Also, when Nineveh repented, God relented from the judgment that He was about to inflict on the Ninevites (Jonah 3:10). Similarly, if our nation repents, God will heal our land of sin and unrighteousness. He may even keep His hand of blessing on the United States of America. Nevertheless, revival in our nation will not necessarily lead to the ultimate end of any plague, economic problem, or civil unrest that may be afflicting our country.

This verse can also be applied to our local church congregations, and the New Testament confirms this principle. In 1 Corinthians 5, Paul dealt with a congregation that was tolerating an open immoral relationship (1 Cor. 5:1). In fact, they were boasting about it (1 Cor. 5:6), perhaps saying something like, "See how open and tolerant we are?" Paul exhorts this community of believers to "clean out the old leaven [a symbol of sin]" (1 Cor. 5:7), so they can be restored to God. Their own tolerance of sin led to the spread of sinful behavior, like yeast in dough, throughout the whole congregation. If the Corinthian church, or any other local congregation, "would humble themselves and pray" and turn from their sinful behavior, certainly God would restore it spiritually and revitalize that community of believers. Spiritual revival will bring spiritual renewal to our local congregations.

Perhaps most important of all, we can apply this verse to ourselves! If we have strayed from the Lord and decide to come back to Him, confessing our sin, we know that the blood of Jesus will cleanse us from all unrighteousness (1 John 1:9). Turning back to the Lord will bring God's restoration. This doesn't mean we'll be protected from getting a disease or that we're promised to recover if we do. It doesn't mean that we will gain material prosperity either. The focus of this truth is that God will heal our lives of sin and restore us spiritually to fellowship with Him (1 John 1:7).

FINAL THOUGHTS

So, should we pray for revival in the United States? Absolutely! The entire Bible confirms this. As the psalmist prayed, "Will You not Yourself revive us again, that Your people may rejoice in You?" (Ps. 85:6). God wants to use the difficulties and distress of our times, whether a worldwide disease, civil crises, or global financial crises, to cause all people to see their need for a Redeemer and turn to the Lord Jesus. He causes all things to work together for our good and for His glory (Rom. 8:28). If we turn back to Him, then our nation, even our world, will be healed of a far greater disease than COVID-19; it will be healed of sin.

I struggle so much with persistent sin and continue to face spiritual and physical problems. Is it possible that I'm under a generational curse?

A number of years ago, a friend of mine told me his twenty-something-year-old daughter was struggling with numerous health problems and asked if it was possible that she was under a generational curse. Other people have asked me if curses from past generations could have been passed down, causing spiritual problems in their lives.

These kinds of questions arise because certain Bible teachers have misinterpreted a few verses and developed a whole theology of generational curses. By generational curses, they mean that a curse that fell on one generation for sins committed in the past has been passed down to the next generation and then on and on. According to these teachers, these types of curses can cause demonic affliction on later generations even though these individuals did not actually commit the sins of the previous generations. As a result, these teachers have developed workshops and seminars on how to break generational curses, usually involving the alleged casting out of demons from believers and other sensational counteractions designed to break the chain of curses. Although their presentations seem powerful, they're actually based on weak and incorrect interpretation of God's Word.

EXAMINING THE CLAIM

As evidence for the existence of generational curses, people frequently cite the biblical commandment against worshiping idols which also states that God would visit "the iniquity of the fathers on the children, on the third and the fourth generations of those who hate Me" (Ex. 20:5). The same idea is stated elsewhere in the Torah (Ex. 34:7; Num. 14:18; Deut. 5:9). But it is a mistake to assume that these passages support the idea of generational curses.

The first reason is that the generational curse interpretations miss the point of these verses. They are all designed to emphasize that God's love and mercy is far greater than His just judgment. For example, after saying that God will visit "the iniquity of the fathers on the children, on the *third and fourth generations* of those who hate Me" (Exod. 20:5, italics added), the very next verse says that God will show "lovingkindness to *thousands*, to those who love Me and keep My commandments" (Exod. 20:6, italics added). The same message of God's greater mercy and love is found in Exodus 34:6–7, Numbers 14:18 and Deuteronomy 5:9–10. By reading these passages in context, we better understand the emphasis on God's mercy and love.

Second, these verses are not about curses caused by sin, but rather the consequences of sin. This is captured much more clearly in the CSB translation, which states that God will bring "*the consequences of the fathers' iniquity* on the children to the third and fourth generations of those who hate me, but showing faithful love to a thousand generations of those who love me and keep my commands" (Ex. 20:5–6, italics added). This passage identifies the reason parents must be careful to bring their sinful behavior to the Lord for forgiveness and transformation by Him. Sadly, studies have shown that alcoholism and substance abuse, adultery, anger, and emotional and physical abuse as well as other sins, cause damage, and too often these sins repeat themselves in the lives of the next generation. Heartbreakingly, children often follow in the footsteps of their parents and pass the consequence of that same sin on to the next generation. It's naïve and harmful to believe that the sinful behavior of one generation won't cause damaging consequences to the next generation and even the following one.

PRESENTING THE COUNTER-EVIDENCE

Old Testament Evidence

Although there are observable consequences of sinful behavior on the following generations, there are four biblical passages which present ideas that contradict the idea of generational curses. To begin, the Torah itself, in a section about capital crimes, declares "Fathers shall not be put to death for their sons, nor shall sons be put to death for their fathers; everyone shall be put to death for his own sin" (Deut. 24:16). The point of this command is that people are to be responsible for their own sins. Moreover, it is forbidden to take vengeance on family members for the sin of another, whether parents or children. If God were to send generational curses, He would be violating His own law.

Second, many years later, the prophet Ezekiel affirmed the above Mosaic commandment, stating, "The person who sins will die. The son will not bear the punishment for the father's iniquity, nor will the father bear the punishment for the son's iniquity; the righteousness of the righteous will be upon himself, and the wickedness of the wicked will be upon himself" (Ezek. 18:20). When a father or mother sinned, God would not respond by breaking His own principle, punishing the next generation with a generational curse for the parent's sin.

New Testament Evidence

A third way the Scriptures contradict generational curses is in the story of the healing of the man who was born blind (John 9). There, the disciples asked Jesus, "Rabbi, who sinned, this man or his parents, that he would be born blind?" (John 9:2). The implication of their question is that it would be possible for the punishment of the parents' sin to fall upon a newborn baby. The Lord Jesus answered, "It was neither that this man sinned, nor his parents; but it was so that the works of God might be displayed in him" (John 9:3). The disciples had adopted the mistaken ideas of Job's friends, that all suffering is a direct result of personal, or even parental, sin. Although suffering is indeed a result of living in a fallen world, caused by Adam's sin, the Lord Jesus makes it plain that the man's blindness was not a result of sin, committed by the parents or the man. Rather, the man was born blind so that God would be glorified in him. In this way, the Lord Jesus Himself repudiates any idea of a generational curse that would cause the man to be born blind.

Fourth, the apostle Paul reminds us that it is impossible for a follower of the Lord Jesus to experience condemnation. He writes, "Therefore there is now no condemnation for those who are in Christ Jesus" (Rom. 8:1). A generational curse would be a punishment and condemnation passing from one generation to the next. Even if that were possible (which all the above Scriptures indicate that it's not), then trusting in Jesus would immediately break any condemnation. To be clear and plain, the idea of generational curses goes against the consistent teaching of Scripture.

BREAKING THE CYCLE

Although the Bible rejects any form of generational curses, it is possible for the consequences of parental sin to be passed from generation to generation. In light of that, is it possible to stop the consequences and break the cycle of sin? Absolutely! A child of alcoholics or drug abusers does not have to relive those issues. The Bible gives hope for breaking the cycle of sin in four ways.

A New Creation

First, when a person comes to know the Lord, trusting in Jesus as their Redeemer and Leader, he or she becomes a new creation. Paul writes, "Therefore if anyone is in Christ, he is a new creature; the old things passed away; behold, new things have come" (2 Cor. 5:17). Coming to know the Lord has a transformational effect—we have a new capacity for obedience to God. God sees us as united to the Messiah Jesus. We really do become new people.

A New Spiritual Power

A second way that God empowers us to overcome the consequences of parental sins is through the indwelling Holy Spirit. The apostle Paul is clear—once we come to know the Lord Jesus, the Holy Spirit dwells in all of us. In fact, Paul says, "if anyone does not have the Spirit of Christ, he does not belong to Him" (Rom. 8:9). Clearly, the opposite must be true—if anyone belongs to Christ, he has the Spirit of Christ dwelling in him.

Paul clarifies the significance of the indwelling Holy Spirit and the patterns of sin into which we may have fallen. He declares, "But if the Spirit of Him who raised Jesus from the dead dwells in you, He who raised Christ Jesus from the dead will also give life to your mortal bodies through His Spirit who dwells in you" (Rom. 8:11). The simple point of this is that the very power that was potent enough to raise the Lord Jesus from the dead dwells in us and will enable us to break the cycle of sinful patterns. As we learn to appropriate the Holy Spirit's power, sin will no longer reign over us and these habitual or even instinctual sins will lose their hold over us. Even though there are no generational curses, there are certainly generational consequences for sin. What God has done by creating us anew and empowering us by the power of the Holy Spirit is strong enough to break harmful family patterns of sin.

A New Community

Third, when we follow Jesus, we are put into a new community, the body of Christ. This community is "built on the foundation of the apostles and prophets" and "growing into a holy temple in the Lord, in whom you also are being built together into a dwelling of God in the Spirit" (Eph. 2:20–22). Not only is the Spirit of God at work in individual followers of Jesus, He is building us into a community that looks more and more like Jesus.

That's why the author of Hebrews encourages us to keep meeting together so that we can "stimulate one another to love and good deeds" (Heb. 10:24–25). It's also the reason being part of a congregation is so vital—it is one way God works to help us break the cycle of sinful patterns we may have learned from our parents. Just as alcoholics need to go to AA meetings to help stay on the path of sobriety, so we, as recovering sinners, need to be in our home congregations to help us on the path to obedience, thereby breaking the cycle of sin.

A Renewed Mind

A fourth way we can break the cycle of parental sins is through the renewing of our minds. Paul urged followers of Jesus to "be transformed by the renewing of your mind" (Rom. 12:2). The Scriptures are central to biblical mind renewal.

This follows the basic computer programming principle of "garbage in, garbage out." When we program our thoughts with the excellence of God's Word, God uses it to produce obedience in us. Therefore, we need to read, memorize, and meditate on the Scriptures to experience transformed lives (Ps. 1:1–3; 119:9–11).

FINAL THOUGHTS

I know a man whose father was violent, angry, and abusive. As a boy, this child vowed never to be like his dad. Many years later, having married and raised a family, a friend asked him how it was that he was able to be such a loving dad and reject his father's behavior, thus breaking this sinful pattern. This man thought for a moment and said, "As a child, I was determined that whatever my dad did, I would do the opposite. But I would never have been able to fulfill that promise, except that as a teenager, I trusted in Jesus as my Redeemer and Lord. He made me into a new creature, gave me His Holy Spirit, and gave me the Scriptures to guide me and fellow believers to encourage and strengthen me. That's how God did it, not me." Clearly, this man demonstrates that the patterns of parental sins need not be replicated in the next generation because God's "divine power has granted to us everything pertaining to life and godliness" (2 Peter 1:3) in order to break the consequences of sin from one generation to another.

Did God allow polygamy in the Old Testament?

I t is not surprising that many people assume that God permitted polygamy in the Old Testament. There are many examples of men with multiple wives, from patriarchs to kings. In fact, some contend that regulations in the Law of Moses endorse polygamy. Why does it seem that God allowed polygamy, when at creation He intended one man for one woman? Let's examine what the Scriptures actually say about this.

GOD'S CREATION OF MARRIAGE

At the time of creation, God fashioned the very first woman, Eve, from Adam's rib, and brought her to the man (Gen. 2:18–22). Upon seeing his wife, Adam burst into a song of joy (Gen. 2:23). Then Moses, the human author of Genesis, breaks into the story, giving the divine perspective on the creation of marriage. He states, "For this reason a man shall leave his father and his mother, and be joined to his wife; and they shall become one flesh" (Gen. 2:24).

This verse explains the God-ordained institution of marriage. Marriage, as God intended, has several components. The first is *independence*. A man leaves his family home and creates a new family unit with his wife. Second, marriage must be *exclusive*, meaning it is between one man and one woman.

There isn't the hint of polygamy in this text. Third, marriage is to be *permanent*, seen in the word "joined" (some versions use the word "cling"). The same Hebrew verb (*dabaq*) is used of Ruth clinging permanently to her mother-in-law Naomi (Ruth 1:14) and referring to Hezekiah's faithful commitment to the Lord (2 Kings 18:6). It has the idea of holding on and not letting go, showing that marriage was designed to be a permanent relationship. The fourth aspect of marriage is *unity*. Although some only see marital sex in the phrase "they shall become one flesh," it actually depicts a couple that had become unified as a new family unit. Therefore, sexual union is merely an expression of the unity between a husband and wife.

The establishment of the institution of marriage as described in Genesis makes it apparent that God's intention for marriage was that it was to be between one man and one woman for life. There was no hint of bigamy or polygamy in God's creation plan.

BIBLICAL EXAMPLES OF POLYGAMY

Despite the evident expectation of monogamy in God's establishment of marriage, Scripture gives numerous examples of men with multiple wives. These examples should not be viewed as an endorsement of bigamy or polygamy but rather as man's rebellion against God's prescriptive will. For example, the very first person to take multiple wives was Lamech (Gen. 4:19), yet this account is found in the midst of the rebellious line of Cain (Gen. 4:17–24).

Other cases include Abram, who succumbed to his wife's idea of taking Hagar as a concubine. Yet, Scripture never portrays this action as a good choice. In fact, Genesis 16 uses language similar to Genesis 3, deliberately associating Sarai's suggestion with Eve's temptation, including the sentence "And Abram listened to the voice of Sarai" (Gen. 16:2), calling to mind Genesis 3:17: "Because you have listened to the voice of your wife . . . ." The rest of the story demonstrates the disastrous consequences of Abram's choice.

Certainly, the example of Jacob taking two wives while living with his pagan Uncle Laban was not intended to be understood as proper behavior (Gen. 29:1–30). Likewise, David's marriage to multiple wives set up his ultimate failure with Bathsheba (2 Sam. 11) and led to his many difficulties later in life. Solomon's decision to marry 700 women and to maintain a harem with 300 concubines was not recorded as an example of someone obeying the Word of God. In fact, these women turned Solomon's "heart away after other gods" (1 Kings 11:3–4). It's plain in Scripture that although people practiced bigamy or polygamy, it was never presented as if these practices were good or obedient to God's intention for marriage.

ALLEGED EVIDENCE FOR POLYGAMY

There are only five passages that seem to support biblical approval for having more than one wife. But do they really endorse polygamy? Let's examine them.

Exodus 21:7–11

The law of Exodus 21:7–11 has to do with a young girl being sold to a man in payment of a debt, initially to serve as a servant girl but in the future, when she comes of age, as a bride. In our culture, selling a young girl to another household to serve as an indentured servant and ultimately as a wife would be morally reprehensible, but in biblical times all fathers received a bride price for giving their daughters in marriage. This law was designed to protect the rights of a young woman sold before reaching marriageable age. The servant girl was not to be released in her seventh year, as was a male indentured servant. Instead, her master could choose to marry her or to have his son marry her. Many modern English versions follow the ancient Greek Bible (the Septuagint) in their translations and therefore misunderstand Exodus 21:8. My own literal translation is, "If she is displeasing in the eyes of her master, who does not designate her (or betroth her), then he must allow her to be redeemed (for a price). He has no right to sell her to a foreign people because of his deceit of her (in not marrying her)." It goes on to say if he does betroth her to his son, he must treat her as he would his own daughter (Ex. 21:9) and not as a servant.

The support for polygamy is often found in verse 10, it being understood that he has taken an "additional wife" (HCSB). But the word translated "wife" could just as well be translated "woman," which fits the context. Since he has not designated this servant girl as his own wife, he chooses "another woman" as his wife. If the servant girl is not redeemed by another so she stays in his household, he may not diminish her "food, her clothing, or her conjugal rights."

Of course, use of the words "conjugal rights" makes it seem as if the man has taken an additional wife. However, the Hebrew word translated this way only appears here in the Old Testament. It's not clear that it even means "conjugal rights." It is translated this way only because the ancient Greek version guessed that it was its meaning, so English versions have followed suit.

Some have suggested that it referred to her daily allotment of ointment or oil.[15] Another, more likely, possibility is that the word is derived from an altogether different Hebrew root meaning "dwelling"[16] and refers to her right to stay in the household even with a different wife there. If the man did not provide these three items (food, clothing, lodging), according to verse 11, the girl was to be released without paying the man a redemption price for her. Admittedly, this passage is fairly difficult to interpret, but, once translated carefully, it really specifies treatment of a servant girl and does not endorse polygamy.

Leviticus 18:18

The prohibition found in Leviticus 18:18 is that a man is not to "marry a woman in addition to her sister as a rival while she is alive, to uncover her nakedness." Some presume that this only prohibits taking a sister-in-law as a second wife while any other woman would be permissible. In light of

God's establishment of marriage as being between one man and one woman (Gen. 2:24), it seems better understood as a prohibition of a specific kind of polygamy. In addition to the general ban on multiple wives, this forbidding of marrying one's sister-in-law would be necessary for the community of Israel to learn this in light of Jacob's marriages to sisters Leah and Rachel (Gen. 29:21–30). The people of Israel were not to consider their patriarch's actions as a valid exception to the prohibition of polygamy and therefore, they were not to practice Jacob's same vexing sin of marrying two sisters.

Deuteronomy 21:15–17

Deuteronomy 21:15–17 describes a man having had sons with two different wives, one loved and the other unloved. If the son of the unloved wife is the firstborn, the father may not prioritize the son of the loved wife over him when making his will. It states, "he cannot make the son of the loved the first-born before the son of the unloved, who is the firstborn. But he shall acknowledge the firstborn, the son of the unloved, by giving him a double portion of all that he has" (Deut. 21:16–17). The presumption of many is that this discussion demonstrates that having two wives was lawful.

Two responses must be considered. First, this law is dealing with inheritance rights, not lawful marriage. While it is dealing with a problem that might come up if someone were to break the law of monogamy, it should not be read as endorsing bigamy. Rather it is seeking to regulate the problems that ensued when God's people disobeyed His command for monogamy.

Second, it need not be assumed that this is discussing a man having two wives at the same time. The Hebrew verb tenses are not concerned with time. Therefore, it could be understood to discuss the problems that might ensue when a man has had two wives in succession and wants to treat the son of the second wife, whom he loves, as if he were the firstborn. Regardless, this passage is certainly not an endorsement of having two wives at the same time and may not even address that issue at all.

Deuteronomy 25:5–10

In Deuteronomy 25:5–10, Moses gives the law of levirate marriage (from the Latin word *levir,* a husband's brother), calling for a brother to marry his dead brother's widow. The purpose of such a marriage was to raise a child to inherit the dead brother's name and property, and thereby keep the inheritance in the family. Some believe that levirate marriage would be required even if the surviving brother was already married and therefore consider it God-ordained bigamy. Others do not see this as a blanket endorsement of multiple wives but a permitted exception to monogamy under these circumstances alone.

It seems better to see levirate law as requiring an *unmarried* brother to raise up the heir for his dead brother. The only examples of levirate marriage in Scripture involved unmarried men (Gen. 38; Ruth 3–4). But what if the brother was married? Then he would be disqualified and another unmarried relative would need to take up the role as kinsman-redeemer. This is perfectly acceptable because the Hebrew word for "brother" is elastic enough to mean "relative." Thus, Boaz, who was only a relative and not a brother, could act as the kinsman-redeemer for Ruth (Ruth 4:6–10).

2 Samuel 12:7-8

After David committed the sin of adultery with Bathsheba, Nathan the prophet came to rebuke him. Speaking for the Lord, he recounted for David all that God had done for him, including "I also gave you your master's house and your master's wives into your care, and I gave you the house of Israel and Judah" (2 Sam. 12:8). Some have taken this to mean that God gave Saul's wives to be David's wives, thereby showing God's approval of polygamy.

This is unlikely because the Law of Moses prohibited kings from having multiple wives (Deut. 17:17). The verse is actually saying that the Lord gave into David's care everything that had been Saul's, including his household, his kingdom, and his women (a more likely translation than wives). Renowned Old Testament scholar Walter C. Kaiser Jr. concludes that this is not saying that the Lord gave Saul's wives to David but rather Saul's women. These included giving David the oversight of Saul's female domestics and courtiers, in fact "everything was placed under the control and supervision of David much as a conquering king exhibited his full victory over a subjugated nation by taking control of the defeated king's household."[17]

FINAL THOUGHTS

God created marriage to be between one man and one woman for life. He didn't create marriage to be monogamous, only to change His mind to allow polygamy in the Law of Moses, and then change it back to monogamy in the New Testament. Rather, God always intended marriage to be monogamous.

Why would the Law of Moses require a woman to marry the man who raped her? This just seems so wrong.

I f you browse atheistic websites or books criticizing the Scriptures, you may hear the allegation that the Law required a woman to marry her rapist. This supposed fact is used to support the claim that the Bible is morally suspect and oppressive to women. But is it true? A careful reading of the Bible will show that the Law of Moses did not require a woman to marry her rapist.

This question comes from a misunderstanding of Deuteronomy 22:28–29: "If a man finds a girl who is a virgin, who is not engaged, and seizes her and lies with her and they are discovered, then the man who lay with her shall give to the girl's father fifty shekels of silver, and she shall become his wife because he has violated her; he cannot divorce her all his days." Various Bible versions (e.g., NIV, CSB) translate the words "seizes her" as "rapes her" and so it certainly may seem that this woman would be forced to marry her rapist.

But a closer reading of Scripture shows that this verse was actually designed as a protection for a young women. It focuses on a woman who has been seduced by a man and engaged in consensual sexual relations with him. A closer look at the original meaning of the phrase "seizes her" shows that this should be understood as referring to seduction, not rape. Here's why:

THE CONTEXT OF THE LAW

The context of this statute indicates that this phrase refers to seduction and not rape. The previous paragraph (Deut. 22:25–27) describes the law about an actual rape and uses a different Hebrew verb (*chazaq*), meaning "forces" or "overpowers." The word used in the passage under discussion has a different word (the Hebrew verb *tapas*), translated "seizes," indicating that there is a distinction in meaning being made with the rape of the previous verse. The word *chazaq* clearly indicates force, but the word *tapas* used here does not imply any kind of forcible attack or assault. The lexical differences of these two different verbs and the nearness of their uses in two adjoining paragraphs indicate that these refer to two different situations—the first to rape and the second to seduction.

Another distinction with the previous paragraph (Deut. 22:25–27) is that rape is treated differently than the situation being discussed in this passage (Deut. 22:28–29). First, in determining whether a rape occurred, the girl cried out but there was no one present to hear her (Deut. 22:27). In the second case, the issue of crying out is not even raised, demonstrating that a forcible attack was not being addressed. Second, the consequences are different in the two paragraphs. In the first case of rape, there was no charge against the woman but the punishment for the rapist would be execution; the crime of rape was viewed as a capital offense (Deut. 22:25). In the case of seduction, the consequence for the man was to marry the woman he mistreated (Deut. 22:29). He was not allowed to love her and leave her. He had to take responsibility for the woman. By reading the passage in context, it is evident that the issue being addressed in Deuteronomy 22:28–29 is seduction and not rape.

THE SENSE OF THE VERB

The verb in Deuteronomy 22:28–29, translated "seizes," literally means "captures" or "takes hold of." Yet, it can have a figurative sense, as it does in Ezekiel 14:5, in the phrase "to lay hold of the hearts". The sense is more of persuasion than assault. The same verb is also used in the story of Potiphar's wife's seduction of Joseph, when she *seized* him, seeking to persuade him to sleep with her (Gen. 39:12). The verb itself can have the idea of capturing a woman's feelings, not forcible sexual assault.

INTERACTION WITH OTHER PASSAGES

Additionally, Deuteronomy 22:28–29 must be read intertextually, meaning in association to other passages of Scripture. First, the parallel law, found in Exodus 22:16–17, uses a different Hebrew verb (*patah*), translated "entice," and plainly refers to seduction, not rape. This is important because the passage in Exodus is referring to the same situation as in Deuteronomy. Exodus contains the first statement of this law, while Deuteronomy is a repetition and exposition of that same law. If the first statement of the law was clearly referring to seduction, so then the second one (Deut. 22:28–29) must also refer to seduction.

Second, when examining all the rape stories found in the Bible (Judg. 19:25; 2 Sam. 13:11–14), they use the verb "over-power," as found in the rape law in the previous paragraph. They never use the verb *tapas* used in Deuteronomy 22:28–29, showing that rape was considered distinct from seduction.

SUMMARY OF THE MATTER

To summarize, the law in Deuteronomy 22:28–29 is about a man who took hold of a virgin, or seduced her, so that she consented to have sexual relations with him. It describes a man's behavior that could include using sweet words or flattery but not physical force (i.e., rape). The resulting danger would be that, after having slept with this young woman, he would cast her aside and bring shame to her. Therefore, as Old Testament scholar Meredith Kline states, the law requires that this "seducer of an unbetrothed virgin was obliged to take her as wife, paying the customary bride price and forfeiting the right of divorce."[18]

FINAL THOUGHTS

Although this law might be offensive to modern sensibilities, it was not designed to be unkind to a young woman but actually to protect her from having a man take advantage of her. It was intended to protect her honor and, even more, to prevent her from destitution. In that culture, marriage was a necessity for economic stability. If she slept with this man consensually and he did not marry her, it would be unlikely that another man would take her as a wife. Moreover, this law provided financial support for a child that might have been born of this illicit union and served as a deterrent against seduction, premarital sex, and abandonment. So rather than see this law as harmful to a woman, it should be viewed as helpful. Moreover, it guarded against the exploitation of women and held men accountable for their sexual behavior.

How is it possible to justify God's command that Israel destroy the Canaanites?

While it may be understandable for us to wonder at God's command that issued such destruction, it is always helpful to look at the event in question in context. This command was given to the people of Israel by God at the end of their 40 years in the wilderness. As they were about to enter the Promised Land, they were told: "When the Lord your God brings you into the land where you are entering to possess it, and clears away many nations before you, the Hittites and the Girgashites and the Amorites and the Canaanites and the Perizzites and the Hivites and the Jebusites, seven nations greater and stronger than you, and when the LORD your God delivers them before you and you defeat them, then you shall utterly destroy them. You shall make no covenant with them and show no favor to them" (Deut. 7:1–2; cf. Ex. 23:32–33; 34:12–16; Deut. 20:15–18).

God's command for Israel to utterly destroy the Canaanites is one of the most commonly raised objections to the God of the Bible as a just and loving God. Atheist Richard Dawkins charges, "The God of the Old Testament is arguably the most unpleasant character in all fiction: jealous and proud of it; a petty, unjust, unforgiving control-freak; a vindictive, bloodthirsty ethnic cleanser; a misogynistic, homophobic, racist, infanticidal, genocidal, filicidal, pestilential, megalomaniacal, sadomasochistic, capriciously malevolent bully."[19] Dawkins's words are clearly over the top, yet they echo the concerns of many. The Lord's requirement that Israel annihilate the Canaanites certainly raises serious issues about the mercy and love of God. How could He tell the Israelites to "show them no mercy" (Deut. 7:2 CSB)? To be blunt, there are no easy answers to this question, but there are several perspectives that help resolve the moral questions raised by the destruction of the Canaanites.

NOT A GENERAL PRINCIPLE
BUT AN ISOLATED CIRCUMSTANCE

The commanded destruction of the Canaanites was not a general principle of war and conquest in Scripture; this appears to be an isolated circumstance. Israel was not told to destroy every other nation they were to encounter. In fact, as a general rule, the Lord told Israel that when they went to war, they were to offer the enemy "terms of peace" (Deut. 20:10). God's command to destroy was limited to the seven nations of Canaan (Deut. 7:1–2; 20:17). Clearly, this command was not a general rule for Israelite warfare in every place and every battle. Rather, it was limited in scope and time only to the conquest of Canaan, a one-time event.

NOT AN ETHNIC GENOCIDE
BUT A DIVINE JUDGMENT

Generally, genocide stems from the ethnic hatred between tribes or nations. But in the case of this one-time destruction of the Canaanite nations, it was not driven by Israel's ethnic hatred for these nations or because of their pent-up desire to murder and destroy. It wasn't ethnic cleansing at all that motivated these actions but divine judgment by the Lord God Himself. The Lord had decided the time had come to judge the Canaanites for their debauchery. This act should not be viewed as genocide but a case of capital punishment, applied on a national scale.

God gave this as His explanation for His actions to Israel, declaring "the land has become defiled, therefore I have brought its punishment upon it, so the land has spewed out its inhabitants" (Lev. 18:25). We must remember that God is just in His judgments and so He demanded, in this case, that Israel be the instrument of His judgment on Canaan. Similarly, acting as a righteous judge, God would bring judgment on Israel and Judah through the Assyrians and Babylonians. As human beings, we tend to object to God bringing His just judgment on ourselves or on anyone else. At those times, we must remember that He is God and we are not. His acts of judgment may not be clear to us from a human perspective; nevertheless, they are just.

NOT ETHNIC IDENTITY,
BUT EXTREME WICKEDNESS

God declared, "It is because of the wickedness of these nations that the LORD your God is driving them out before you" (Deut. 9:5). As mentioned earlier, God was acting in righteous judgment against the wickedness of the Canaanites. But were they really that bad? Actually . . . yes. Even by ancient standards, the Canaanites were especially morally depraved. Their idolatrous fertility cults led to debauched sexuality to the extreme. I was especially struck by this when visiting the Israel Museum's archaeology wing, seeing the display of ancient Canaanite idol figurines, both male and female, with grotesquely enlarged genitalia. The worship of these false gods produced all sorts of sexual perversity, including adultery, temple prostitution, pederasty, bestiality, and incest. They also practiced divination, witchcraft, and human sacrifice. These sins were so severe that God said He would spew them out of the land as a consequence (Lev. 18:19–25). When God commanded Israel to destroy the Canaanites it was not because they were an unfavored people group or because of Israel's ethnic hatred for them. It was the God of justice coming to the end of His patience with these morally corrupt peoples and finally bringing them to judgment.

NOT IMPATIENT OR INTEMPERATE,
BUT LONGSUFFERING PATIENCE

Was God impatient or intemperate with the Canaanites, suddenly exploding with rage without expectation or warning? Certainly not! If you go back to God's confirmation of the Abrahamic Covenant in Genesis 15, the Lord told Abraham that his descendants would spend 400 years in Egypt prior to their return to the Promised Land. God could easily have granted Abraham possession of Canaan immediately. He did not do so because, as He told Abraham, "the iniquity of the Amorite[20] is not yet complete" (Gen. 15:16). God would patiently tolerate the sins of the Canaanites until Abraham's descendants would bring retributive justice upon them with the conquest under Joshua.

The longsuffering patience of God is similar to His attitude toward pagans found in Romans, saying that "God gave them over" to their lusts, to degrading passions, and to a depraved mind (Rom. 1:24, 26, 28). In this case, God did not launch immediate judgment but rather tolerated their dreadful behavior, allowing them to go farther and farther into sin than was even imaginable. An impatient or intemperate God would have destroyed all the Canaanites when Abraham entered the land. His patience allowed them to expand their revolt against the Lord until their iniquity was complete, hundreds of years later.

NOT DIVINE VINDICTIVENESS
BUT DIVINE PROTECTION

Despite God's patience, some might object that He could have granted Israel access to Canaan without necessarily destroying the Canaanites. Couldn't they have simply shared the land? Perhaps so, but God was concerned about protecting Israel and keeping them from the ungodly influence of the Canaanites' sins. He told Israel that His policy of destroying the Canaanites was "so that they may not teach you to do according to all their detestable things which they have done for their gods, so that you would sin against the LORD your God" (Deut. 20:18). The legitimacy of this concern is evident in that the Israelites did not obey the Lord and "did not drive out the inhabitants" of the land (Judg. 1:27–33). The horrific consequences of this were that "the sons of Israel lived among the Canaanites . . . and they took their daughters for themselves as wives, and gave their own daughters to their sons, and served their gods. The sons of Israel did what was evil in the sight of the LORD, and forgot the LORD their God and served the Baals and the Asheroth" (Judg. 3:5–7). Israel's failure to carry out the Lord's command led to the very danger from which the Lord sought to protect them. As a result, the *Canaanization* of Israel led to the disasters of the days of the judges, when "every man did what was right in his own eyes" (Judg. 17:6; 21:25).

But why destroy the children? As painful as this must have been, it was a needed protection for Israel. First, because these children would grow up, pursue the same abominable practices as their parents, and then influence Israel to abandon the Lord. Second, it was necessary because as adults, they would pursue vengeance against the people of Israel for having carried out the destruction of their parents. God was protecting Israel from nations of men who would live to execute vengeance against the nation that killed their fathers.

FINAL THOUGHTS

Walter C. Kaiser Jr. suggests one last thought about the destruction of the Canaanites. He says all prophecies or forecasts of doom have "a suppressed 'unless' attached to them."[21] When Jonah proclaimed, "Yet forty days and Nineveh will be overthrown" (Jonah 3:4), there was an implied "unless you repent" appended to that prediction. And repent Nineveh did, so "when God saw their deeds, that they turned from their wicked way, then God relented concerning the calamity which He had declared He would bring upon them. And He did not do it" (v. 10).

The Canaanites, like the Ninevites, were warned of their impending doom. Had they responded as Rahab did (Josh. 2:8–14), with faith in the God of Israel and repentance for their abominable deeds, there certainly would have been a better outcome for them. Just as Rahab, along with her family, was spared in the destruction of Jericho (Josh. 6:25), it's likely that there would have been a brighter and better end for the Canaanites.

Did Jephthah actually offer his daughter as a human sacrifice (Judg. 11:29–40)?

In the book of Judges, we read the story of a great warrior named Jephthah. Asking God for victory, Jephthah made an impulsive vow. Many believe that this promise led to Jephthah sacrificing his only daughter as a burnt offering. This account is certainly troubling on many levels. But the most basic is that human sacrifice was explicitly forbidden under God's Law: "There shall not be found among you anyone who burns his son or his daughter as an offering" (Deut. 18:10 ESV). How could a judge of Israel, commended for his valor (Judg. 11:1) and faith (Heb. 11:32), commit such a heinous sin? The answer is: he didn't. Keep reading.

JEPHTHAH'S STORY

Jephthah was the illegitimate son of a prostitute. This fact caused his half brothers, the sons of Gilead, to disown him. Nevertheless, he became a great warrior. Later on, after the Ammonites made war with Israel, the leaders of Gilead, the very ones who had cast him out, appealed to Jephthah to lead them in battle. If Jephthah led them to victory, they promised to make him their leader (Judg. 11:1–11). Therefore, Jephthah sought to negotiate with the Ammonites but they refused him. So Jephthah battled the Ammonites, and the Lord granted Jephthah a great victory (Judg. 11:12–28, 32–33). Thus, he became the eighth judge of Israel.

JEPHTHAH'S VOW

Despite his military success, Jephthah's one major failure was the rash vow he made as he went to battle the Ammonites. He swore that if the Lord enabled him to defeat the Ammonites, "then it shall be that whatever comes out of the doors of my house to meet me when I return in peace from the sons of Ammon, it shall be the Lord's, and I will offer it up as a burnt offering" (Judg. 11:30–31). Much to his sorrow, Jephthah's daughter was the first to approach him when he returned home after his victory. As a result, many conclude that Jephthah, a man honored in Scripture for his faith, actually engaged in the forbidden practice of human sacrifice.

JEPHTHAH'S SACRIFICE

That Jephthah would have practiced human sacrifice is extremely unlikely. Another but superior view of this troubling issue is that Jephthah sacrificed his daughter by giving her to lifetime service in the tabernacle, not as a burnt offering. Several lines of evidence support this alternative view.

First, the Hebrew conjunction in the verse that contains

Jephthah's rash vow could be translated with the word "or" to reflect two alternatives. It would then read, "whatever comes out of the doors of my house to meet me . . . it shall be the Lord's *or* I will offer it up as a burnt offering" (Judg. 11:31). This translation is legitimate. If this is correct, the vow would distinguish the resulting action between a human or an animal coming out to meet the victorious judge. If it were human, it would be offered up to serve God in the tabernacle. But if an animal came out, it would be given as a burnt offering.

Second, Jephthah's statement that whatever met him "shall be the LORD's" is similar to the phrase used of the Levites in the Pentateuch. The Lord declared that the Levites would be separated out for God's own service in the tabernacle, saying "the Levites shall be Mine" (Num. 3:12, 45; 8:14). Jephthah's words use the same Hebrew verb and Hebrew particle as these phrases in Numbers. This is no accident. It demonstrates that Jephthah was saying that he would give someone over to belong to the Lord's service, just as the Levites were given for God's service.

Third, the description of Jephthah's daughter hints at her being offered to serve in the tabernacle. She came out to greet him "with tambourines and with dancing" (Judg. 11:34). This phrase was deliberately designed to remind readers of the virgins who were dedicated to serving God in the tabernacle. For example, Psalm 68:24–25 describes the procession of worshippers entering God's sanctuary, the tabernacle. The depiction of the worshippers calls to mind the behavior of Jephthah's daughter: "The singers went on, the musicians after them, in the midst of *the maidens beating tambourines*" (Ps. 68:25, italics added).

Fourth, Jephthah's daughter's request indicates that she realized that, as a maiden serving in the tabernacle, she would never marry and have children. She accepted her father's vow but only asked that she be allowed to "go to the mountains and weep because of [her] virginity" (Judg. 11:37). If she was going to be killed, she would have far more to lament than her virginity. She did indeed go to the mountains and wept there "because of her virginity" (v. 38). After the two months were completed, Jephthah "did to her according to the vow which he had made; and *she had no relations with a man*"(v. 39, italics added). The text does not say, "and she was sacrificed as a burnt offering."

This threefold emphasis on the unmarried, virginal status of Jephthah's daughter was tragic for him because "she was his one and only child; besides her he had no son or daughter" (v. 34). It seems that the women who served in the tabernacle never married and remained virgins all their lives. In Psalm 68:25, the verse about maidens with tambourines at the tabernacle discussed above, the word translated "maidens" is the Hebrew word *alamoth,* the plural form of the same word used in Isaiah 7:14 for "virgin." Although a word study would be too long for this discussion, the word can be understood to refer to a virginal and pure maiden.[22] Seemingly, the young women given over to the service of God in the tabernacle were virgins. In light of Jephthah's daughter mourning for her virginity, it appears that she believed she was going to become one of those virginal maidens serving in the tabernacle for life. Jephthah did not offer his daughter as a burnt offering, but rather gave her to the Lord by giving her to tabernacle service. In doing so, he gave up his only hope of having an heir.

FINAL THOUGHTS

The story of Jephthah's foolish and unthinking vow is a great warning for followers of Jesus to be careful before making promises to the Lord. Solomon warned, "When you make a vow to God, do not be late in paying it; for He takes no delight in fools. Pay what you vow! It is better that you should not vow than that you should vow and not pay" (Eccl. 5:4–5). Believers need to take the vows we make to the Lord seriously because, like Jephthah, we are responsible to keep them, even if it brings us loss. Although Jephthah did not carry out a human sacrifice, he did have to sacrifice his dream and desire for his posterity to continue through an heir. This was no small matter in that culture and it certainly broke his heart. Nevertheless, Jephthah paid his vow and in so doing, he taught us an important lesson: Be careful about the promises we make to the Lord.

Why is God not mentioned in the book of Esther? How can a biblical book not speak of God?

C an you imagine someone writing a history of the birth of the United States, including the Revolutionary War, the constitutional convention, and the first federal government, and omitting any mention of George Washington? That would be inconceivable!

So, it cannot go unnoticed that in the biblical book of Esther, God, who is central to the entire story, is not mentioned even one time. The book tells of a Jewish girl, Esther, who became the queen of Persia, her cousin Mordecai who advised her, and Haman who plotted to destroy the Jewish people. Haman's scheme was ultimately thwarted and, to this day, Jewish people celebrate *Purim* (the festival of "Lots") every late winter/early spring because of this great deliverance.

PROPOSED EXPLANATIONS
FOR THE BOOK OF ESTHER

Why was God not explicitly mentioned in the book of Esther? Four proposals have been suggested:

"Esther Is a Profane Book"

Some view the book of Esther as morally bankrupt. According to Old Testament commentator Lewis Bayles Paton, the book is too *profane* for God to be in it. According to Paton's view, the king in the book, Xerxes, was a sensual oppressor and Esther is a manipulator who used her beauty to advance herself, Mordecai was insolent in refusing to bow to Haman, and the whole book was merely about vengeance. Paton writes, "There is not one noble character in this book . . . Morally Est. falls far below the general level of the OT., and even of the Apocrypha."[23]

According to this view, the scroll of Esther is bankrupt of any virtue. It's as if God would be too embarrassed to be found in it. But, if so, why would Esther have been included in the biblical canon? So, we are back to the original question—where is God in the book of Esther?

"Esther Is a Book of Propaganda"

Some view the scroll of Esther as merely nationalistic *propaganda*. One author, Arthur Waskow, dates the book in the Hellenistic period (in between the Old and New Testaments), long after the alleged events of the book. According to Waskow, Esther was intended as a fictional explanation of the Jewish holiday of Purim. He interprets the book as an illustrative tale of national defense and struggle against Hellenism. In his view, "God forbid that God should appear in such a story!"[24]

But no evidence exists that the biblical account is historically unreliable. In fact, there is ample evidence supporting the historicity of the book. Ahasuerus (Xerxes), the king whose drinking parties and fits of rage are recorded in the book of Esther, is verified by extra-biblical ancient histories. These works also confirmed other features of court life found in the book, such as the palace in Susa and the large harem.[25] There is little support to this view that the book is mere propaganda.

"Esther Is a Book of Parables"

Still others view the book of Esther as a *parable*, or rather typology, in which God is hidden in the book through the various characters. Bible expositor Ray Stedman takes this approach. Although he accepts the historicity of the book, he sees it as a parable or allegory of the spiritual life. In this view, Mordecai represents the Holy Spirit, the king represents the believer's flesh, Esther represents the redeemed believer, and Haman represents Satan. While it may be intriguing, this allegorical view is far too subjective to be accepted as the author's literary purpose for not mentioning God explicitly.[26]

"Esther Is a Book of Providence"

The correct explanation is that the book of Esther is about divine *providence*. The book conceals the name of God as a deliberate literary strategy in order to reveal God's providential actions. Providence means that God lovingly guides all of history for His good purposes and intentions. Providence refers to the way God works behind the scenes of our lives, orchestrating events to accomplish His good plan. There are no miracles (suspensions of natural law) in providence. Rather what appears to be normal human events (from our limited viewpoint) are actually under God's sovereign control. What appear to be amazing coincidences are not coincidences at all, but products of divine design.

This view is made all the more significant because the scroll of Esther reveals that the Jewish people had adopted the Persian culture and forgotten their God. The message of this book is that even when Israel forgot God, God always remembered His people. So, God is deliberately left out of this record to reflect the way the Jewish people of Persia had left Him out of their lives. Despite that, the book of Esther is a clear and powerful reminder that God never forgets His promises or plans! God is actively working even when we do not acknowledge Him.

EXAMPLES OF PROVIDENCE
IN THE BOOK OF ESTHER

God's providence is evident throughout the book of Esther. I'll give you a few examples, but I would encourage you to read it for yourself and you'll find many more:

- Esther "just happens" to find favor with the royal official in charge of the beauty contest (2:9).
- Mordechai "just happens" to overhear the plot against the king (2:21–22).

- The king "just happens" to welcome and point his scepter at Esther (5:2).
- The king "just happens" to have insomnia and read the story of Mordecai saving his life (6:1–2).
- Haman, the genocidal maniac and hater of Jews, "just happens" to perish on the very gallows that he had prepared for Mordecai (7:10).

This emphasis on providence is reflected in the words of Mordecai when he challenged Esther to go to the king about Haman's plan: "For if you remain silent at this time, relief and deliverance will arise for the Jews from another place . . . and who knows whether you have not attained royalty for such a time as this?" (Est. 4:14).

THE APPLICATION OF THE BOOK OF ESTHER

God's Providential Care for the Jewish People

What does Esther's story have to do with today? First of all, we can be assured that God is providentially active in preserving and protecting the Jewish people. God promised in the book of Jeremiah:

This is what the LORD says:

he who appoints the sun
to shine by day,

> who decrees the moon and stars
> to shine by night,
> who stirs up the sea
> so that its waves roar—
> the LORD Almighty is his name:
> "Only if these decrees vanish from my sight,"
> declares the LORD,
> "will Israel ever cease
> being a nation before me."

This is what the LORD says:

> "Only if the heavens above can be measured
> and the foundations of the earth below be searched
> out
> will I reject all the descendants of Israel
> because of all they have done,"
> declares the LORD.

(Jer. 31:35–37 NIV)

This verse is clear: Israel can only be destroyed as a people if the sun, moon, stars, and the roaring seas can be destroyed. Moreover, Israel will only cease to be a nation if the heavens can be measured and the core of the earth explored. All of these things are impossibilities.

God's promise is plain: The Jewish people can never be destroyed because God will providentially protect them. So, whether the avenger is Haman, or Hitler, or the Ayatollah Khomeini of Iran, the God of Israel will ultimately preserve the people of Israel, even if they forget or neglect Him.

God's Providential Care for Followers of Jesus

We can also be certain that God is providentially caring for every individual follower of the Lord Jesus. God is not just concerned with nations—He cares for individual people. If God's eye is on every sparrow that may fall, He will also care for us (Matt. 10:29). The Bible states that He numbers the hairs on our heads and nothing takes Him by surprise (Matt. 10:30–31). When bad things happen to us, we may mistakenly assume that God has somehow overlooked or ignored us. Nothing could be further from the truth! God has a purpose and plan for our lives. When amazingly good things happen to us, we sometimes write off such events as luck or coincidence. We cannot dismiss good or bad events in our lives as mere coincidences. Esther teaches us that God is at work in our lives in a specific and intentional way, caring for His people in good times and bad.

God's Providential Plan in Sending the Messiah Jesus

Finally, God was acting with providence when He sent the Messiah Jesus. God promised to bless the whole world through the seed of Abraham, Isaac, and Jacob (Gen. 12:1–3; 22:18; 26:4; 28:14). Had Haman succeeded in destroying the Jewish people, the Messiah Jesus would not have been born.

But God preserved His chosen people so the Messiah Jesus could come as promised. Not only was God active in physically delivering His people, but He also sent the Lord Jesus to die and be raised again and to deliver us all spiritually from our own failures and sins.

FINAL THOUGHTS

God is not excluded from the scroll of Esther because He was too embarrassed to be there. Nor was the book a piece of unhistorical propaganda. God is not hidden as an allegory in the book of Esther. Rather, His seeming absence was a deliberate literary strategy to remind us that even when we do not acknowledge or remember God, He is active in caring for us. How should we respond to that message? By acknowledging God in all our ways, thanking Him for His providence, and trusting in the Messiah Jesus.

Does the Old Testament predict the Messiah or is this just an idea invented by New Testament authors?

Although most followers of Jesus believe that the Old Testament predicted the future Messiah, there is a challenging view that has gained popularity. Some Bible teachers are saying that the New Testament authors just picked Old Testament verses out of context and tried to make them sound as if they were about the Messiah.

For example, I once went to an academic conference and heard a paper read by an Old Testament professor from one of the world's leading Bible-believing seminaries. His paper was about whether or not the Old Testament prophets really predicted the Messiah. I sat there in shock as this biblical scholar made the case that there wasn't even one verse in the Hebrew Bible that predicted a messianic figure. In fact, he argued that the whole idea of the Messiah was made up in the time period between the Old Testament and the New Testament. Since the New Testament maintains that Jesus is the fulfillment of Old Testament prophecy, this scholar needed to come up with some sort of explanation, some way of dealing with that issue. And he did. He argued that the human authors of the Old Testament only wrote about what was going on in their own day but that the Holy Spirit had a deeper and fuller meaning. He believed the Divine Inspirer of Scripture intended it to mean something more than the human authors understood. Similarly, another scholar I've read says the New Testament authors were engaged in "creative exegesis," finding meanings in the Old Testament that weren't really there.

THE PERSPECTIVE OF THE PROPHETS

To me this "creative exegesis" approach has numerous flaws. First, it seems to maintain that the Hebrew prophets didn't know they were writing about the Messiah. This idea is rooted in a mistaken interpretation of 1 Peter 1:10–12. In this passage it says the Old Testament prophets "made careful searches and inquiries, seeking to know what person or time the Spirit of Christ within them was indicating as He predicted the sufferings of Christ [the Messiah] and the glories to follow." However, the passage doesn't say the prophets didn't know that they were writing or speaking of the Messiah. It says they didn't know *when* the Messiah would come or who He would be. It is similar to our situation as believers today. We know there is a future false messiah, the Antichrist, coming. But we don't know *when* he will come or *who* he will be. The passage goes on to say that it was revealed that they weren't writing about their own day but about the Messiah's arrival in the distant future.

THE PERSPECTIVE OF DIVINE INSPIRATION

Another problematic aspect of this view is an unusual perspective on biblical inspiration. The Bible is an inspired text (2 Tim. 3:16) because human authors were moved by the Holy Spirit to write the words God intended, using their own ideas, personalities, and styles (2 Peter 1:21). In other words, both the Divine Author and the human author had the same meaning when they wrote; they had the same intention. In fact, the Holy Spirit's superintending of the human author guaranteed the truth of the human author's intentions and words. The Holy Spirit is the one who enabled biblical prophets to predict the future Messiah. This is what Peter meant when he wrote, "no prophecy was ever made by an act of human will, but men moved by the Holy Spirit spoke from God" (2 Peter 1:21).

THE PERSPECTIVE OF JESUS THE MESSIAH

Yet another difficulty with this view is that the Lord Jesus, the Messiah Himself, disagrees with it. Think about when the Messiah Jesus met Cleopas and his friends on the road to Emmaus (Luke 24:25–27). He told them that the only limitation that kept them from believing in messianic prophecy was that they were "foolish men and slow of heart to believe in all that the prophets have spoken!" (v. 25). The resurrected Lord goes on to say that the Scriptures taught that it was necessary for the Messiah to suffer before entering into glory (or being resurrected; v. 26). Then, Luke says, "beginning with Moses and with all the prophets, He explained to them the things concerning Himself in all the Scriptures" (v. 27).

Just a short time later, the Lord Jesus had a resurrection appearance with His disciples (Luke 24:44–46). He met them in the upper room and told them, "These are My words which I spoke to you while I was still with you, that all things which are written about Me in the Law of Moses and the Prophets and the Psalms must be fulfilled" (v. 44). And what did He say was written? That "the Christ would suffer and rise again from the dead" (v. 46). Clearly, the Lord Jesus taught His disciples that the Old Testament Scriptures were messianic and that they pointed to Him.

Additionally, just to be clear that the Old Testament authors understood their words, remember what Jesus told Israel's leadership in John 5:45–47? There He said, "Do not think that I will accuse you before the Father; the one who accuses you is Moses . . . for if you believed Moses, you would believe Me, for he wrote about Me." Jesus' point was that, at the final judgment, Moses himself would convict them because they should have believed in his predictions of the Messiah. How could Moses do that if he himself did not understand that he was writing about the Messiah? According to Jesus, the authors of the Hebrew Bible understood they were predicting the Messiah.

FINAL THOUGHTS

Last century, biblical scholar A. T. Robertson commented on Luke 24, saying, "Jesus found himself in the Old Testament, a thing that some modern scholars do not seem to be able to do."[27] Robertson was jabbing the critical scholars of his own day, whose anti-supernaturalism kept them from recognizing any direct predictions of the Messiah in the Hebrew Bible (Old Testament). Unfortunately, the views of these critics have become so influential that they have infiltrated even committed Bible-believing scholars today.

God used messianic predictions to lead me to faith in the Messiah Jesus and to have confidence in the inspiration of Scripture. As followers of Jesus, we need to reclaim messianic prophecy as one of the great evidences that Jesus is indeed the Messiah and that the Bible, both Old and New Testaments, is supernaturally and divinely inspired.

What specific Old Testament predictions reveal Jesus to be the Messiah?

How can someone be convinced that Jesus truly is who He claimed to be—the Messiah of Israel and the world? One of the ways that Jesus Himself proved this was by citing the Hebrew Bible's (my favorite term for the Old Testament) prophecies of the Messiah and how He fulfilled them. For example, Jesus said, "These are My words which I spoke to you while I was still with you, that all things which are written about Me in the Law of Moses and the Prophets and the Psalms must be fulfilled" (Luke 24:44).

So, to which prophecies was Jesus referring? Probably not merely specific isolated messianic texts, but to the Hebrew Bible as a whole. Even so, there are numerous specific predictions about the coming of the Messiah that Jesus fulfilled. In fact, the entire life of the Messiah can be found in the Hebrew scriptures, demonstrating that Jesus is actually the Promised One.

THE MESSIAH'S BIRTH

The Hebrew Bible contains several predictions of the locations or circumstances surrounding the Messiah's birth. Micah, the

Old Testament prophet, foretold that Messiah would be born in Bethlehem when he wrote, "Bethlehem Ephrathah, you are small among the clans of Judah; One will come from you to be ruler over Israel for Me" (Mic. 5:2 HCSB) .

Also, Genesis 49:10 predicted that the Messiah would come in the first century. It says, "The scepter shall not depart from Judah, nor the ruler's staff from between his feet, until Shiloh comes, and to him shall be the obedience of the peoples." Some understand the word "Shiloh" as a proper name and messianic title but it's best to be understood as a phrase meaning "He to whom it belongs," referring to the Messiah as the rightful ruler. Besides plainly stating that the Messianic King would come from the line of Judah, it also says He would come before the "scepter" and "staff" depart from Judah. The word *scepter* in Hebrew, as used here, refers to tribal identity (note the same word is translated "tribe" in 49:16). The word *staff* means a "judge's staff" and refers to judicial authority. The prediction is that Messiah would come before Judah would lose its tribal identity (lost in AD 70 with the destruction of the temple) and judicial authority (lost in AD 6 or 7 when the Romans replaced Herod Archelaus with a Roman governor). Based on these two elements, the Messiah needed to come by the first century.

Additionally, Isaiah predicted that the Messiah would be born of a virgin. King Ahaz and Judah were under a threat from an alliance of the northern kingdom of Israel and the nation of Aram (Syria). These two kingdoms wanted to remove the Davidic king, which would jeopardize the Messianic promise. The Lord directed Isaiah to take his son Shear Jashub and bring a message of hope to King Ahaz—an offer that Ahaz rejected. At this point, Isaiah gave two predictions. The first, a far prophecy (7:13–15), directed to the whole Davidic house (note the pronoun "you" in these verses is plural) assured the enduring nature of the Davidic house until the coming of the Messiah. Isaiah wrote, "Therefore, the Lord Himself will give you a sign: Behold, a virgin will be with child and bear a son, and she will call His name Immanuel." The sign of hope would be the Messiah's supernatural birth by a virgin in the distant future.

The second prediction (7:16–17) related to the near situation and was directed again to King Ahaz (note the pronoun "you" in these verses is singular). It foretold that by the time "the boy" Shear Jashub (whom Isaiah had brought along, cf. Isa. 7:3) reached an age to know right from wrong, the imminent threat of the two northern kings would be removed. This happened when Assyria defeated both these kingdoms in 732 BC, just two years after Isaiah's prophecy. So, the Hebrew Bible predicted that the Messiah would be virgin born in Bethlehem by the time of the first century.

THE MESSIAH'S NATURE

Although some have thought that Messiah would be merely a glorious human king, the Scriptures foretold that Messiah would have a unique nature. For example, the same prophecy that predicted that the Messiah would come from Bethlehem (Mic. 5:2) also said that His origin would really be "from long ago, from the days of eternity" indicating His eternal nature.

Isaiah also foresaw that the Messiah would have a divine nature. In a birth announcement of the Messiah, Isaiah gave the royal names of the future messianic king: ". . . . Wonderful Counselor, Mighty God, Eternal Father, Prince of Peace" (Isa. 9:6). These glorious titles of deity indicate that the Messiah would be God Himself.

THE MESSIAH'S LIFE

Isaiah foretold specific characteristics of the Messiah's life. In the messianic age, "the eyes of the blind will be opened and the ears of the deaf will be unstopped. Then the lame will leap like a deer, and the tongue of the mute will shout for joy" (Isa. 35:5–6). So, when the Messiah would make His appearance, He was to be a miracle worker. Isaiah also predicted that Messiah's teaching would "bring good news to the afflicted . . . [and] bind up the brokenhearted" (Isa. 61:1). Despite these many signs, Isaiah foretold that Messiah would also be "despised and forsaken of men" and that His own people would confess that "we did not esteem Him" (Isa. 53:3).

THE MESSIAH'S DEATH

Daniel predicted the time of the Messiah's death (Dan. 9:26). He said Messiah would be "cut off" before the Romans would "destroy the city [Jerusalem] and the sanctuary [the temple]." Since this destruction took place in AD 70, the Messiah would have to die sometime before.

King David foretold that Messiah would die by crucifixion, saying in a first-person poem about the Messiah, "they pierced my hands and my feet" (Ps. 22:16) . David's prediction about the Messiah's crucifixion was written in 1,000 BC, more than 300 years before crucifixion was even a known manner of execution.

More significant than the time or manner of His death, Isaiah predicted that the Messiah's death would be as a substitution for humanity's sin. The Servant of the Lord would die a disfiguring death (Isa. 52:14); He would be "pierced through for our transgressions [and] crushed for our iniquities" (Isa. 53:5); the Lord would punish Him for "the iniquity of us all" (v. 6). The Servant would have "poured out Himself to death" and, as a result, "He Himself bore the sin of many" (v. 12).

THE MESSIAH'S RESURRECTION

The prophets not only foretold the Messiah's death—they anticipated His resurrection as well. In Isaiah 52:13–53:12, after describing Messiah's substitutionary death, Isaiah promised that the Lord would "prolong His days" (Isa. 53:10) and that Messiah would see "the light of life" (Isa. 53:11 NIV). David, speaking for the Messiah in the first person, also expressed the Anointed One's own confidence that God would "not abandon me to Sheol" because the Messiah, God's "faithful one" would not "see decay" (Ps. 16:10 CSB).

THE MESSIAH'S RETURN

The Hebrew scriptures present the Messiah in two ways: as a suffering servant and as a victorious and righteous King. Although these two vastly different presentations have confused many, the difficulty is resolved by recognizing that the prophets anticipated two appearances of the Messiah. First, He would come as an atoning sacrifice for sin. Second, He would come to establish His righteous kingdom. One of the passages that links the two comings is Zechariah 12:10. It speaks of Messiah coming to deliver Israel at the last battle and then "they will look on Me whom they have pierced." These verses depict Messiah's second coming as the victorious King but also recognize His first appearance as the pierced one. Then, when He returns, He will fulfill Isaiah's prediction that He will reign "on the throne of David and over his kingdom, to establish it and to uphold it with justice and righteousness from then on and forevermore" (Isa. 9:7).

FINAL THOUGHTS

Although there are many more predictions of the Messiah in the Hebrew Bible, the passages mentioned above show that Jesus did indeed fulfill the messianic expectation of the Hebrew Bible.[28] Mathematician Peter W. Stoner calculated the probability of one person fulfilling not all the messianic predictions of the Bible, or even the ones mentioned above, but just eight of the messianic predictions. He found that the probability would be 1 in 10^{17} or 1 in 100,000,000,000,000,000! The likelihood of this occurring is comparable to covering Texas with 10^{17} silver dollars, marking only one of them, stirring the mass of dollars, and then having a blindfolded man randomly pick up the marked silver dollar.[29] This is the likelihood of Jesus of Nazareth randomly fulfilling only eight of the Messianic predictions of the Hebrew Bible.

Clearly, Jesus did fulfill every one of the messianic expectations of the Old Testament. It's why Andrew, having met Jesus, told his brother Simon Peter, "We have found the Messiah" (John 1:41) and Philip declared to his friend Nathanael "We have found Him of whom Moses in the Law and also the Prophets wrote—Jesus of Nazareth" (John 1:45).

QUESTIONS

about

JESUS

THE MESSIAH

Did Jesus really turn water into wine at the wedding in Cana (John 2:1–11)?

I once heard famed atheist Richard Dawkins interviewed on a secular radio program, and he was shocked to discover that his interviewer actually believed in Jesus. His response was to ask whether the host of the program sincerely believed that Jesus turned water into wine. He was stunned when the answer was, "Yes." Dawkins's attitude reflects the approach taken by many skeptics—they question how anyone could believe it possible for Jesus to have carried out this miracle.

Some followers of Jesus ask the same question, but with a very different intent. They find it hard to believe, in light of all the damage caused by alcohol abuse, that the Lord Jesus would actually turn water into wine with genuine alcohol content. To them, it's inconceivable that the Lord Jesus would provide real wine, and, by doing so, condone social alcohol consumption or possibly even partake of it Himself. So, it's vital to address these questions, posed both by the skeptic and the teetotaler, in that order.

THE REALITY OF THE MIRACLE

The denial of miracles presupposes a naturalistic point of view. Skeptics argue that Jesus could not have turned water into wine because it's simply not scientifically possible for a miracle to have taken place. This approach is problematic for a couple of reasons. First, it has the wrong premise, confusing naturalism with scientific fact. Naturalism states that only nature exists and there is nothing transcendent beyond it. By contrast, a truly scientific person would accept the evidence that there is a Creator who established the laws of nature and who then could transcend those laws. That's why famed former atheist Anthony Flew came to believe that "a superintelligence is the only good explanation of the origin of life and of the complexity of nature."[30] If God does exist, then miracles are not only possible but absolutely necessary in order to explain the historical record.

Pure naturalism denies the historical record of events like turning water into wine at the wedding of Cana. But critics should consider the number of people who were present at the wedding of Cana. All of those in attendance attested to the remarkable miracle of Jesus turning water into wine. John declared that his purpose for including these miraculous signs in his gospel was to convince people to "believe Jesus is the Messiah, the Son of God [deity], and by believing you may have life in His name" (John 20:30–31 HCSB). The miracle at Cana was well known and gave evidence of the deity of Jesus. Denial of the miracle not only rejects the testimony of John but of every other person present at that time. The critic, by denying these first-person validations, is saying, "My mind is made up—don't confuse me with the facts."

Josh McDowell compares the rejection of eyewitness testimony to explorers going to Australia and discovering an animal that seemed to deny all the zoological categories previously known. It was a semi-aquatic, egg-laying mammal with webbed feet, a broad, flat tail, and a flat bill similar to a duck. At first, people rejected the eyewitness report of this discovery and considered it a hoax because it didn't fit their previously conceived notions. When the explorers returned from Australia a second time, carrying the hide of a duck-billed platypus, they were again accused of fabricating a fraud.[31] This modern-day example demonstrates the danger of only trusting our preconceived ideas rather than believing reliable firsthand testimony.

John's purpose for including this miracle was to prove the deity of Jesus. Only God could turn water molecules into wine molecules. Those who are followers of Jesus fully accept the ability of Jesus to do this and much more! Many, though, have a different issue related to the suitability of that miraculous wine.

THE QUESTION OF THE GRAPES

The wisdom writer states categorically, "Wine is a mocker, strong drink a brawler, and whoever is intoxicated by it is not wise" (Prov. 20:1). He also gave an extended description of the woes, sorrows, contentions, complaints, and wounds of those "who linger long over wine" (Prov. 23:29–35). The danger of alcohol abuse has caused many to question why the

Lord Jesus would actually turn water into wine with alcoholic content. It seems to them that this would be contrary to His love and concern for people. They try to explain away this miracle. Yet all the biblical evidence seems to indicate that Jesus did indeed create wine out of water.

The Lexical Evidence

When the wine ran out at the wedding in Cana, Jesus had the pots filled with water. Afterwards, the headwaiter tasted the liquid in the pots and the water "had become wine" (John 2:9). The Greek language has perfectly good words for both juice and wine. In this paragraph, the word *oinos* plainly means wine. Southern Baptist Greek scholar A. T. Robertson has written, "It is real wine that is meant by *oinos* here. Unlike [John] the Baptist, Jesus mingled in the social life of the time, was even abused for it (Matt. 11:19 = Luke 7:34)."[32] The plain sense of the word used here is actual, real wine.

The Contextual Evidence

It's not only the word used in John 2:9 that points to real wine, but also the very next verse. The headwaiter who had tasted the wine told the bridegroom, "Every man serves the good wine first, and when the people have drunk freely, then he serves the poorer wine; but you kept the good wine until now" (John 2:10). These words indicate what was (and maybe still is) standard operating procedure at weddings. In particular, it was normal to serve the better wine first. Then, when people became drunk (the literal translation of "drunk freely;" cf. NET Bible), they would offer the lesser quality wine. However, in this case, clearly the best wine had been made available late in the celebration.

This verse is not saying anyone had yet become drunk—only what was normally done at weddings. The important detail to note is that the sort of wine offered at weddings was the kind that could cause drunkenness. Imagine the headwaiter saying, "Normally, the name brand grape juice is brought out first, and then, when the senses are dulled, the store brand quality is released." This would make no sense. The only way to understand the headwaiter's words would be if he were talking about real wine.

The Cultural Evidence

We must consider that the miracle took place at a first-century Jewish wedding. All Jewish festivals and weddings at that time were consecrated and celebrated with real wine. It would make no sense for Jesus to go against the cultural tradition and turn water into grape juice. Clearly the miracle involved Jesus turning the water into actual wine with alcoholic content.

The Historical Evidence

Prior to the modern era, there was no question that this was a miracle with real wine. It was only in nineteenth-century America, with its rampant abuse of wine and other alcohol, that followers of Jesus began to reject drinking wine whatsoever. This in turn led many to question the alcoholic content in the miraculously made wine of Jesus. However, to deny the alcoholic content of the wine in this miracle and in this setting is to read the Bible through the lens of our modern-day culture and emotions.

SO WHAT?

What should we make of Jesus turning water into wine at the wedding of Cana? To begin, the passage shows that Jesus approved of drinking wine. Master educator Gilbert Highet, in a book about methods of instruction, pointed out that Jesus taught in ways other than by lecturing. He states, "The first miracle told of him in John's gospel was the creation of wine to help the festivities at a wedding. He could not have said more plainly that he approved of both marriage and [wine]-drinking."[33] Bishop Ryle similarly comments, "If our Lord Jesus Christ actually worked a miracle in order to supply wine at a marriage feast, it seems to me impossible, by any ingenuity, to prove that drinking wine is sinful."[34]

Second, the Bible includes clear warnings about the danger and destruction of drunkenness. The book of Proverbs (cited previously) warns about the abuse of alcohol. The Bible teaches that the damage caused by drinking alcohol should be a caution against ever imbibing too much. Moreover, the abuse of alcohol by many in our culture should give us pause. We can agree that if we never took a drink of wine or any other sort of alcohol, we would never be able to abuse it. Certainly, this could be the wisest course for many of us.

Third, we are cautioned by Paul to consider the effect of our alcohol consumption on others. Paul's teaching about meat sacrificed to idols can easily apply to the drinking of wine. Even if we are able to drink wine temperately without abusing it, Paul taught believers to limit our liberty in doubtful things, so as not to cause "a stumbling block to the weak" (1 Cor. 8:9–10). To cause someone to stumble does not mean we are annoying a legalist. Rather, it refers to causing others to behave in a way that is contrary to their conscience. If a believer drinks wine, and by doing so causes someone else who is struggling with resisting wine to drink it, then we "sin against Christ" (1 Cor. 8:12).

FINAL THOUGHTS

What can we conclude? We need balance when it comes to our attitude and behavior toward wine and other types of alcohol. While we do not want to become legalists, condemning brothers and sisters in the faith who have the freedom and control to drink wine, we must also not behave so carelessly that we cause a stumbling block for brothers and sisters "for whose sake Christ died" (1 Cor. 8:11). Remember the words of Paul: "Therefore, if food [or drink] causes my brother to stumble, I will never eat meat [or drink wine] again, so that I will not cause my brother to stumble" (1 Cor. 8:13).

Some of the statements made by Jesus sound harsh and confusing. They make me feel uncomfortable. For example, why did Jesus curse a fig tree for not having fruit when it wasn't even the season for figs (Mark 11:12–14)? Or, why did He call a needy Gentile woman a dog (Matt. 15:21–28) or prohibit a man from burying his father (Luke 9:59–60)? Why did He promise to cause war (bring a sword) if He was the Prince of Peace (Matt. 10:34)? How do you explain these statements of Jesus?

31

The main reason that first-century Jewish people didn't recognize Jesus as their Messiah was that He didn't fit their expectations. They were looking for a conquering King and political deliverer, but Jesus, in His first coming, arrived instead as a suffering servant and as a spiritual deliverer. In much the same way, twenty-first-century people have a hard time recognizing the real Jesus of the Gospels because He doesn't fit their cultural or societal expectations.

It should not be shocking that some of the statements made by Jesus surprise us. Even so, by taking a closer look at the four examples mentioned in this question, we see there are good and simple explanations.

THE CURSING OF THE FIG TREE

Critics have objected to the story of the cursing of the fig tree (Mark 11:12–14, 19–25) because to them, it makes Jesus appear vindictive and selfish. On the surface, it appears that just because Jesus was hungry, He cursed a fig tree finding no fruit on it, "for it was not the season for figs" (v. 13). After He cursed it, the tree withered (vv. 20–21).

The confusion comes from a failure to understand the horticulture of first-century Israel. Fig trees in that part of the world sprout unripe figs before growing leaves. These unripe figs were often eaten by the poor and others when hungry. So, by the time Jesus saw the fig tree (which had leaves on it), it should have already produced edible, unripe figs. The absence of fruit proved that this tree was barren; it would never provide fruit at all.

The cursing of the fig tree was not a vindictive, selfish act, but rather one used by Jesus to teach two spiritual lessons.

The first was about the danger of religious hypocrisy. This is evident from the events that occurred between the cursing of the fig tree and when the disciples saw the tree had withered. In between those two events, the Lord Jesus went to the temple and declared that it had become a business operation rather than, as intended, a place of worship (Mark 11:15–17). The object lesson was clear: Just as the tree had leaves but no fruit, so the religious leadership at the temple looked holy but was not producing spiritual fruit. Jesus was demonstrating that this kind of religiosity would wither and die, just like the barren fig tree.

The second lesson concerned prayer. Jesus did not cause the tree to wither because He exercised His divine power as the Son of God but rather as a result of faithful prayer. So the next day, when the disciples were amazed that the fig tree had withered already, Jesus taught them that they too could pray, and if they believed, they could move mountains (Mark 11:22–24). Mountain moving was an illustration of the power of prayer, not a literal exercise in moving Mount Rushmore into the Pacific Ocean. The Lord's point was that mountain-moving prayer is a privilege given to all followers of Jesus who trust God completely.

The cursing of the fig tree was not about Jesus being selfish and vindictive but was intended to teach His followers the importance of authentic spirituality and the need for mountain-moving faith in our prayers.

THE GENTILE WOMAN CALLED A DOG

Critics frequently ask, since the Lord Jesus is the perfect model of love, why did He call a Gentile woman a dog (Matt. 15:21–28)? While the Lord Jesus was in the area of Tyre and Sidon (Syro-Phoenicia), a Canaanite woman was begging the Lord Jesus to heal her demonized daughter. The Lord Jesus responded that He needed to minister to the people of Israel before serving Gentiles. Then He gave the illustration that one does not give the children's bread to the dogs. She persisted, saying even dogs receive crumbs. In response, the Lord Jesus delivered her daughter.

At first glance, it does seem rude for Jesus to compare this woman to a dog. But while Jesus' response may appear harsh to our modern ears, it was actually gentle. The Greek word used in this passage is *kunarion* which is a diminutive term, meaning "a little dog, doggie, or house pet." Jesus did not use the word *kuon*, a Greek word commonly translated "dog" but used for "wild, dog packs." It is helpful to note that Paul used this harsh term, saying "Beware of the dogs" (Phil. 3:2), when warning the Philippians about false teachers.

So what can help us better understand this interaction between the Messiah Jesus and the Canaanite woman? First, the Lord Jesus was merely expressing God's divine priority, not His own bigotry. As the Messiah of Israel, Jesus was called to present Himself to the Jewish people first. That is why He told the Samaritan woman, "Salvation is from the Jews" (John 4:22).

Similarly, Paul told the Jewish people of Pisidian Antioch, "It was necessary that the word of God be spoken to you first" (Acts 13:46) and declared the gospel to be "to the Jew first and also to the Greek" (Rom. 1:16). The message of the Messiah was founded in Israel and promised to the Jewish people. The gospel is an especially Jewish message, and it was essential for the Jewish Messiah to be presented to the Jewish people first since they took priority.

Second, in order to explain this divine program, the Lord Jesus was merely offering an illustration to help this woman understand. His point was that just as a parent has a priority for caring for children before a beloved pet (as evident in His use of the diminutive "doggie" or "puppy"), so the Lord Jesus needed to minister to the Jewish people before caring for a dear Canaanite woman.

Third, notice that the Canaanite woman did not take offense but rather accepted God's divine priority. Still she did not get discouraged, but persisted. She used the Lord's illustration to ask for "bread crumbs," thereby expressing her great faith in the mercy of the Messiah Jesus.

Finally, when the woman persisted, the Lord Jesus commended the woman for her faith ("O woman, your faith is great," v. 28), and He healed her daughter. This demonstrated that the Messiah Jesus was ready to respond to the humble faith of any person, Jewish or Gentile.

FORBIDDING A MAN TO BURY HIS FATHER

When the Lord Jesus called a man to follow Him, the man requested, "Lord, permit me first to go and bury my father," The Lord Jesus responded in a way that may surprise and concern us: "Allow the dead to bury their own dead; but as for you, go and proclaim everywhere the kingdom of God" (Luke 9:59–60). This reply to a grieving son seems callous and unkind. How could Jesus have been so harsh?

The answer is that the man's request was not to go to his father's funeral or perhaps, to attend to a deathly sick dad who would die soon. More likely, this was the oldest son in the family and he wanted to return home, wait for his perfectly healthy father to die, bury him, and then collect his inheritance. The request was not for a brief delay but an open-ended postponement of the call to follow and serve the Messiah Jesus.

The response of the Lord Jesus illustrates the urgency of following Him. We're not to wait until it's convenient or comfortable for us to serve the Lord. Rather, we are to obey and serve Him immediately, even if doing so might require a loss of personal benefits.

THE MESSIAH AND WAR AND PEACE

According to Isaiah 9:6, one of the throne-titles of the future Messiah is "Prince of Peace." That's why Jesus' words seem so shocking: "Do not think that I came to bring peace on the earth;

I did not come to bring peace, but a sword" (Matt. 10:34). Was Jesus endorsing war? Actually, He was doing no such thing, but He was being deliberately controversial. When the Lord says "Do not think . . ." He was intentionally shaking up the perspective of His listeners. The following three insights help us understand what Jesus was actually saying.

First, the context reveals that the Lord Jesus was speaking of family division, not holy war. He quotes Micah 7:6 which describes the division between fathers and sons, mothers and daughters, and enemies within families (Matt. 10:35–36).

Second, the Lord Jesus' use of the word "sword" is figurative for division, not literal for a weapon of war. In the first century, a sword, as used in the Roman Empire, was a two-edged weapon used for cutting or cleaving. Jesus was not speaking of war here but using the figure of a sword which would divide families.

Finally, the Lord Jesus' description of division was predictive, not prescriptive. He was not demanding that families divide over their faith in Him, but He was foretelling that they might face separation. Anyone who has heard of a spouse leaving a husband or wife when one of them became a follower of Jesus or a parent disowning a child over belief in Jesus understands the reality of this prediction. In fact, this happened to me. When I became a follower of Jesus, contrary to my deepest desire, my Dad, an observant Jewish man, disowned me, and even said the Jewish prayer for the dead for me. Although the Lord Jesus did not prescribe this kind of separation, He certainly predicted it. Understanding this passage as a prediction is certainly correct when understood in the context of this passage and in Scripture. In the following paragraph (Matt. 10:37–39), the Lord emphasized the importance of prioritizing love for Him even over love for family.

FINAL THOUGHTS

Would the Messiah really make such shocking statements? Absolutely! The Lord Jesus requires His followers to be fully devoted to Him. He may say things that challenge and surprise us. Nevertheless, His words, when understood within context, are never vindictive, harsh, unkind, or warlike. They are consistent with what we expect from the Lord of lords and King of kings.

Why did the Lord Jesus quote Psalm 22:1, "My God, My God, why have You forsaken Me?" (Matt. 27:46)? Did Jesus not understand why He was dying?

The most common explanation of the Lord Jesus' cry on the cross is that, at that very moment, all the sins of humanity for all time came upon Him and He became sin. Therefore, some have said, the Father could no longer look upon the Son and so fellowship between God the Father and God the Son was broken for the first and only time throughout eternity. According to this view, the crucifixion shocked the Messiah Jesus to such an extent that He exclaimed, "Why have you forsaken Me?" So widespread is this interpretation that we even find it in contemporary worship hymns. For example, Stuart Townend's beautiful worship song "How Deep the Father's Love for Us" contains these lyrics (emphasis added):

How great the pain of searing loss –
The Father turns His face away[35]

Clearly, it has become normative to believe that the Father turned away from His Son and the eternal fellowship of the Godhead was broken (at least for that moment) at the cross.

PROBLEMS WITH THE BROKEN-FELLOWSHIP EXPLANATION

Jesus Was Not Shocked

So, what's wrong with this explanation? First, the Lord Jesus clearly knew that He was going to suffer and die. He would not have been shocked. He told His disciples, "The Son of Man will be handed over to the chief priests and the scribes, and they will condemn Him to death. Then they will hand Him over to the Gentiles, and they will mock Him, spit on Him, flog Him, and kill Him, and He will rise after three days" (Mark 10:33–34 HCSB). Not only did the Lord Jesus know that He would die, He also knew the reason for His death: to be a sacrifice for sin and to provide "a ransom for many" (Mark 10:45).

God *Can* Look at Sin

A second problem with this explanation is that it is founded upon a misinterpretation of Habakkuk 1:13. That verse states that God's "eyes are too pure to look on evil" (CSB). Therefore, it is said that when all humanity's sins rested upon Jesus, the Father could no longer look at the Son. According to this view, God literally abandoned the Messiah when the sin of all the world fell upon Him at His crucifixion and the eternal fellowship of the Father and the Son was broken. The problem with this is that Habakkuk 1:13 is not saying that God cannot look at sin. If so, how could He see us? What the verse actually means is that God is too pure to look with approval at sinful actions. That's why the NASB correctly translates this verse as "Your eyes are too pure to approve evil."

He Bore, Not Became, Our Sin

Third, this traditional explanation is problematic because the Lord Jesus never *became* sinful for us. Although 2 Corinthians 5:21 says God "made Him who knew no sin to be sin on our behalf," it is best to understand this phrase as God made the Lord Jesus "to be *a sin offering* on our behalf." The Lord Jesus did not become sinful or morally culpable for our sins but rather He bore the penalty for our sin as our substitute.

For example, in the Old Testament Day of Atonement liturgy, Aaron, acting as high priest, was to "lay both of his hands on the head of the live goat, and confess over it all the iniquities of the sons of Israel and all their transgressions in regard to all their sins; and he shall lay them on the head of the goat and sent it away into the wilderness.... The goat shall bear on itself all their iniquities to a solitary land ..." (Lev. 16:21–22). The scapegoat (literally, "the go-away goat") did not actually become morally sinful but symbolically demonstrated the removal of Israel's sins. Similarly, with the sin offering (Lev. 4), the sinful party was to lay a hand on the sacrificial animal as a symbolic transfer of guilt before the animal was sacrificed.

Nevertheless, it was impossible for an animal to become morally culpable but was a substitutionary offering. Likewise, in 2 Corinthians 5:21, the Lord Jesus did not become morally culpable for our sins, causing the Father to break fellowship with the Son. Rather, He became a substitutionary sacrifice, bearing our punishment and taking our sin away.

Fellowship Cannot Be Broken

Fourth and finally, it is theologically impossible and inconceivable for fellowship within the Godhead ever to be broken. The Father, Son, and Holy Spirit were always united, from eternity past to the eternal forever. Nothing could ever alter that, not even the Messiah Jesus' death for the penalty of our sin.

The Reasons for Quoting Psalm 22:1

So why does the Lord Jesus quote Psalm 22:1 regarding God's forsaking of Him? There are three reasons. First, the Messiah is using the psalm to express His prayer to the Father. As Dietrich Bonhoeffer has said, the book of Psalms "is the prayer book of Jesus Christ in the truest sense."[36] Second, He is using this quotation from Psalm 22 to draw attention to that messianic psalm and identify Himself as its subject. In this way, the Lord is demonstrating that He is the fulfillment of this messianic prophecy. Third, the Messiah Jesus quotes Psalm 22:1 as a rhetorical question, not a literal one. A rhetorical question is a figure of speech in which the questioner knows the answer but asks anyway for dramatic effect or to make a point. The Lord Jesus knew why He was dying and He knew the Father was not literally forsaking Him. It just felt that way.

My students through the years have asked a rhetorical question when they see how much reading I require in the course syllabus. They ask, "Why did I take this course?" knowing all the while that they registered for it because it was needed to graduate. The question expresses how they feel. And, similarly, as He was suffering for the sins of the world, the Lord Jesus felt forsaken by His Father, although He knew it was not literally so.

FINAL THOUGHTS

The Lord Jesus' words at His death are a great reminder for us that redemption was not cheap or easy. Rather, the glorious Messiah, the eternal Son of God, left His throne in heaven, emptying Himself of the rights of deity, and experienced the horrific suffering of crucifixion to provide atonement for our sin (cf. Phil. 2:5–9). Even so, knowing how painful this would be, the Lord Jesus said, "No one takes my life from me. I give it up willingly!" (John 10:18 CEV). This voluntary sacrifice of His life was an expression of His love for us, just as He said, "Greater love has no one than this, that one lay down his life for his friends" (John 15:13).

Jesus said He would be in the grave for three days and three nights (Matt. 12:40). But if we count the days from Good Friday to Resurrection Sunday, it seems there was insufficient time in the grave. Should we recalculate the Passion Week, with the crucifixion actually taking place on Thursday?

33

When people attempt to recalculate Passion Week, they often do so with the best motive, namely, they want to take the Bible literally. These people understand that the time from the crucifixion of Jesus to His resurrection must be a literal 72 hours, as understood by Jesus' words in Matthew 12:40 ("just as Jonah was three days and three nights in the belly of the sea monster, so will the Son of Man be three days and three nights in the heart of the earth"). Therefore, they would conclude that the Last Supper actually took place on Wednesday of Passion Week, the crucifixion on Thursday, and the resurrection on Sunday.

A THURSDAY CRUCIFIXION?

Support for a Thursday Crucifixion

Several reasons are given to support a Thursday crucifixion of Jesus. First and most obviously, this would allow Jesus' burial in the tomb to be literally three days and three nights. Second, it is maintained that the day of preparation and the Sabbath described in John 19:31 ("because it was the day of preparation, so that the bodies would not remain on the cross on the Sabbath (for that Sabbath was a high day)") refer to Passover and not the weekend Sabbath. In this argument, the day of preparation would refer to the day before Passover, and the Sabbath refers to cessation of work on the first day of Passover, and therefore it was a high day. Third, the Greek word for *Sabbath* in Matthew 28:1 is actually plural, so it describes Resurrection Sunday literally as "after the Sabbaths." This would indicate that the resurrection took place after two Sabbaths, the first on the first day of Passover (Friday) and the second on the regular Sabbath (Saturday).

Problems with a Thursday Crucifixion

Although this interpretation appears to solve the problem by allowing for three full days and nights in the tomb and a literal understanding of Jesus' prediction in Matthew 12:40, it does pose some problems. First, the phrase "day of preparation" *always* means the Friday before the weekly Sabbath ("it was the preparation day, that is, the day before the Sabbath"; Mark 15:42). This is true both in the Bible (Matt. 27:62; Luke 23:54;

John 19:14, 31, 42) and in writings of the first century Jewish historian Josephus (*Antiquities,* 16.6). The only reason John 19:14 uses the phrase "the day of preparation for the Passover" is because, in this case, Friday, the normal day of preparation, was also the day before Passover. And, John 19:31 refers to this Sabbath as a high day because it marks the convergence of both the first day of Passover and the Sabbath.

Second, Passover is nowhere called a Sabbath in the Bible. The Law of Moses says the first day of Passover is to be a day without any work (Lev. 23:7; Num. 28:16) but never uses the word "Sabbath" to describe the festival, as it does the Day of Atonement (Lev. 23:32).

Third, the use of the plural form for Sabbath (Matt. 28:1) is totally irrelevant because the word "Sabbath" is commonly in the plural form in the New Testament, even when only one normal Sabbath day is in view (Matt. 12:1, 5, 10–12; Mark 1:21; 2:23–24; 3:2, 4; Luke 4:16, 31; 6:2; 13:10; Acts 13:14; 16:13). This is also true in Josephus (*Antiquities,* 12.274) and the Jewish philosopher Philo (*On Abraham,* 28).

Fourth, the Bible specifies that the crucifixion and burial of Jesus took place on Friday ("the preparation day," Mark 15:42; see also Matt. 27:62; Luke 23:54, 56; John 19:31, 42) and that Jesus was raised on the first day of the week or Sunday (Matt. 28:1; Mark 16:1–2; Luke 24:1; John 20:1). So, a literal reading of these verses indicates a Friday crucifixion and Sunday resurrection. Either this contradicts Matthew 12:40 or there must be a better explanation.

A Friday Crucifixion

The better alternative to recalculation is to recognize that when Jesus said He would be in the grave for three days and three nights, He was using a common Jewish cultural expression called *inclusive time reckoning*.

In ancient times, Jewish people used inclusive time reckoning when speaking of any part of a day as referring to a full day (day and night). An example of inclusive time reckoning in the Hebrew Scriptures is when Esther called for a fast "for three days, night or day" (Est. 4:15–16) but then saw the end of the fast "on the third day" (Est. 5:1). Rabbinic literature gives this example from the Mishnah: Rabbi Eliezer ben Azariah (about AD 100, a contemporary of the Apostle John) taught, "A day and a night are an Onah ('a portion of time') and the portion of an Onah is as the whole of it" (Shabbat 9:3). Clearly, inclusive time reckoning was a common practice among Jewish people in the first century.

We often use idiomatic expressions today when speaking of time. Someone might say, "I did yard work all weekend" but not really mean every minute from Friday night to Sunday night. Nevertheless, a listener would still get the point that much of the weekend was taken up with yard work.

Therefore, I believe we are right to retain the biblical chronology of Passion Week: Jesus shared His Last Supper with His disciples on Thursday night, was crucified on Friday, and raised from the dead early Sunday morning. This time in the tomb includes parts of three days (Friday night, all day Saturday, and early Sunday), a period of time idiomatically described with inclusive time reckoning as "three days and three nights."

FINAL THOUGHTS

Even more important than calculating precisely how many hours the Lord Jesus was buried in a tomb is to recognize the reason for His death and resurrection. He died to pay the penalty for our sin (2 Cor. 5:21) and was raised to give us new life (Rom. 6:4). Too often we fall into the trap of arguing over what is least important and ignoring what is absolutely crucial.

Did the Lord Jesus descend to hell between Good Friday and Resurrection Sunday?

The idea that the Lord Jesus went to hell between the crucifixion and the resurrection has been around since ancient times. In fact, the Apostle's Creed affirms this position when it says, "He suffered under Pontius Pilate, was crucified, died and was buried; *he descended into hell*; on the third day he rose again from the dead" (emphasis added).

WHAT HAPPENED AFTER JESUS DIED?

The Scriptures actually teach that when the physical body of the Lord Jesus died, His spirit went to His Father immediately. One of several verses that supports this is Luke 23:43, where Jesus assures the thief on the cross: "Today you will be **with me** in paradise" (emphasis added). Paradise is the term used in first-century Judaism to describe what we call heaven. Here the Lord Jesus did not say He needed to descend to hell but that He would be in heaven and bring the thief with Him on that same day. Furthermore, the Lord Jesus was not merely saying He would be with the thief in paradise as a consequence of His own omnipresence as God the Son. Rather, He was telling the thief that they would be present together in heaven.

A second verse that teaches that the spirit of the Lord Jesus went to the Father immediately upon physical death is Luke 23:46. Luke records Jesus' words at the point of death, saying, "Father, into Your hands I entrust My spirit" (HCSB). This indicates that upon death, although the Lord's physical body would go to the grave, His spirit would go into the presence of His Father in heaven. Nowhere is there any mention of needing to descend to hell.

Some people believe that Jesus descended to hell only to proclaim victory over Satan, while some others believe that Jesus descended to hell to experience the suffering of humanity for sin. As for suffering in hell for us, John 19:30 demonstrates that He did not need to do this for us. That verse includes Jesus' last words before His death: "It is finished!" In declaring this, the Messiah Jesus was not just saying that His life was over but that His suffering was complete. He did not need to go to hell to suffer; instead, His spirit would go to His Father immediately.

RESOLVING QUESTIONABLE PASSAGES

Ephesians 4:9

The belief that the Lord Jesus descended to hell between His death and resurrection is based on the misinterpretation of several passages. One passage is Ephesians 4:9, which states that the Lord Jesus "descended into the lower parts of the earth." Some have interpreted Jesus' descent to the "lower parts of the earth" as referring to His descent to hell. Yet there is nothing in the context to support this. Others see the descent as referring to the death of the Lord Jesus and His burial "in the lower parts of the earth." However, this would not be an appropriate way to describe burial in a tomb.

The best interpretation is to view Ephesians 4:9 as a reference to the incarnation, when the Son of God became a man, not a descent to hell or to His burial. The phrase "lower parts of the earth" is called a genitive of apposition, a grammatical expression with two nouns, in which the second describes the first. An English example of this is "the city of Chicago" which means, "the city, namely Chicago." So, the translation "he descended to the lower regions, namely, the earth" (NET Bible) better captures the meaning of Ephesians 4:9, showing it refers to the incarnation when the eternal Son of God became a man (cf. John 1:14).

Matthew 12:40

Second, Jesus' words in Matthew 12:40 are mistakenly used to support His alleged descent to hell. There the Lord Jesus compares Jonah's three days and nights in the great fish to His own burial, saying, "so will the Son of Man be three days and three nights in the heart of the earth." But this verse says nothing of a descent to hell. Jonah is said to have descended to "the heart of the seas" (Jonah 2:3), so that "the great deep engulfed" him (Jonah 2:5). This is merely a reference to Jonah's time in the water, likely before the great fish swallowed him, and not a reference to Jonah descending to the abyss or hell. Similarly, Jesus is merely describing the amount of time His body would be in the grave—He is predicting that He would be buried in the heart of the earth for three days. This comparison is not teaching a descent to hell.

John 20:17

A third passage that is frequently misunderstood is John 20:17 which records Jesus' words to Mary Magdalene in the early morning of Resurrection Sunday. In the King James Version, the words of Jesus are, "Touch me not; for I am not yet ascended to my Father." This translation has led many to believe that the Lord Jesus was in hell from Good Friday until His resurrection and had not yet been in His Father's presence. However, this is not at all what the words mean. The NASB captures the meaning best: "Stop clinging to Me, for I have not yet ascended to the Father." This is not saying that Jesus' spirit had not yet been to His Father, but rather that Mary should stop clinging to Him. Imagine Mary's joy and excitement at seeing her risen Lord. She grabbed hold of Him and did not want to let go. The Lord Jesus tells her she could stop holding on to Him because His bodily ascension was yet future. In other words, Jesus is saying, "You can let go of me, Mary. I will be with you for the next 40 days because I have not yet made my final ascension to the Father" (cf. Acts 1:9–11).

Acts 2:27–31

Yet a fourth misinterpreted passage is Acts 2:27–31, a section of Peter's sermon at Pentecost. There Peter quotes

Psalm 16:10, a messianic Psalm predicting the resurrection of the Messiah. The psalm says the Messiah's body would not be abandoned in Sheol (a Hebrew word that means the abode of the dead or the grave), nor would it undergo decay. Although the KJV incorrectly translated the word "Sheol" as "hell," the better translation would be "the grave." Similarly, the Greek word used in Acts 2:27 is "Hades," leading some to think that Jesus descended to hell. However, Hades is just the Greek equivalent of the Hebrew term "Sheol," and only means the realm of the dead. The point of Psalm 16:10 and its use in Acts 2:27–31 is to show that the Messiah Jesus did not decay in the grave but was resurrected from the dead. It says nothing of a descent to hell.

Romans 10:6–7

Fifth, some have mistakenly maintained that Romans 10:6–7 teach Jesus' descent to hell. There Paul, quoting from Deuteronomy 30:12–13, forbids asking these questions: "'Who will ascend into heaven?' (that is, to bring Christ down), or 'Who will descend into the abyss?' (that is, to bring Christ up from the dead)." The word "abyss" means "the deep" and usually refers to the depths of the sea but it also is used in the Greek translation of the Old Testament to refer to the place of the dead (Ps. 70:20 LXX; 71:20 in the English Bible). Only in the book of Revelation is the word used to mean the abode of demons or the bottomless pit. In Romans 10:7 it refers to "the place of the dead" (NLT). The point in Romans 10:6–7 is that it is not necessary to try to bring Jesus near from heaven via the incarnation—that would be pointless because heaven is inaccessible to us and the incarnation has already taken place. Nor are we to go to the grave to bring Jesus close to us because the abode of the dead is inaccessible to us and He has already been resurrected. The Messiah Jesus is already near to us, as close as believing in Him and confessing faith with our mouths (Rom. 10:9). These verses are teaching about the nearness of Jesus to us by faith, not a descent to hell.

1 Peter 3:19–20

The last and most commonly cited passage about Jesus' alleged descent to hell is 1 Peter 3:19–20. It says, "He went and made proclamation to the spirits *now* in prison, who once were disobedient, when the patience of God kept waiting in the days of Noah, during the construction of the ark." Different interpreters have taken this to mean that Jesus descended to hell for three separate reasons: (1) Some say Jesus descended to hell to proclaim judgment to fallen angels; (2) Others believe Jesus descended to hell to proclaim judgment to lost people, specifically those from the days of Noah before the flood; or (3) Yet a third view is that Jesus descended to hell to liberate Old Testament believers from the abode of the dead.

None of these explanations fit the context of 1 Peter nor do they make much sense. First, it couldn't have been to proclaim judgment to Satan and the other fallen angels because the passage is not discussing fallen angels. Rather it is referring to people who disobeyed in the days of Noah. Moreover, the passage speaks of God patiently waiting for the people in Noah's day to repent, specifically saying that "the patience of God kept waiting in the days of Noah." God never waited patiently for fallen angels to repent. Second, it can't be about proclaiming judgment to lost people from the days of Noah. It doesn't make sense that Jesus would descend to hell to proclaim judgment only to lost people from the days of Noah instead of to lost people from all time. Third, it couldn't be to liberate Old Testament believers because the Scriptures nowhere teach that Old Testament believers needed liberation from hell (rather, like Lazarus, the Old Testament faithful went to heaven immediately upon physical death and were comforted there; Luke 16:19–31).

If this passage is not about proclamation in hell, to what does it refer? First, the word "spirits" refers to the immaterial parts of lost people from the days of Noah. The NASB rightly translates it "spirits *now* in prison." They had been alive in the days of Noah but now were dead and their spirits were imprisoned awaiting final judgment. They had heard Noah's preaching, calling them to repentance, back when Noah was building the ark. Noah was considered "a preacher of righteousness" in both the New Testament (2 Peter 2:5) and Jewish literature of the first century AD. Moreover, in context, it is saying that just as the Lord Jesus was raised in the sphere of the Spirit (1 Peter 3:18), similarly, through the Holy Spirit, the Lord Jesus preached through Noah. That is, Noah's message to his contemporaries was through "the Spirit of Christ" (1 Peter 1:11), speaking through Noah as He did to ancient prophets. Simply put, this passage is actually saying that Jesus preached through Noah to people who were alive in the days of Noah but because they rejected Noah's message, were now "spirits in prison" awaiting final judgment. This fits the context of the passage—Peter's hearers were to proclaim the gospel boldly by Messiah's power (1 Peter 3:14–17), just as Noah proclaimed salvation in ancient days.

FINAL THOUGHTS

There is no compelling biblical basis for believing in the descent of Messiah Jesus to hell between His physical death and resurrection. The phrase "He descended to hell" was not included in the earliest versions of the Apostle's Creed. The Apostle's Creed developed gradually from about AD 200 to 750. Rufinius is the first to use the expression in AD 390 but he most likely understood it to mean only that Jesus descended to the grave or was buried. Only in AD 650 was it included to mean that Jesus descended to hell.[37] Theologian Wayne Grudem says that the only argument supporting the doctrine that Jesus descended to hell is that it "seems to be the fact that it has been around so long. But an old mistake is still a mistake."[38]

This is a reminder that the suffering and death of the Lord Jesus is all that is necessary for our atonement for sin. The

Bible teaches that God's attribute of righteousness required a payment for human sin. So God the Son became a man and died (and rose again) to pay that penalty. In this way, according to Paul, God can be both "righteous and declare righteous the one who has faith in Jesus" (Rom. 3:26 HCSB). The Messiah Jesus did not have to pay the debt further by going to hell in our place—His death alone was entirely sufficient for our forgiveness.

Who is responsible for the death of Jesus? I'm troubled by Matt. 27:25 which seems to place all the blame on the Jewish people: "And all the people said, 'His blood shall be on us and on our children.'" Does this mean all Jewish people are guilty of killing Jesus?

35

Sadly, throughout church history, this verse has been wrongly used to accuse the Jewish people of deicide, that is, the murder of God (also called the Christ-killer accusation). This false allegation became the basis of the church's history of hatred for the Jewish people. For example, an influential church father, John Chrysostom, wrote,

> The Jews are the most worthless of all men. They are lecherous, greedy, rapacious. They are perfidious murderers of Christ. They worship the devil; their religion is a sickness. The Jews are the odious assassins of Christ and for killing God there is no expiation possible, no indulgence

or pardon. Christians may never cease vengeance, and the Jew must live in servitude forever. God always hated the Jews. It is incumbent on all Christians to hate the Jews.[39]

A clear definition of the deicide charge against the Jewish people is "that only Jews and all Jews for all time, are guilty of having killed Jesus and in doing so, murdering God."[40] But the New Testament does not actually teach this. Before examining Matthew 27:25, let's consider what the Bible actually says about human guilt in the death of the Lord Jesus.

A CONSPIRACY OF GUILT

The greatest of the church fathers, Augustine of Hippo, wrote, "The Jews held Him, the Jews insulted Him, the Jews bound Him, they crowned Him with thorns, they dishonored Him by spitting upon Him, they scourged Him, they heaped abuse upon Him, they hung Him upon a tree, they pierced Him with a lance."[41] This great theologian mistakenly charged that Jewish people alone carried out the crucifixion of Jesus. Augustine's charge contradicts both the Lord Jesus and the apostles who taught a conspiracy of guilt consisting of some Jews and some Gentiles.

A Conspiracy of Guilt Predicted—Mark 10:33-34

The Lord Jesus Himself actually predicted His crucifixion when He said, "Behold, we are going up to Jerusalem, and the

Son of Man will be delivered to the chief priests and the scribes; and they will condemn Him to death and will hand Him over to the Gentiles. They will mock Him and spit on Him, and scourge Him and kill Him, and three days later He will rise again" (Mark 10:33–34). With these words, the Lord indicated that both Jewish people and Gentiles would be responsible for His death. First, He identified the Jewish leadership (the Sanhedrin) as responsible for condemning Him to death. Then, the Messiah Jesus identified the Gentiles as those who would carry out the mocking, flogging, and murder of the Messiah, clearly referring to the Romans. This prediction demonstrates that responsibility for the crucifixion would not lie solely with Jewish people. Rather, both Jewish people and Gentiles would carry out the predicted unjust execution of the Lord Jesus.

A Conspiracy of Guilt Remembered—Acts 4:27–28

In addition to the Lord Jesus, an unnamed disciple, while praying, recalled the conspiracy of guilt in the crucifixion of Jesus (Acts 4:27–28). His prayer was offered following Peter and John's release from prison for preaching the good news and identifies those responsible for the crucifixion. With regard to human culpability, the prayer states, "For truly in this city there were gathered together against Your holy servant Jesus, whom You anointed, both Herod and Pontius Pilate, along with the Gentiles and the peoples of Israel . . ." (Acts 4:27). First, the phrase "gathered together" is a Greek idiom for "conspired together," showing that the crucifixion was a conspiracy undertaken by both Jews and Gentiles. Second, both a Jewish and a Gentile ruler (Herod Antipas and Pontius Pilate) were guilty of failing to exonerate the innocent Lord Jesus. Third, the conspiracy also included both Gentiles (Roman soldiers) and Jews (the Sanhedrin that condemned Jesus and the crowd that called for Barabbas to be released). As A.T. Robertson has said, "There is guilt enough for all the plotters in the greatest wrong of the ages."[42]

Beyond human guilt, the prayer of this unnamed disciple also recognized God's sovereign plan. He states that those who conspired to kill the Lord Jesus did "whatever Your hand and Your purpose predestined to occur" (Acts 4:28). The death of the Messiah was part of God's purpose and plan. For this reason, the Lord Jesus said, "No one takes my life away from me. I give it up of my own free will. I have the right to give it up, and I have the right to take it back. This is what my Father has commanded me to do" (John 10:18 GNT).

A MISUNDERSTANDING OF JEWISH GUILT

Guilt of the Crowd—Matthew 27:25

Although the church has historically failed to recognize the conspiracy of guilt between Jewish and non-Jewish people, it has also completely misunderstood the Jewish component of guilt. This is evident in the failure to interpret Matthew's statement, "All the people said, 'His blood shall be on us and on our children'" (Matt. 27:25). It is frequently alleged that this verse demonstrates that all Jewish people for all time were guilty. In response, two concepts must be remembered.

First, the phrase "all the people" does not mean "all the Jewish people" universally but refers only to the actual crowd assembled before Pilate. Since it was 6 a.m. on Good Friday when they made this declaration, the crowd could not have been very large. In fact, these people were likely "ringers," gathered at the behest of the Sanhedrin to help convince Pilate to crucify Jesus.

Second, the crowd did not have the authority to bring guilt on their children. As Ezekiel writes: "The person who sins will die. The son will not bear the punishment for the father's iniquity, nor will the father bear the punishment for the son's iniquity; the righteousness of the righteous will be upon himself, and the wickedness of the wicked will be upon himself" (Ezek. 18:20). In context, Pilate washed his hands and declared "I am innocent of this Man's blood" (Matt. 27:24). We know that all the water in the Roman Empire would not have enabled Pilate to wash away his guilt in executing Jesus. In the same way, all the words of the crowd could not bring guilt on their own children or other generations of Jewish people. Although the crowd actually said those words, God certainly did not hold their children guilty.

Guilt of A Few Jewish People—1 Thessalonians 2:14–15

Another portion of Scripture, when taken out of context, has been used to claim that Jewish people are universally guilty of killing Jesus. Paul wrote, "For you, brethren, became imitators of the churches of God in Christ Jesus that are in Judea, for you also endured the same sufferings at the hands of your own countrymen, even as they did from the Jews, who both killed the Lord Jesus and the prophets, and drove us out" (1 Thess. 2:14–15).

The phrase, "the Jews, who both killed the Lord Jesus and the prophets, and drove us out" has been taken to mean that all Jewish people are guilty of killing Jesus. It is important to consider this verse in context. Paul is comparing the sufferings of the Gentile believers at the hands of Gentile leadership in Thessalonica to the suffering of Jewish believers in Judea, at the hands of Jewish leaders. These Jewish leaders, the Sanhedrin, are the same Jews who Paul identified as having participated in the death of Jesus. He is not blaming all Jewish people for all time, but a select group of leaders at that particular time.

A RECOGNITION OF IGNORANCE

Throughout history, Jewish people have been charged with knowingly and deliberately killing their own Messiah. Yet the Lord Jesus Himself, while dying, prayed, "Father, forgive them; for they do not know what they are doing" (Luke 23:34). This statement of forgiveness did not just apply to the Roman soldiers but to all the Jewish people involved in condemning Jesus.

Another recognition of Jewish ignorance is found in Peter's words to a crowd in Jerusalem. It seems that many who cried

"Crucify Him" were present (Acts 3:14). Peter said, "And now, brethren, I know you acted in ignorance, just as your rulers did also" (Acts 3:17).

Paul reiterated the ignorance of those involved in the crucifixion, writing that those leaders who condemned Jesus did not understand who He was, "for if they had understood it they would not have crucified the Lord of glory" (1 Cor. 2:8). Although ignorance does not mean they were innocent, it certainly shows that this was not a deliberate and knowing murder of the Son of God.

THE FINAL WORD ON WHO KILLED JESUS

So, what does the New Testament actually teach about human responsibility in the death of the Lord Jesus? We can clearly conclude, by considering the biblical text and historical facts, that some Jewish people and some Gentiles conspired together to kill the Lord Jesus. But theologically speaking, the responsibility extends much further. The Bible teaches that "all have sinned and fall short of the glory of God" (Rom. 3:23).

Our sin is the reason the Lord Jesus died, to be a substitutionary sacrifice for all of us. So who killed Jesus? We have to recognize that we all played a part in this death. I did. You did. In fact, we all did, because Jesus died for all of us. Our sin put Jesus to death and God's power raised Him to life again. Instead of pointing fingers of guilt toward others, we need to recognize our own part in this crime.

FINAL THOUGHTS

Agatha Christie's mystery *Murder on the Orient Express* follows her standard approach in that every character seems to be the likely murderer. There is a twist at the end, however, when Hercule Poirot proves that all the suspects are guilty, that they all joined together to murder their victim. A detective investigating the murder of Jesus of Nazareth would find a similar result. Who killed Jesus? Was it Judas Iscariot? The Jewish leaders? Or maybe the mob was responsible? But what about Pilate who condemned Him? Or, was it not the Roman soldiers who actually crucified Him? All of the above may be true, but ultimately, it was all of us. Our sins placed the innocent Lord Jesus on that tree, and He went willingly to be our Savior (John 15:13).

I find some parts of Colossians to be confusing. Why does Paul seem to say that Jesus is not God but a created being and that believers fill up His sufferings?

36

I f Colossians actually taught that Jesus was not fully God or that His atonement was not complete, the book would never have been accepted as part of the Bible. Yet, there are verses in Colossians that, when read out of context, might lead to those wrong conclusions. Let's examine what Paul actually teaches about two of these troubling issues.

THE SUPREMACY OF THE LORD JESUS

The Deity of the Lord Jesus

You ask why Paul writes that Jesus was a created being? This question refers to Colossians 1:15b which calls the Lord Jesus "the firstborn of all creation." Before even discussing what this phrase means, we need to observe the context. First, Paul is clearly stating that Jesus is fully God. To begin, the very same verse just mentioned begins by saying that Jesus "is the image of the invisible God" (Col. 1:15a). The word *image* means "an exact representation." The Lord Jesus knew He was the exact representation of God. This is demonstrated by what He told Philip the disciple: "He who has seen me has seen the Father" (John 14:9).

The rest of this section in Colossians describes the Lord Jesus with attributes of deity. He is the creator of and sustainer of all things (vv. 16–17) and He existed before all creation (v. 17), demonstrating His eternal nature. Not only is He the head of the Lord's universal congregation (the church) but He has "supremacy" (v. 18, NIV) over everyone and everything. Above all, "God was pleased to have all his fullness dwell in him" (v. 19 NIV). The word translated *fullness* means completeness. Paul is saying that deity, fully and completely, is permanently present in the Lord Jesus. This whole paragraph clearly states that the Lord Jesus is fully God and not a created being.

In the next chapter in Colossians, we see another clear statement about the full deity of the Lord Jesus. It states, "For in Him all the fullness of Deity dwells in bodily form" (2:9). This simple sentence is filled with several important truths about Jesus. First, the phrase "fullness of Deity" uses the strongest words possible to say that Jesus is completely God. Second, the word *dwells* can be translated "lives" and is in the present tense. This means that deity did not come to reside in Jesus temporarily but it is His permanently. The deity of the Lord Jesus did not come upon Him at the incarnation and leave at His crucifixion. He existed from eternity past to the forever future, the eternal God, the Son. Third, the deity of the Son lives "in bodily form," indicating the full humanity of Jesus. In Colossae, the false teachers were denying the full deity of Jesus, presenting Him as merely an important angel. They also said His body was not real but only appeared to be so. So, in Colossians 2:9, Paul sharply repudiates both of those false ideas and establishes that the Lord Jesus is fully God and fully man, the eternal God-Man.

The Meaning of Firstborn of Creation

Now, in light of Paul's clear teaching in Colossians that the Lord Jesus is fully God, how should we understand the phrase "firstborn of all creation" (Col. 1:15b)? Although the word *firstborn* can mean "first in order of birth," it can also have a figurative sense of "pre-eminence" or "superior,"[43] indicating "supremacy in rank."[44] This is how the word is used in Psalm 89:27, describing the future Davidic (messianic) king as "My firstborn, the highest of the kings of the earth." The phrase "of all creation" should really be translated "over all creation," and the entire verse (Col. 1:15) is saying that the Lord Jesus, as the exact representation of God, is pre-eminent over all creation.

The context supports the idea of this phrase indicating the supremacy of the Messiah Jesus. The following three verses all express the supremacy of the Lord Jesus, showing that "all things have been created through Him and for Him. He is before all things, and in Him all things hold together. He is also head of the body, the church; and He is the beginning,

281

the firstborn from the dead, so that *He Himself will come to have first place in everything*" (vv. 16–18, italics added). Far from teaching an inferior view of Jesus the Messiah, Paul's letter to the Colossians presents the Lord Jesus as exalted above all and the supreme ruler over all creation.

THE AFFLICTIONS OF THE LORD JESUS

The second part of the question raised about Colossians is whether the atonement of Messiah Jesus is sufficient or do His followers, like Paul, need to fill up "what is lacking in Christ's afflictions" (Col. 1:24)? Some have understood Paul to be saying that the suffering of the Lord Jesus was deficient or incomplete. It is impossible for Paul to have meant that because it would contradict the rest of Colossians and the entire teachings of Scripture.

The Sufficiency of the Lord's Atonement

In the next chapter, Paul describes the death and resurrection of Jesus as making us "alive together with Him" and that He forgave us "all our transgressions" (Col. 2:13). Then, Paul says that Jesus "canceled out the certificate of debt consisting of decrees against us . . . having nailed it to the cross" (v. 14). These verses clearly demonstrate that the Lord Jesus' atonement for us is utterly and completely sufficient to provide forgiveness. We have no need to add to His offering for us. This squares with the rest of Scripture concerning the atoning offering of Jesus. The author of Hebrews declares that the body of Jesus was offered as a "once for all" (Heb. 10:10) sacrifice and its provision is "for all time" (Heb. 10:12; cf. 7:26–27).

The Continuation of the Lord's Afflictions

When Paul speaks of the Messiah Jesus' "afflictions," he uses the Greek word *thlipsis,* a word never used to refer to the death of Jesus. It generally means "troubles," "distress," or "oppression"[45] and refers to the trials and tribulations in His life, not the suffering of His death. We should understand that when Paul says "Christ's afflictions," he is not referring to His priestly suffering and death on our behalf but to His earthly sufferings, identifying with our humanity. Isaiah described the Messiah as being "despised and forsaken of men, a man of sorrows and acquainted with grief" (Isa. 53:3).

The afflictions of Paul, or of any follower of Jesus on the basis of our union with Messiah Jesus, continue the earthly afflictions of the Lord Jesus, and in that sense, complete them. The body of the Messiah (the church) is so identified with the Lord Jesus that He asked Saul on the Damascus road, "Why are you persecuting Me?" (Acts 9:4), not "Why are you persecuting My people?"

So, in what sense were Jesus' earthly afflictions lacking? Only in the sense that the people for whom He suffered don't understand His afflictions and may not even be aware of them. So Paul is saying, his own suffering for the Colossians and others is done so that they may begin to grasp Jesus' identification with their affliction and pain. Simply put, Paul's point is that because of his union with Messiah Jesus, his own afflictions mimic and continue what the Lord Jesus had done, and extend and communicate the Messiah's sufferings to others.

FINAL THOUGHTS

What do these teachings in Colossians about the supremacy and afflictions of the Messiah Jesus have to do with us today? First, we need to adopt a daily commitment to worship the Lord Jesus, our exalted and supreme Lord of all the earth. Second, we should not fear affliction or suffering because it identifies us with the sufferings of Jesus in life. Moreover, it extends a living example of the sufferings of the Lord Jesus to those who need to know it most.

QUESTIONS

about

THE JEWISH

PEOPLE

Since most Jewish people don't believe in Jesus, are the Jewish people still God's Chosen People?

Since the second century, Christians have frequently asserted that the church has become the new people of God and that the Jewish people are no longer a part of God's plan. They hold their view because the leadership of Israel rejected Jesus as the Messiah. And, most of the Jewish nation has followed that decision. This point of view is called "replacement theology" or supersessionism. But is this view valid? Are the Jewish people no longer God's chosen nation? Let's look at what the Scripture says.

GOD'S FAITHFULNESS TO ISRAEL

It seems that the New Testament-era church in Rome may have been the first to develop an early form of replacement theology. That's why Paul corrects that view and clarifies the status of the Jewish people in his letter to the Romans. In several places within that epistle, the apostle reminds his readers of God's faithfulness to Israel.

God Is Faithful Despite Israel's Unbelief—Romans 3:3–4

Paul begins by reminding the church at Rome of the advantages God gave the Jewish people, specifically that God entrusted them with "the oracles of God" (Rom. 3:2) or the Scriptures. Then, he turns to the problem of Jewish unbelief in Jesus. He asks and answers, "What then? If some did not believe, their unbelief will not nullify the faithfulness of God, will it? May it never be! Rather, let God be found true, though every man be found a liar" (vv. 3–4). The apostle's point is that although most Jewish people did not believe in Jesus, God would always remain faithful to His promises. God will not abandon the Jewish people. He will protect and preserve them and, ultimately, fulfill every promise He ever made to them.

God's Promises Still Belong to Israel—Romans 9:4–5

In context, these verses indicate that Paul is speaking of unbelieving Israel, his deep compassion for them, and his desire for them to believe in the Messiah Jesus. Nevertheless, in Romans 9:4–5, Paul describes the blessings and promises God has granted to the Jewish people, saying they "are Israelites, to whom belongs the adoption as sons, and the glory and the covenants and the giving of the Law and the temple service and the promises, whose are the fathers, and from whom is the Christ according to the flesh, who is over all, God blessed forever. Amen." These verses are governed by the present-tense verb "are," indicating that all these gifts from

God still belong to the Jewish people, even those who do not believe in Jesus the Messiah. This means that every blessing God gave to Israel still belongs to them, with the greatest one being that God the Son became incarnate in Jewish humanity.

God Has Not Rejected Israel—Romans 11:1–5

It might seem logical that, since Israel as a nation rejected Jesus as the Messiah, God would reject them. In response to that conjecture, Paul exclaims "May it never be!" or "Absolutely not!" (Rom. 11:1). To prove his point, Paul uses himself as an example of a Jewish believer in Jesus. He then points to history. In Elijah's time, God worked through a believing remnant to preserve 7,000 faithful Israelites (vv. 2–4). So, Paul argues, "In the same way then, there has also come to be at the present time a remnant according to God's gracious choice" (v. 5). God has not abandoned or rejected the Jewish people, claims Paul. In every age, from the Old Testament to the present day, there will be a remnant (a small part of the whole) of Israel that will remain faithful to the Lord, until the day when the entire nation turns in faith to their Messiah Jesus (v. 26).

God Chooses and Loves Israel Despite Unbelief— Romans 11:28–29

The most significant passage about the status of the Jewish people is found in Romans 11:28–29. At the outset, it asserts that "from the standpoint of the gospel they are enemies for your sake." This does not say that Jewish people are enemies of God or of Christians. It does acknowledge that they are opposed to the gospel. Except for a remnant of Jewish people who have become followers of Jesus (cf. Rom. 11:1–5), tragically most Jewish people do not believe in Jesus and reject the good news that Jesus is the Redeemer of Israel. What is so sad about this rejection is that Jewish people need Jesus to experience God's eternal forgiveness. Nevertheless, this verse is plainly describing Jewish people who do not believe in Jesus.

Despite their unbelief in Jesus, verses 28 and 29 also say Jewish people will continue to hold a special status as God's people. This unique national identity (which is different than their spiritual status) has three important aspects:

First, despite their unbelief in Jesus, the Jewish people remain God's chosen nation. Romans 11:28 continues by saying "but from the standpoint of God's choice they are beloved for the sake of the fathers." The word *choice* refers to God's choice of the people of Israel. This goes all the way back to God's choice of Abraham, Isaac, and Jacob (Gen. 12:1–3; 26:3–4; 28:10–14) and their physical descendants to be the people through whom God would make His name known throughout the earth.

We might wonder, *Aren't all believers in Jesus chosen?* Clearly, Ephesians 1:4 says that believers were chosen before the foundation of the world. But this verse refers to God's spiritual choice for salvation, not God's national choice of Israel. The Jewish people remain God's chosen nation.

Second, the Jewish people remain God's beloved nation. They are loved not because of anything intrinsic in themselves (Deut. 7:7–8), but because of God's choice and His commitment to the patriarchs, Abraham, Isaac, and Jacob. We might ask, *Doesn't God love Gentiles too?* Of course, He does. John 3:16 says "God so loved the world." But throughout Scripture it is clear that God has a special love for the Jewish people. This is similar to me saying that I love all my students (and I do), but I have a special love for my own sons.

Third, despite their unbelief, Jewish people retain God's unbreakable promises. Romans 11:29 says "for the gifts and calling of God are irrevocable." God's gift of special blessings and His call to the Jewish people to represent Him to the world are irrevocable. The gifts God gave Israel include the Scriptures (Rom. 3:1–2) and those mentioned in Romans 9:4–5 (the adoption as sons, the glory, the covenants including the land covenant, the law, the temple worship, the promises of the Abrahamic covenant, and Jesus, the Messiah of Israel). This means that every promise that God made to Israel still belongs to the people of Israel. One day, the whole nation of Israel, alive at the return of the Lord Jesus, will believe in Him, and the whole nation at that time will be saved (cf. Rom. 11:26). God intends to fulfill every promise He ever made to the Jewish people.

The question remains, if Romans is so clear that God is faithful to Israel and has not rejected His people, why do people think otherwise? To answer, let's consider two central passages which are used to argue that the identity of Israel was changed from the Jewish nation to the church.

THE IDENTITY OF ISRAEL

There are two main passages that are often cited as supporting the alleged change of meaning of Israel from the ethnic Jewish people to all followers of Jesus, Jewish or Gentile. However, both actually speak of ethnic Jewish people.

The True Israel—Romans 9:6

Immediately after pointing out that God's national promises still belong to Israel (Rom. 9:1–5), Paul comments, "But it is not as though the word of God has failed" (Rom. 9:6a). Despite Israel's failure to believe in the Messiah Jesus, God's word remains true. The evidence is in the righteous remnant of Israel, the Jewish followers of Jesus. Paul describes them when he says, "For not all who are descended from Israel are Israel" (Rom. 9:6b HCSB). Although some have taken this to mean that God has expanded Israel into a spiritual Israel, consisting of both Jewish and Gentile believers, that is not what Paul means. Rather, he is speaking of a sub-group within Israel, the Jewish believers (or the remnant of Israel). Jewish followers of Jesus are Abraham's descendants by both physical and spiritual descent, and so they are considered the true Israel. The context of this passage helps us understand this as a narrowing of Israel, referring to Jewish believers, rather than an expansion of Israel to include Gentiles.

This position is supported by the use of the word *Israel* in the New Testament. It is used 73 times, and in 71 of these uses it is undisputed that *Israel* refers to ethnic Jewish people and not Gentiles. It seems extremely unlikely that Paul would use the word *Israel* here to include Gentiles. In context, understanding this passage as speaking of Jewish followers of Jesus makes more sense.

So we can deduce that Paul views Jewish believers in Jesus as the true Israel because of both their physical descent and their spiritual relationship with God by faith in Jesus the Messiah. A good paraphrase of Romans 9:6 would be, "God's word is true—there is a faithful, believing Israel, the faithful remnant, within collective Israel." Consequently, according to Paul, God keeps His promises to the Jewish people through the true Israel, the Jewish followers of Messiah Jesus.

The Israel of God—Galatians 6:16

The only other passage in the New Testament that allegedly uses the word *Israel* to describe the church is Galatians 6:16. But this verse (just as Rom. 9:6) also refers to Jewish followers of Jesus, not to a combination of Jewish and Gentile believers in the church. At the end of Galatians, Paul pronounces a blessing on those who follow his teaching about justification by faith alone, saying, "And those who will walk by this rule, peace and mercy be upon them, and upon the Israel of God" (v. 16).

There are three reasons this passage can be understood as referring to Jewish believers and not the church. First, we should take careful note of the simple conjunction "and" in the phrase, "**and** upon the Israel of God." Some take this word in an explanatory sense, translating it as "even" as if it were explaining that all that walk by Paul's rule (Jew and Gentile alike) are the Israel of God. This would then be describing the church as the Israel of God. On the other hand, this same conjunction in Greek is most commonly used in its simple sense of "and," meaning "to give additional information." If understood this way, Paul is blessing all who follow his teaching *and additionally*, "the Israel of God." Renowned New Testament Greek scholar S. Lewis Johnson, when commenting on this verse, said, "We should avoid the rarer grammatical usages when the common ones make good sense."[46] It makes sense for Paul to bless all who follow his teaching **and** to bless Jewish believers. This view fits the purpose of the book of Galatians.

Second, understanding this verse as a special blessing for Jewish believers fits better within the context of Paul's letter. In the book of Galatians, Paul was dealing with some Jewish teachers who were calling for Gentiles to convert to Judaism and be circumcised. Paul rebukes them for adding a work to God's grace. Some might have considered Paul's sharp rebuke as a condemnation of all Jewish followers of Jesus. So here at the end of the book, Paul gives a blessing to all believers, with an added special blessing for the Jewish believers who were faithful to the truth.

Third, the New Testament uses the word *Israel* 73 times; 72 of these refer to ethnic Israel. It seems highly unlikely that in just one case, Galatians 6:16, the word *Israel* would refer to the church. In the Old Testament and the New Testament, the word *Israel* refers to ethnic Jewish people.

FINAL THOUGHTS

Once, during the Q & A part of a lecture I was giving, someone asked, "Why is it so important to understand God's faithfulness to Israel?" In response, I pointed the audience to Paul's letter to the Romans, particularly chapters 9–11. Romans 8 ends by stating that nothing can ever separate believers from the love of God (vv. 31–39)! Paul frequently answers the challenges of an unseen objector in the book of Romans and here he anticipates what the objection might be: If God rejected Israel, certainly He could reject a disobedient and unfaithful follower of Jesus! Paul's answer in Romans 9 to 11 is designed to vindicate God's faithfulness. His point is that despite Israel's failure to believe in Jesus, God would remain faithful to the national promises He made to Israel. Even better, one day He will bring the nation to faith in Jesus! God's faithfulness to Israel should bring assurance to all believers today. Just as God is faithful to Israel, so He'll be faithful to all followers of Jesus. Even if we fail Him, He will never fail us.

Do Jewish people and Christians worship the same God?

38

Once, while I was standing in Jerusalem surrounded by devout Jewish people, I listened to a talk an American pastor was giving to the people visiting Israel with him. "Don't think for a second that these Jewish people worship the same God as you and I do," he said. "They don't! Jewish people don't believe in the Triune God we believe in. They don't believe in the true God of the Bible. They believe in a different god."

Maybe you have also wondered if Jewish people worship the same God as Christians. I believe that this issue is so important that we should look at what the Scriptures actually say. A close look at the New Testament reveals that Jewish people and Christians do worship the same God. To help us understand why this is true, we'll look closely at some biblical passages found in Paul's defenses given near the end of the book of Acts and then at the heart of Paul's theology of Israel in the book of Romans.[47]

PAUL'S DEFENSES

The Same God—Acts 22:3

The first verse to consider is Acts 22:3. In the context (Acts 21:27–40), Paul had been falsely accused of bringing a Gentile beyond the court of the Gentiles into the Jerusalem temple. It was alleged that Paul brought Trophimus of Ephesus to an area forbidden for non-Jews to enter and to worship (Acts 21:29). Rather than accept his arrest quietly, Paul asks and receives permission to address the crowd (Acts 21:40). In chapter 22, he begins to tell his faith story and says in verse 3, "I am a Jew, born in Tarsus of Cilicia, but brought up in this city, educated under Gamaliel, strictly according to the law of our fathers, being zealous for God just as you all are today." Speaking to this Jewish crowd, Paul didn't say that he is zealous for God (referring to the God of the Bible with a capital G) but that they were zealous for a different god (with a small g). By saying that he was zealous for God just as they were, Paul indicated that both he and the Jewish people worship the same God.

The Same Hope—Acts 24:14-15

Not only did Paul and the Jewish people worship the same God, they also held the same hope of the resurrection. In Acts 24:14–15, Paul is on trial for the same alleged offense of bringing a Gentile into a forbidden area of the temple (Acts 24:5–9). However, this time he is being judged by the Roman governor Felix. Addressing Felix, Paul says of those Jewish people who accused him of wrongdoing: "But this I admit to you, that according to the Way which they call a sect I do serve the God of our fathers, believing everything that is in accordance with the Law and that is written in the Prophets; having a hope in God, which these men cherish themselves, that there shall certainly be a resurrection of both the righteous and the wicked" (Acts 24:14–15). Paul is saying that his faith and expectation is that God will raise the dead and that his Jewish accusers share that same faith and expectation in God. Since they both share the same hope, it would lead to the conclusion that their hope is in the same God as Paul's.

The Same Worship—Acts 26:6-7

In addition to sharing the same hope, Paul and the Jewish people observed the same worship. In Acts 26:6–7, Paul is still on trial for the same alleged offense (Acts 25:23–27). This time, however, he presents his case to the Jewish King Agrippa, saying, "And now I am standing trial for the hope of the promise made by God to our fathers; the promise to which our twelve tribes hope to attain, as they earnestly serve God night and day. And for this hope, O King, I am being accused by Jews" (Acts 26:6–7). When saying that Jewish people earnestly serve God, the word Paul uses, "serve," actually is a Greek word used in Scripture to mean "worship." The verse is speaking of the God who made a covenant with Abraham and it clearly states Jewish people worship Him. Paul and the Jewish people shared the same worship.

PAUL'S THEOLOGY

In Romans chapters 9 to 11, Paul articulates his theology of Israel and the Jewish people. Specifically, in Romans 10:2, after expressing a heart of compassion for his Jewish brothers who don't yet believe Jesus is the Messiah, Paul says, "For I testify about them that they have a zeal for God, but not in accordance with knowledge." The word "zeal," according to the standard Greek lexicon, means to have "intense positive interest in something . . . ardor."[48] It's the very same word used in John 2:17 to describe the enthusiasm of the Lord Jesus for God's temple: "Zeal for Your house will consume me." Based on this usage, I would define this word to mean "having passionate activism." Therefore, Paul identifies his Jewish brothers as passionate activists, not for being Jewish, but for the God of Israel, the same God for whom Paul was zealous.

This verse is helpful because it reveals that Jewish people worship the same God, but, nevertheless, have an incomplete view of Him. Their zeal is "not in accordance with knowledge." Although there are some Jewish believers in Jesus (see Rom. 11:1–5), most Jewish people who believe in the God of Abraham, Isaac, and Jacob do not realize that He is the God and Father of the Lord Jesus (2 Cor. 11:31). They do not acknowledge that He is triune, nor do they recognize that Jesus is the promised Lord and Messiah.

The Bible makes it clear that this incomplete knowledge leads to incomplete worship. Therefore, in Romans 10:1, Paul says his "heart's desire and . . . prayer to God" for the Jewish people is that they might be saved. Jewish people worship the same God but in an incomplete way. They still need to know Jesus and experience forgiveness by believing in Him. So we must pray for them and tell them lovingly of the good news that the Messiah of Israel has come, and that He is Yeshua (Jesus) of Nazareth.

FINAL THOUGHTS

One last thought: We may very well be thinking about this question incorrectly. Instead of asking, "Do Jewish people worship the same God as Christians?," we might want to turn that question around and acknowledge that Christians worship the God of Israel. When Christians worship the God of the Bible, they are worshiping the God of Abraham, Isaac, and Jacob. Christians worship the Holy One of Israel, as Isaiah called Him (for example, Isa. 12:6, one of 29 times this title is used in Isaiah). Instead of portraying Jewish people as worshiping a different false god, Christians should acknowledge that their faith is in the God revealed in the Hebrew Bible, the God of Israel. And if Christians truly appreciated that, it might lead to greater respect for the Jewish people and also a deeper determination to present the Good News to our Jewish friends. Realizing that Gentile Christians are standing on the Rock of Israel (2 Sam. 23:3; Isa. 30:29), they will have greater resolve to proclaim lovingly that the Messiah of Israel has come and His name is Yeshua, the son of David, the son of Abraham (Matt. 1:1).

QUESTIONS

about

SEEMING CONTRADICTIONS AND MYSTERIES

The recorded suicide of Judas seems to have several contradictions and problems. What really happened to Judas?

I t's not surprising that critics of the Bible like to point out alleged contradictions or presumed errors of fact. Books and websites love to charge that the Bible is full of mistakes. So we should also not be surprised that they raise issues about the biblical record of the suicide of Judas.

In Matthew's account (Matt. 27:3–10), Judas is recorded as committing suicide by hanging himself (27:5). But according to Luke in the book of Acts, Judas fell headlong and his guts spilled out (Acts 1:18). Another apparent contradiction is when Matthew says the chief priests bought a potter's field (Matt. 27:6–7), but Luke says it was Judas who purchased the field (Acts 1:18). Finally, Matthew says the actions of Judas fulfilled Jeremiah's prophecy (Matt. 27:9–10) but then he quotes from Zechariah 11:12–13, not from the book of Jeremiah.

But, in Matthew 27:3–10, as in other passages which critics use to challenge biblical accuracy, there are fairly simple explanations that will both address the problems and (more importantly) give us confidence in Scripture. Let's take a look at how to unravel these alleged problems about the death of Judas.

THE DEATH OF JUDAS ISCARIOT

Matthew presents the account of the death of Judas Iscariot, who betrayed the Lord Jesus, in a straightforward way. He writes, "And he [Judas] threw the pieces of silver into the temple sanctuary and departed; and he went away and hanged himself" (Matt. 27:5). Then, in Luke's account in Acts, when the apostles were explaining the need to name a twelfth apostle to replace Judas, Peter says, "Now this man [Judas] acquired a field with the price of his wickedness, and falling headlong, he burst open in the middle and all his intestines gushed out" (Acts 1:18).

HARMONIZING THE ACCOUNTS

How Did Judas Die?

The first element that needs to be harmonized relates to how Judas died. The story in Matthew records Judas hanging himself (Matt. 27:5) but Acts 1:18 says he fell headlong and his guts spilled out. Although the text doesn't state where Judas carried out his suicide, we can imagine him attaching a rope to a branch of a dead tree in an isolated area. Why does the account in Acts 1:18 seem to differ? It would be reasonable to understand that, as Judas's body hung from the tree, a gust of wind or some sort of earthly upheaval caused the branch to break. In fact, at the moment when Jesus died, besides the veil of the temple tearing, "the earth shook and the rocks were split" (Matt. 27:51). Many things could easily have caused the breaking of the branch from which Judas hung. When the swollen corpse fell, it burst open and its intestines poured out. When understood in this way, the two accounts are easily harmonized.

Who Purchased the Potter's Field?

The second apparent contradiction relates to the account of what Judas did with the money he received for betraying Jesus. According to Matthew, Judas "threw the pieces of silver into the temple sanctuary" (Matt. 27:5). The temple authorities, not wanting to put the money into the temple treasury, used it to buy a potter's field (vv. 6–7). But, according to Luke's record, Judas acquired the field with that money (Acts 1:18). Which account is true? The answer is both are true. The authorities didn't want the money back in the temple treasury, so they used the betrayal money to purchase the field *in the name of Judas*. The reason that the Acts record identifies Judas as the purchaser is because the temple leadership bought the potter's field in Judas's name and with his money.

Explaining the Accounts

The harmonization of these two accounts is actually secondary to the real question: Why did the two biblical authors report the accounts differently? The simple reason is that the authors each wanted to communicate distinctive ideas to their respective audiences. Matthew was writing to a Jewish audience and Luke was writing Acts to a Greco-Roman audience.

So, with respect to the chief priests not allowing the blood money paid to Judas to be returned to the temple and purchasing a potter's field in the name of Judas, Matthew wanted to emphasize the guilt and hypocrisy of these leaders. They were willing to pay blood money but not willing to receive it back. Although this should not be misconstrued as supporting the anti-Jewish Christ-killer accusation that has been the basis of so much persecution of the Jewish people, it does recognize that the chief priests were conscious of their wrongdoing.

On the other hand, in Acts 1:18, Luke's quotation of Peter was designed to emphasize the guilt of Judas in purchasing a field. When discussing that Judas acquired the plot of land with the money received from wrongdoing, Gleason Archer suggests that Peter's words are to be taken ironically: "Judas acquired a piece of real estate all right, but it was only a burial plot."[49] This emphasized, in a sarcastic way, the culpability of Judas. Despite his hollow remorse, he was still the son of perdition (John 17:12).

As for Matthew stating that Judas hanged himself and Luke recording that he fell headlong and burst open, both accounts emphasize that Judas was accursed for his behavior. Matthew was writing to a Jewish audience who would have been aware of the Torah's statement, "He who is hanged is accursed of God" (Deut. 21:23). They would have understood Judas hanging himself was a sign that God had condemned him.

This recognition would not have been so clear to Luke's Greco-Roman audience. In that culture, someone who was guilty of wrongdoing was thought to redeem themselves by committing suicide. Thus, Judas hanging himself would have led Luke's audience to conclude that he had undone his evil and thus expunged his guilt. On the other hand, the Hellenistic world had adopted a great adoration of the human body. By saying that Judas had fallen headlong, bursting his body and spilling his intestines, the Greco-Roman audience would have seen that defacing of the body as a sign of Judas being cursed. Luke emphasized this aspect of the death of Judas to make clear to his readers that Judas was the son of perdition. The two accounts of the death of Judas can be easily harmonized but, more importantly, they can be shown to emphasize the message of each individual author.

Quoting from the Old Testament

The second major issue in the account of the death of Judas is found in Matthew's quotation from the Old Testament. Matthew states that these events fulfilled the words of Jeremiah. The problem is that the quotation that Matthew gives is actually from Zechariah 11:12–13.

This alleged error has been explained a number of ways. Some critics say that Matthew may have had a memory lapse and confused Jeremiah with Zechariah. However, that explanation would contradict the inspiration and inerrancy of Scripture. Some say it was an oral statement by Jeremiah not recorded in Scripture. While this may seem plausible, it cannot be proven. Others say these verses were removed from

Jeremiah by Jewish scribes. But, again, that is highly unlikely for two reasons: (1) Jewish veneration of the Bible preserved the text of Scripture; and (2) these very same verses were kept in Zechariah, showing that Jewish scribes had no objection to the passage—we'd have to ask why would scribes take it out of Jeremiah and leave it in Zechariah?

Another common explanation given involves finding passages in Jeremiah using similar words (Jer. 18:2; 19:1, 11) and alleging that Matthew is conflating them with Zechariah and saying it is a quotation from Jeremiah, the more significant prophet. The problem with this solution is that the verses in Jeremiah do not contain a prophecy of Judas and the potter's field as do the verses in Zechariah.

The simplest and most reasonable explanation is that in ancient times, Jeremiah was at the head of the Prophets section of the Bible and it was a common Jewish practice to cite the entire section with the name of the first book. Similarly, the Lord Jesus cited the Law, the Prophets, and "the Psalms," citing the first book to represent the whole section. The ancient book of Jewish wisdom and law, the Talmud, notes the order of the latter Prophets as "Jeremiah, Ezekiel, Isaiah, and the Twelve" (Bava Batra 14b). This is evidence that ancient Jews ordered the latter Prophets with Jeremiah at the head. Therefore, Matthew quoted the passage from the scroll of the Prophets, citing it by its first book, Jeremiah.

FINAL THOUGHTS

We can conclude that the two passages recording the death of Judas (Matt. 27:3–10; Acts 1:18–19) are not filled with contradictions and errors. In actuality, they focus their attention on those who were truly guilty for the travesty that led to the death of Jesus. Moreover, it shows that all of these details were always part of the plan of God. The actions of the chief priests and Judas were predicted in Zechariah 11:12–13. A careful reading of these texts leads us not to doubt, but to greater confidence in Scripture with regard to both history and prophecy.

What happens when followers of Jesus die? Do they immediately go to the presence of the Lord or do their souls sleep until the resurrection?

Rhoda was a committed follower of Jesus and a member of a congregation I served. Although only 42 years old, she was diagnosed with stage four cancer and quickly succumbed to the ravages of the disease. I sat at her hospice bedside and saw her intense physical pain. Although Rhoda was barely conscious because of her painkilling medications, she was still able to communicate to me that she longed to be with her Lord Jesus. Her hope reflected the desire of all followers of Jesus—that someday, we'll be ushered into the presence of the Lord Jesus, when all the pain and difficulties of this life will have passed and we will be in glory. This isn't just pie in the sky but our actual confident expectation.

Is this view of the afterlife valid or should believers expect an extended period of soul sleep before the resurrection from the dead, when we will at last see the Lord Jesus? What do the Scriptures have to say about this?

THE REASON FOR CONFUSION ABOUT HEAVEN

The source of any confusion about heaven versus soul sleep arises from 1 Thessalonians 4:13–18. This passage was intended to comfort those who were concerned that their loved ones who had already died in the Lord would therefore miss the return of the Lord Jesus and not be with Him forever.

Three times Paul describes those who have died as being "asleep" (1 Thess. 4:13–15). The phrase "those who have fallen asleep" does not actually teach some sort of doctrine of soul sleep. Rather, the word "sleep" is a euphemism for death. It describes the condition of the physical body of a Jesus follower who has died. Upon physical death, the inner, immaterial person goes to be with the Lord immediately. But our bodies become empty vessels, separated from our spirits and even look as if they are sleeping.

The comfort Paul gives is that when the Lord returns, we will be "caught up" to be with Him (1 Thess. 4:16–17).[50] We will not precede those who have died when entering the Lord's presence. Rather, those who have died in the Lord will be resurrected before those who are caught up to be with the Lord. At that time, the bodies of those who have died ("fallen asleep") will reunite with their spirits which have been present with the Lord since physical death. The believers who are alive will then be snatched up and receive glorified bodies without ever dying. Then, we will be together forever, both the resurrected believers and those who were taken up by the

Lord Jesus. At that time, we will be reunited and have glorified, immortal bodies, just like the resurrected body of the Lord Jesus (cf. 1 Cor. 15:42–49).

THE BIBLICAL CASE FOR IMMEDIATE HEAVEN

So what do the Scriptures say will happen when a follower of Jesus dies? The Bible clearly states that those who have believed that Jesus died (taking the punishment for their sins) and was raised from the dead (proving He is God) will go to be with the Lord immediately upon death.

"Today You Will Be with Me in Paradise"

How do we have this assurance? The first passage that comes to mind contains the words of the Lord Jesus to the thief on the cross, "Truly I say to you, today you shall be with Me in Paradise" (a first-century Jewish word for heaven; Luke 23:43). Clearly, the Lord was promising that the penitent thief would go to heaven immediately upon death.

Those who hold to soul sleep argue against the simple meaning of this verse, saying (correctly) that the original Greek did not have commas. Therefore, it's only the English translators who put the comma after the phrase "Truly I say to you" and not after the word "today." They contend that the correct translation of the Lord's words are: "Truly, I say to you today, you shall be with me in Paradise (someday after the resurrection from the dead)." In summary, some assert that the word "today" refers to the time when the Lord was speaking and not to the time of the thief's arrival in heaven.

There are two basic problems with this interpretation. First, although the Lord frequently uses the word "Truly" to begin a statement, nowhere else does He say "Truly I say to you today." If the Lord Jesus only meant that He was saying something on that day, He certainly would have used that expression elsewhere. Second, placing the comma after the word "today" results in a meaningless redundancy. Of course, Jesus was saying it that day. When else would He be saying it? Placing the comma after "I say to you" and beginning the next clause with "today" makes an important point of emphasis— that very day the thief would be with Him in heaven.

To Depart and Be with Messiah

A second support for believers in Jesus going to be with Him immediately upon death is found in Philippians 1:21–25. This passage describes the tension Paul feels about life and death, saying "I am hard-pressed from both directions, having the desire to depart and be with Christ, for that is very much better; yet to remain on in the flesh is more necessary for your sake" (Phil. 1:23–24). Paul "was torn by a win-win situation."[51] On the one hand he wanted "to depart [die] and be with Christ," plainly indicating that at the moment of death, he would immediately go to be with Jesus. In the apostle's view, this would be far better than any other experience. On the other hand, Paul saw the necessity and benefits of remaining "on in the flesh" to minister to the Philippians. That's why he wrote, "For to me, to live is Christ and to die is gain" (v. 21). Paul's earthly life was filled with joyful service for Jesus the Messiah but dying would be even better because he would see his Lord face to face.

Home with the Lord

A third passage that teaches that followers of Jesus go to be with the Lord upon death is 2 Corinthians 5:6–8. There Paul describes circumstances of life and death. While we are alive in this life ("at home in the body," 2 Cor. 5:6), we are not in the immediate presence of the Lord Jesus ("we are absent from the Lord," 2 Cor. 5:6). Alternatively, the apostle wrote that his preference was "to be absent from the body and to be at home with the Lord" (2 Cor. 5:8). By this he meant that when we leave this life, we go directly into the presence of the Lord in heaven, our true home. The testimony of both the words of Jesus and Paul confirm that followers of Jesus go to be with the Lord immediately when they die.

FINAL THOUGHTS

We need never fear death nor grieve uncontrollably for Jesus followers who have died. We who believe that Jesus died and rose again (1 Thess. 4:14) can have the confident expectation that at the moment of physical death, our immaterial part (soul, spirit, mind, heart) will enter into the presence of the

Lord. All followers of Jesus who have died ("fallen asleep") will immediately be in heaven and stay with Him until His return. When the Lord Jesus does return, two events will take place. Those who have died in Jesus will be resurrected, uniting their bodies and spirits in new glorified, immortal bodies. Those who are still alive will then be caught up to Him, their bodies being translated to glorified, immortal bodies as well. That will be a great reunion of all believers in Jesus, together with Him. This hope of "the mortal putting on immortality," is so great that Paul declared, "Death is swallowed up in victory. . . . O death, where is your sting?" (1 Cor. 15:54–55). Death, which we mortals fear most, will give way to glory, once and for all.

Will we see God when we die and go to heaven? Will we spend eternity being able to see the face of God?

I f we love the Lord Jesus, one of our great frustrations is that we have not yet seen Him. Of course, the Lord promised a special blessing for us, telling a doubting Thomas, "Because you have seen Me, have you believed? Blessed are they who did not see, and yet believed" (John 20:29). Nevertheless, it is only natural that we should long to look upon the face of God once we are with Him for eternity. Will that be possible?

The simple answer is "yes." Believers will spend eternity with the Lord and we will see our God. The clearest verse about this is Revelation 22:3–4: "The throne of God and of the Lamb will be in it, and His bond-servants will serve Him; *they will see His face*, and His name will be on their foreheads" (italics added). This states that in the New Jerusalem in the New Creation, the redeemed will spend eternity looking upon their God. However, this does not resolve how this will be possible in light of all the Scriptures have to say about seeing God.

THE NEW TESTAMENT TEACHING:
NO ONE CAN SEE GOD

The problem is that the New Testament is emphatically clear that no person has seen or can see God the Father. Jesus taught "God is spirit" (John 4:24), meaning He is immaterial and so cannot be seen. In John 1:18 it says "No one has seen God at any time; the only begotten God who is in the bosom of the Father, He has explained Him." The Lord Jesus taught no one "has seen the Father, except the One who is from God; He has seen the Father" (John 6:46). John reiterates this in 1 John 4:12: "No one has seen God at any time." So plainly, according to John in both his Gospel and epistle, no one has seen God or can see Him except for the Lord Jesus, who is God the Son incarnate.

This idea is not limited to John's writing but is stated by Paul as well. The apostle Paul described the Father as "the King eternal, immortal, *invisible*, the only God" (1 Tim. 1:17, italics added). Since God is invisible, Paul goes on to say that He "dwells in unapproachable light, whom *no man has seen or can see*" (1 Tim. 6:16, italics added). Plainly, the New Testament asserts that it is not possible for a mortal person to see God.

THE OLD TESTAMENT TEACHING:
NO ONE CAN SEE GOD

The Old Testament answer to this question is the same as the New Testament. When Moses asked God to show him

His glory (Ex. 33:18), God told Moses, "You cannot see My face, for no man can see Me and live!" (Ex. 33:20). Clearly, the Old Testament teaches that the God of Israel revealed in the Old Testament could not be seen by any person.

Yet in this very same passage (Ex. 33:21–22), God puts Moses in the cleft of the rock, covers him, and says, "Then I will take My hand away and you shall see My back, but My face shall not be seen" (Ex. 33:23). Is this saying that it's possible to see God's back but not His face? Not really. The point of this passage is that God showed Moses a glimpse of His presence. As God passed by, Moses caught sight of His glory. Seeing a glimpse of God's glory is similar to how we can see the rays of the sun, but we can't look at the sun directly or we will be blinded. Moses didn't see God—he only saw a reflection of His glory.

What about other examples from the Old Testament of those who have seen God? For example, when Moses brought Aaron, Nadab, Abihu, and the 70 elders of Israel to Mount Sinai, the text says "they *saw* the God of Israel; and under His feet there appeared to be a pavement of sapphire, as clear as the sky itself. Yet He did not stretch out His hand against the nobles of the sons of Israel; and they *saw* God, and they ate and drank" (Ex. 24:10–11, italics added). How can they have seen God and lived? The most likely explanation of their encounter with God is in the nuance of the Hebrew verb *chazah*, translated "saw" twice in these verses. It generally means to see in a vision (cf. Num. 24:4, 16). In other words, they did not literally see God Himself, but only saw a vision of Him.

Similarly, in Isaiah 6, when Isaiah saw the Lord, although a different Hebrew verb is used, it is plain that this is a prophetic vision and not an actual sighting of God. Also, when Daniel saw the Ancient of Days (Dan. 7:9ff), he describes all that he saw as part of a night vision (Dan. 7:2). Similarly, Ezekiel describes seeing God in all His radiance and glory (Ezek. 1:26–28). However, at the beginning of the chapter, the prophet said "I saw visions of God" (Ezek. 1:1). So, plainly Ezekiel only had a vision of the Lord and didn't literally see God.

WE WILL SEE GOD THE SON!

So how is it that we will be able to see God in our forever future? For you and I, it will be possible to see God, but only God the Son, the Lord Jesus. In response to Philip's request that the Lord Jesus show them the Father, He said, "The one who has seen Me has seen the Father" (John 14:9 HCSB).

Also, in the Old Testament, there is the mysterious Angel of the Lord. In numerous passages, the Angel of the Lord is used interchangeably with Yahweh, the God of Abraham, Isaac and Jacob (e.g., Ex. 3:2, 6–7). This has led many to conclude that these appearances of the Angel of the Lord are theophanies—visible manifestations of God. Since John 1:18 states that no one has ever seen God but that the Lord Jesus has revealed Him, it has led to the conclusion that Old Testament theophanies were actually Christophanies, or pre-incarnate manifestations of the Messiah Jesus, God the Son.

So, when the Angel of the Lord appeared to Hagar (Gen. 16:7–14), she marveled at seeing God: "Have I even remained alive here after seeing Him?" (Gen. 16:13). She had indeed seen God but it was a pre-incarnate appearance of God the Son. Similarly, when Samson's parents were visited by the Angel of the Lord and they saw His wonders, Manoah was frightened and exclaimed, "We will surely die, for we have seen God" (Judg. 13:22). They did not die because, once again, this was a pre-incarnate appearance of God the Son.

FINAL THOUGHTS

This is the great hope that we have. One day, the Lord Jesus will return and we will look at His face directly. John describes it like this: "We know that when He appears, we will be like Him, because we will see Him just as He is" (1 John 3:1–2). The Lord Jesus will transform us into His righteous image and we will finally be without sin and entirely holy.

Although Revelation 22:3–4, mentioned above, says that the throne of God and of the Lamb will be in the eternal city, a better translation would be, "The throne of God, *even* of the Lamb, will be in it (the New Jerusalem), and His servants will serve Him. *They will see His face.*" This indicates that it is the Lamb, the Lord Jesus, the Son who is fully God, whom we will look upon forever. It is the face of Jesus the Messiah we will see. And when we see Him, I guarantee, we will never be disappointed.

Why does God allow so much evil and suffering?

A friend of mine recently posted a statement on her Facebook page. In short, it said, "Life is unfair." She was heartbroken over her 40-year-old sister-in-law, a new mom, being diagnosed with stage four colon cancer. Besides this kind of individual suffering, people frequently ask, "Where is God when there are earthquakes, tsunamis, hurricanes, terrorist attacks, mass shooters, pandemics, you name it?" Why does God allow all of this human suffering?

Since this is such a common question, you'd think I'd have a good answer. I don't. There is no one simple and satisfying answer for such a painful and complex question. But I do have some thoughts that have helped me when I struggle. Here are several concepts that we can embrace when we wonder why a good God allows evil and suffering.

GOD'S SOVEREIGNTY

First, when considering life's challenges, we must recognize the absolute truth that God is sovereign over everything, including suffering. No natural disaster or personal struggle or any evil experience we may encounter can ever cause God to be surprised. God knows it all. He says in Isaiah 45:7: "I form light and create darkness, I make success and create disaster; I am the LORD, who does all these things" (CSB). Just as God is the sovereign Creator, He is sovereign over disasters.

HUMAN LIMITATIONS

Second, as humans, we are bound by our own limitations. We are limited by our lack of understanding—we don't know what God's purposes are in allowing suffering. It is a terrible mistake to assume that God's purposes are knowable to us. That's why God declared through Isaiah: "'For My thoughts are not your thoughts, nor are your ways My ways,' declares the LORD. 'For as the heavens are higher than the earth, so are My ways higher than your ways and My thoughts than your thoughts'" (Isa. 55:8–9). God's omniscient plans and purposes are far beyond our finite human ability to understand them.

A FALLEN WORLD

Another problem we face is that we live in a fallen world. We need to remember that tragic events are not necessarily related to the specific behavior of nations or individuals. This world is corrupt because Adam and Eve chose to rebel against God's command. Of course, some might object that God is still culpable because He created a world in which Adam and Eve could sin. Yet, if God had made a world in which Adam and Eve could not choose to obey (or disobey) God, then He would have been creating a mechanized world with human robots. God made Adam and Eve with moral responsibility so they could choose to love and obey Him. Robots can't have a relationship with God, but people, created with moral responsibility, can. Unfortunately, Adam and Eve chose to disobey. As a result, we live in an evil and fallen world where bad things happen. Every day we see this. People get terminal diseases, planes crash, young people die, and tidal waves overwhelm communities. This is not because of direct divine judgment, but because we live in this fallen world. Paul identified this problem when he wrote, "We know that the whole creation groans and suffers the pains of childbirth together until now" (Rom. 8:22). This world is groaning because it is fallen and as a result, we also groan under its pain of suffering.

GOD'S REMINDERS

God sometimes uses suffering as a reminder in our lives. This is seen in Jesus' teaching that disasters, whether natural or man-made, are *a reminder of God's mercy*. In Luke 13:1–9, responding to the question of why God allowed evil, Jesus told the parable of the unproductive fig tree (Luke 13:6–9). Although the tree was not producing fruit, the vineyard keeper decided not to cut it down in order to give it more time to bear fruit. Jesus' point was that if God were to act based on our behavior, disaster and devastation would be the norm, not the exception. We all sin, and if God responded based on what we deserve, we'd all be devastated all the time. This is what Jeremiah meant when he wrote, "Because of the LORD's great love we are not consumed, for his compassions never fail" (Lam. 3:22 NIV). It is only God's loving mercy that prevents Him from destroying all of us instantaneously. So when we see evil events happening around us, we should remember God's mercy which prevents every terrible circumstance possible from falling upon every person.

God may use suffering to remind us to turn to Him. When we see natural disasters or personal suffering strike others, Jesus said this was the reminder for us to turn to God before we perish as well (Luke 13:3–5). That's the reason the psalmist wrote, "In my trouble I cried to the LORD, and He answered me" (Ps. 120:1). Author C. S. Lewis explained it well: "God whispers to us in our pleasures, speaks to us in our conscience, but shouts in our pains: It is His megaphone to rouse a deaf world."[52] God sometimes uses our pain and sorrow to get our attention and to remind us to turn to Him for comfort.

God also uses tragic events to remind us that we're not home yet. It's easy for us to get overly comfortable here on earth and to never want to leave, as if this temporal life is all that God has for us. But God has given us eternity. Suffering on this earth serves as a reminder that God has prepared a far better home for us in the future. The "sufferings of this present time are not worthy to be compared with the glory that is to be revealed to us" (Rom. 8:18). Suffering and adversity remind us not to allow ourselves to become overly comfortable here. It's God's great reminder that this world is not our real home. Suffering makes us remember that, if we know the Lord Jesus, we're citizens of a far better future world, where every tear will be wiped away and all pain and sorrow will be removed.

FINAL THOUGHTS

English writer Dorothy Sayers said that when it comes to human sufferings, sorrow, and death, God had "the honesty and the courage to take His own medicine."[53] In the Messiah Jesus, God entered this world as a fully human person. He not only suffered for us, but also suffered with us that through His death and resurrection we can have life forever.

Why is the God of the Old Testament so severe while the God of the New Testament is loving and gracious? The Law of Moses seems unnecessarily harsh, calling for an eye for an eye and a tooth for a tooth. This seems so primitive and callous.

It's fairly common to think that the God of the Old Testament was harsh and vindictive but the God of the New Testament, as revealed through Jesus, is gentle, loving, and kind. As a result, people often call out the "eye for an eye" concept in the Law of Moses as proof that the God of Israel was harsh. In the New Testament, the Lord Jesus seems to reflect a more forgiving approach, saying "He who is without sin among you, let him be the first to throw a stone . . ." (John 8:7). Nevertheless, the God who gave the laws through Moses is the same God who gave His one and only Son for the sins of the world. We need to take a deeper dive to better understand the alleged law of retaliation and what seems like two very different portrayals of God in the Old and New Testaments.

THE LAW OF RETALIATION

This law, frequently called the "law of retaliation" (*lex talionis*), is deeply misunderstood. The same "eye for an eye" commandment is found in Exodus 21:23–25, Leviticus 24:19–20, and Deuteronomy 19:16–21. This commandment is part of the Law of Moses, a document designed to be the constitution of the people of Israel living in the land of Israel. Therefore, this commandment is talking about governmental authority, not personal behavior. The Deuteronomy rendering of the law is as follows: "then both the men who have the dispute shall stand before the LORD, before the priests and the judges who will be in office in those days. The judges shall investigate thoroughly.... Thus you shall not show pity: life for life, eye for eye, tooth for tooth, hand for hand, foot for foot" (Deut. 19:17–18, 21).

Judicial, Not Personal

The misunderstanding about this statute is that it is often perceived as vengeful and excessive when it was actually designed to restrain vengeance and excessive punishment. There are two reasons for this perspective. First, the law required that retribution was to be *judicial, not personal*. In Exodus 21:22, it states that fines should be paid "as the judges decide" while in Deuteronomy 19:18 it says that the dispute is to be brought to the judges who "shall investigate thoroughly." The Law of Moses made no allowance for personal vendettas, vigilante justice, or individual acts of vengeance. Disputes and criminal actions were brought to judges and the government was to carry out punishment. This law did not mean that if someone hurt my eye, I was permitted to hurt his eye. Rather, the courts would determine appropriate justice, thereby avoiding long-term feuds like the Hatfields and the McCoys.

Equal, Not Excessive

Second, these laws required that punishment should be *equal to the crime, not excessive*. In other words, the punishment was to fit the crime. If someone was liable for injuring my eye, the punishment would not be the death penalty. The consequence had to be equivalent to the injury done. Moreover, the context of Exodus is about paying monetary fines (cf. Ex. 21:19, 22), so it appears that the "eye for an eye, tooth for a tooth" command was not to be taken literally but referred to the appropriate financial restitution for an injury. If these words were taken literally, then it would lead to a blind, toothless society. What good does it do for a sightless person to have the person who blinded him also become blind? Rather, the court was to determine the appropriate compensation to help the person who was disabled.

CAPITAL PUNISHMENT

The only exception to the financial application of these laws appears to be the death penalty for deliberate homicide. Since people are made in the image of God, deliberate murder of someone required the courts to carry out capital punishment as the only appropriate justice. That's why Genesis 9:6 says, "Whoever sheds man's blood, by man his blood shall be shed, for in the image of God He made man." Clearly the Law of Moses was not primitive or harsh. Rather, it provided for appropriate justice and restricted the sinful human desire for excessive vengeance and personal retaliation.

One last thought about this command: this idea is not limited to the Old Testament but a similar concept is mentioned in the New Testament as well. In Romans, Paul calls believers to be subject to legitimate governmental authority (Rom. 13:1–7). Moreover, he warns the person who does evil to "be afraid; for it [the government] does not bear the sword for nothing; for it is a minister of God, an avenger who brings wrath on the one who practices evil" (Rom. 13:4). So governmental punishment was not just part of the Old Testament Law but included in the New Testament, even to the point of capital punishment. Note that Paul talks about the government bearing the sword—this would refer to using it to put to death, not to slap someone's bottom.

THE SAME GOD

Just as God affirms governmental authority in both the Old and New Testaments, He is also portrayed as just and loving in both. Here are some ways God is both gracious and fierce in both Testaments.

A Loving and Forgiving God in the Old Testament

In the Old Testament, we see that God is loving and merciful as He forgives sin. For example, David, who committed adultery and set up the death of Uriah the Hittite, is shown mercy when David repents and God forgives him. In Psalm 32:5, David said, "I acknowledged my sin to You, and I did not hide my guilt; I said, 'I will confess my wrongdoings to the Lord'; and You forgave the guilt of my sin" (nasb). The Old Testament describes God this way: "The Lord, the Lord God, compassionate and gracious, slow to anger, and abounding in lovingkindness and truth; who keeps lovingkindness for thousands, who forgives iniquity, transgression and sin . . ." (Ex. 34:6–7).

A Just and Wrathful God in the New Testament

And while we may see the sterner side of God in the Old Testament, those characteristics are evident in the New Testament as well. Throughout the Bible, God is a God of justice. He holds people accountable for their sin and sometimes exercises discipline in seemingly severe ways. For example, when Ananias and Sapphira lied about how much they were giving to the congregation, Peter rebuked Ananias first, saying he had "not lied to men but to God," and then God struck him dead. The same then happened to his wife Sapphira (Acts 5:1–11), reminiscent of instant justice sometimes seen in the Old Testament. The New Testament also describes the end of days, when God's judgment would fall on the earth at the hands of Jesus, the Lamb of God. This is how people will respond in that day: "They said to the mountains and to the rocks, 'Fall on us and hide us from the presence of Him who sits on the throne, and from the wrath of the Lamb; for the great day of their wrath has come, and who is able to stand?'" (Rev. 6:16–17).

FINAL THOUGHTS

Here's the main point to remember: God is always the same. He is perfect and infinite in holiness and justice and in His love and mercy. These attributes explain the very reason the Lord Jesus came to redeem humanity. In His holiness and justice, God demanded that all sin be punished, but in His love, He Himself provided the One who would take that punishment. The Lord Jesus died for our sins to satisfy God's just anger at sin and then was raised from the dead. God did this because He loved the world and provided the means of our forgiveness and eternal life (John 3:16). In this way, God "would be just and the justifier of the one who has faith in Jesus" (Rom. 3:26). That is the essential message of the Good News: that the holy and just God redeemed us in love through Jesus the Messiah.

Can you give a simple explanation of the Trinity?

I wish I could! Unfortunately, there is no simple or easy explanation of the Trinity. This theological concept is what Ken Boa calls an antinomy. Although "antinomy" literally means a conflict between two equally valid principles, the term is used theologically to refer to God's revelation in Scripture going beyond "the level of human reasoning and comprehension by stating as fact two things which [human beings] cannot reconcile."[54] The basis of biblical antinomies is found in Isaiah 55:8–9, "'For My thoughts are not your thoughts, nor are your ways My ways,' declares the Lord. 'For as the heavens are higher than the earth, so are My ways higher than your ways and My thoughts than your thoughts.'" It's not that the Trinity is contrary to logic and reason, but rather it's beyond the human ability to comprehend fully. God understands the Trinity just fine; we human beings don't.

Nevertheless, the Trinity is clearly expressed as a fact in Scripture; it just doesn't explain exactly how it works. Later theologians have developed explanations that have come to us as the accepted understanding of this biblical teaching. We'll examine what the Bible and theologians have said and hopefully get a better grip on the Trinity.

THE SIMPLE DEFINITION

You may be surprised to hear that the word "Trinity" is not found in the Bible. This is a fact frequently pointed out by people who don't believe in it. The absence of the word is actually irrelevant since the concept of the Trinity is certainly found in Scripture. The word refers to God being three in one, with the "tri" indicating His threeness and the "nity" indicating His unity or oneness. I actually prefer to use the term "triunity" of God because it seems so much clearer. But where does the Bible teach that God is three in one?

THE BIBLICAL DATA

God's Oneness

The Old Testament clearly teaches monotheism (the belief that there is only one God), indicating that God alone is the one and only true God. The most foundational verse supporting God's oneness is called the Shema (the Hebrew word meaning "hear"), the basis of monotheism in Judaism: "Hear, O Israel! The LORD is our God, the LORD is one!" (Deut. 6:4). The oneness of God is presented throughout the Old Testament, not just in this verse. For example, God declared through Isaiah, "For I am God, and there is no other; I am God, and there is no one like Me" (Isa. 46:9, cf. Ex. 20:3; Deut. 4:35; 5:7; 32:39; Ps. 83:18; Isa. 43:10–11).

The New Testament also affirms monotheism. For example, Paul states explicitly, "For there is one God" (1 Tim. 2:5) and again, "There is . . . one Lord . . . one God and Father of all" (Eph. 4:4–6; cf. 1 Cor. 8:6). James also says, "You believe that God is one. You do well" (James 2:19). Of course, in Mark 12:29, the Lord Jesus affirmed the oneness of God, declaring that the foremost commandment was Deuteronomy 6:4 (cited above). There is no doubt that both the Old and New Testaments teach monotheism.

God's Threeness

Although there is no one specific verse explicitly declaring that God is triune, both Testaments provide evidence of this fact. The Old Testament implies that there is a plurality in the one God, while the New Testament speaks of Father, Son, and Holy Spirit more explicitly.

Old Testament Evidence

The very first Old Testament hint of God's plurality is when God says, "Let Us make man in Our image, according to Our likeness" (Gen. 1:26). Some believe this is a mere use of the plural pronoun to express God's majesty (the royal "We"), which is possible. Others say that this is God speaking to the angels; however, humanity was not made in the image of angels. Yet, it most likely refers to the mysterious plurality in the Godhead because of the verse that follows. It states that God "created man in His own image . . . male and female He created them" (Gen. 1:27). This shows that one aspect of human likeness to their Creator is that, just as God is one and also has plurality in His nature, so humanity has one essence (humanity) but also has plurality, both male and female.

The Old Testament also points to the deity of the future Messiah in several ways. It has a unique figure, called the Angel of the Lord, who is identified as the Lord and yet distinct from the Lord (e.g., Gen. 22:15–16; Ex. 3:2–9), describing the pre-incarnate appearances of the Lord Jesus. Also, David calls the Messiah his Lord, declaring, "The LORD says to my Lord: 'Sit at My right hand . . .'" (Ps. 110:1). Isaiah gave four throne titles indicating the deity of the future Messiah: Wonderful Counselor, Mighty God, Eternal Father, and Prince of Peace (Isa. 9:6).

The Old Testament also describes the Holy Spirit as possessing certain attributes that belong to God alone, such as omnipresence (Ps. 139:7) and omnipotence (Job 33:4). Additionally, the Old Testament identifies the Holy Spirit's deity by revealing His divine work in creation (Gen. 1:2).

Perhaps the clearest Old Testament passage indicating plurality in the Godhead is Isaiah 48:12–16. At the beginning of the paragraph, God clearly identifies Himself, saying, "I am the first, I am also the last. Surely My hand founded the earth, and My right hand spread out the heavens" (Isa. 48:12–13). Then, at the end of the paragraph, God says, "And now the *Lord GOD* has sent *Me*, and His *Spirit*" (Isa. 48:16, italics added). This verse presents the mysterious threeness within the oneness of God.

Some might object that the Old Testament teaching of plurality in the Godhead somehow contradicts Deuteronomy 6:4, which says that "the LORD is one." However, the Hebrew word for one is *echad* and can carry the meaning of a "composite unity." For example, when God established marriage, He declared that when married, a man and a woman "shall become one flesh" (Gen. 2:24), indicating a composite unity.[55] Although the use of *echad* in Deuteronomy 6:4 does not demand this meaning, it does permit it, allowing for these hints of plurality in God's oneness in the Old Testament.

New Testament Evidence

The New Testament does not have one verse that says "God is triune"[56] but it does explicitly identify the Father, the Son and the Holy Spirit as deity. To begin, the Father is plainly called God. For example, the Gospel of John speaks of the Son, on whom "the Father, God, has set His seal" (John 6:27). Paul also recognizes the deity of the Father, calling Him "one God and Father of all who is over all" (Eph. 4:6).

In addition to the Father, the Son, the Lord Jesus the Messiah, is called God in the New Testament. For instance, when Thomas finally believed that Jesus has been raised from the dead, Thomas called Him, "My Lord and my God!" (John 20:28). Paul described the Second Coming as "the blessed hope and the appearing of the glory of our great God and Savior, Christ Jesus" (Titus 2:13). He also declared that in the Lord Jesus, "all the fullness of Deity dwells in bodily form" (Col. 2:9) and that Jesus is "the Messiah, who is God over all, praised forever" (Rom. 9:5 HCSB). The New Testament describes Jesus with attributes that only belong to God, such as omniscience (John 2:24–25; Matt. 9:4), omnipotence (Matt. 28:18; Heb. 1:3), and eternality (John 17:5). It also attributes the divine work of creation to Him (John 1:3; Col. 1:16). The deity of the Lord Jesus the Messiah, God the Son, is one of the clearest teachings of the New Testament.

Also, the New Testament identifies the Holy Spirit as God. For example, the Holy Spirit possesses omniscience (1 Cor. 2:10–12), an attribute that belongs exclusively to God. The Spirit also performs divine works such as regeneration (John 3:5–6, 8), conviction (John 16:8), and the inspiration of Scripture (2 Tim. 3:16; 2 Peter 1:21). The most obvious passage indicating the deity of the Holy Spirit is Acts 5:3–4, where lying to the Holy Spirit is equated with lying to God ("Why has Satan filled your heart to lie to the Holy Spirit? . . . You have not lied to men but to God.").

Frequently, the New Testament speaks of Father, Son, and Holy Spirit as equals in their work. For example, Paul gives praise for the entire Godhead's work in salvation: First the Father who chose us (Eph. 1:3–6), then the Son who redeems us (Eph. 1:7–12), and also the Holy Spirit who secures us (Eph. 1:13–14). Similarly, Peter describes believers as "chosen according to the foreknowledge of *God the Father*, by the sanctifying work of *the Spirit*, to obey *Jesus Christ* and be sprinkled with His blood" (1 Peter 1:1–2, italics added; cf. 2 Cor. 13:14).

Perhaps the strongest statement of the triune nature of God is found in the command of the Lord Jesus for His followers to baptize "in the name of the Father and the Son and the Holy Spirit" (Matt. 28:19). While identifying the three persons, indicating the "threeness" of God, the noun "name" is singular where a plural would be expected grammatically, indicating God's oneness.

It is plain to see that the whole Bible supports the idea that God is one and that there is a mysterious threeness or plurality in that oneness. This led many theologians to attempt to explain how this could be.

THE THEOLOGICAL EXPLANATIONS

The Mistaken Explanations

One erroneous explanation affirms that the Father is fully God but denies or depreciates the deity of the Son and the Holy Spirit. This interpretation contradicts the testimony of Scripture. Another mistaken approach is a form of Tritheism, affirming the deity of Father, Son, and Holy Spirit but denying the biblical teaching that there is only one God. A third incorrect explanation, called Modalism, sees the Father, Son, and Holy Spirit as three forms or modes of the One God. So, God is the Father in the Old Testament, the Son in the Gospels, and the Holy Spirit after the giving of the Holy Spirit in Acts 2. Yet, at the baptism of the Lord Jesus, the Son was baptized, the Holy Spirit descended from heaven, and the Father declared His love for the Son (Matt. 3:16–17), showing all three persons present at once. These wrong views led to other theologians providing a better explanation.

The Orthodox Explanation

There is an explanation of the trinity that has been considered correct and agreed upon (what we mean by "orthodox") by the church leaders since ancient times. Certain church fathers affirmed both the oneness and threeness of God and sought to explain how this could be using a Greco-Roman philosophical perspective. They adopted two terms, essence (*ousia*) and person (*hypostasis*), explaining that there is but one essence of God, and that the three distinct persons of the Godhead each fully had the essence of deity. This satisfied the need for an explanation and was accepted as the correct meaning of the triunity of God. Some have objected to using the word "person" because it may imply three separate individuals. It might be better to say that the essence of deity exists in three personal self-distinctions. Once again it gets awfully hard to understand. The difficulty in understanding led to this helpful (and common) depiction of the triune nature of God.

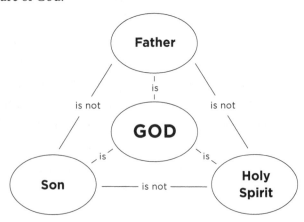

Although certainly helpful in explaining the triunity of God, it still remains a hard concept to grasp. As a result people have proposed a variety of illustrations. Some say God is like water (H_2O), which can be solid (ice), gas (steam), or liquid, and given the right conditions, all three can exist in equilibrium. Others have proposed an egg, with shell, yolk, and albumen (egg white) all being fully egg and yet distinct. These and other illustrations may help but ultimately are not fully adequate for explaining God's triunity.

FINAL THOUGHTS

At the outset, I wrote that the theological concept of the tri-unity of God, although biblical, is certainly hard to grasp. It's why my predecessor as Jewish Studies professor at Moody Bible Institute, Dr. Louis Goldberg, a brilliant philosophical scholar, would always speak of "the mystery nature of God." He would often tell us in class that God's plurality in His one-ness is the infinite mystery of God's being. It's what Ken Boa meant when he spoke of the triune nature of God as an antinomy, writing, there are "many things about God [which] are mysterious, incomprehensible, and superrational. God in his existence as the three-in-one is beyond the limits of human comprehension."[57] We can affirm that the Trinity is certainly taught in Scripture but it's beyond our finite human minds. So, although we may not be able to explain the Trinity completely, we must certainly believe in it absolutely.

Why pray if God has already decided the outcome of all circumstances?

Consider the following situation: A man's young wife, the mother of their two small children, has been diagnosed with advanced cancer. As someone who believes in God, will he not pray for her healing? Why would anyone think that since God has a good and providential plan for all, that this husband would not pray for his wife to be healed? Certainly, he'd pray for her to experience healing, either directly by God or by divine providence through medical treatment. Even when he realizes that only God knows the eventual outcome of their situation, he'll seek God, asking for Him to spare his wife. I can't imagine any other response.

Still, we believe that God is sovereign. As the psalmist said, "But our God is in the heavens; He does whatever He pleases" (Ps. 115:3). This may cause an issue for some. How do we pray in light of God's sovereignty? This is another example of an *antinomy*, an apparent contradiction that God fully understands but we, in our human understanding, cannot. So, even though we serve a sovereign God who ordains all that comes to pass, we should still pray. Here are three reasons to bring everything to God in prayer.

PRAYER IS COMMANDED

To begin, we are commanded to pray. When the Lord Jesus taught His disciples to pray, using His model prayer, He said, "Pray, then, in this way . . ." (Matt. 6:9). The verb "pray" is a command, not an option. Before the parable of the persistent widow, Luke says Jesus' purpose was "to show that at all times they ought to pray and not to lose heart" (Luke 18:1), indicating that prayer was not an option but an expectation God has for us. Paul commanded, "Pray without ceasing" (1 Thess. 5:17) and "in everything by prayer and supplication with thanksgiving let your requests be made known to God" (Phil. 4:6). The verbs in both these verses are imperatives, showing that prayer isn't a choice but a requirement for us. Yet these are just general commands to pray; there are also commands to pray for specific requests. Some of these include, for example, praying for workers in God's harvest (Matt. 9:38), for governmental leaders (1 Tim. 2:1–2), for fellow believers (Eph. 6:18), for deliverance from temptation (Matt. 26:41), even for the peace of Jerusalem (Ps. 122:6). The Bible does not say "pray if you understand how it works." Scripture just commands us to pray.

PRAYERS ARE ORDAINED

A second reason to pray is that the sovereign God has ordained all things, including our prayers. There are numerous biblical examples of God answering prayer. He gave water to Israel in answer to the prayers of Moses (Ex. 15:22–25; 17:4–7); the Lord gave Hannah a child in answer to her prayers (1 Sam. 1); God caused a drought and then sent rain in answer to the prayers of Elijah (1 Kings 18–19); God opened the eyes of a servant to see the Lord's army in answer to the prayer of Elisha (2 Kings 6:17). There are many more examples in Scripture. Our presumption too often is that God only ordained these results.

But we must also presume that God, who knows the end from the beginning (Isa. 46:10), also ordained these prayers. Of course, we believe in a God who determines all things but we are not fatalists. God not only determines the end result, He also determines every step on the way to the end, including prayer. So, if God chose to heal through medical treatment the cancer-stricken wife of the man mentioned above, we can also say that God determined to have her husband and others pray for her as well. God also, before time, ordained the training and development of her surgeon and oncologist. God's providence works *all things together* for good for those who love Him and are called according to His purpose (Rom. 8:28).

PRAYER CHANGES US

Yet another reason to pray is that prayer changes us for the better. Unfortunately, people are overly concerned that somehow prayer changes God, or perhaps the mind of God. That can't be true because God is unchangeable. He declares, "For I, the LORD, do not change" (Mal. 3:6). Unlike people, God adheres to His plans: "God is not a man who lies, or a son of man who changes His mind. Does He speak and not act, or promise and not fulfill?" (Num. 23:19 HCSB). It's not God who changes when we pray—the big transformation actually comes about in us when we pray.

Some people like to object that God does indeed change His mind. They point to biblical examples where it seems God changed His mind in response to prayer, such as when God said He would destroy Israel and begin a new chosen nation through the descendants of Moses. Moses prayed, asking God to relent and "the LORD changed His mind about the harm which He said He would do to His people" (Ex. 32:14). Since God, in His sovereignty, had already determined this outcome, it is better to understand this phrase as an anthropomorphism, helping us to grasp the infinitely difficult concept of God's sovereign response to human prayer. The Lord accommodates our inability to grasp this by using this figure of speech which attributes human attributes, like changing one's mind, to God. Nevertheless, it is we who are truly changed by prayer.

When the Lord Jesus taught us to pray, "Give us this day our daily bread," (Matt. 6:11), His purpose was to teach us dependence on the Lord for our sustenance. Also, when He taught us to persist in prayer (Matt. 7:7–11), He reminded us that no earthly father would give a stone to a child who asks for bread or a snake to one who asked for fish. "If you then, being evil, know how to give good gifts to your children, how much more will your Father who is in heaven give what is good to those who ask Him!" (Matt. 7:11). The Lord Jesus is making the point that through prayer we can learn to trust God to do what is good and best for us. Similarly, the psalmist cried to the Lord in distress (Ps. 18:6), and when God answered and delivered him (Ps. 18:48), he was transformed. His experience in prayer moved him from fear and dread to a person of thankfulness and praise, saying, "Therefore I will give thanks to You among the nations, O Lord, and I will sing praises to Your name" (Ps.18:49).

Many times, when my children were young, they would ask me for a special treat or to take them to a Yankees baseball game or for some item, like a new bicycle. In fact, I always wanted to give those good gifts to my kids (if it was good for them). Yet I was glad that they asked me because this way they could learn to depend on me to be loving and to provide for them. Similarly, God has a good plan ordained for us but He wants us to learn to ask of Him, and in that way, we learn to depend on the kindness and love of our heavenly Father. Prayer transforms us into people who depend on our Lord for all that we need in life.

FINAL THOUGHTS

The last piece of advice I'd give about prayer is that we should stop trying to figure out how it works and instead trust that God hears us and wants what's best for us. I learned this when someone very close to my wife and I, a young husband and father, suffered a life-threatening aneurysm. We cried out to God and begged for the Lord to intervene. I specifically prayed for a doctor that would know what to do and for this surgeon to be able to locate the bleed and close it. I prayed for this young man's life. Amazingly, in this circumstance, God answered by instantly sending the right physician and providentially using her to save his life.

What I didn't do at that moment was try to solve how prayer works. I wasn't concerned with wondering what outcome God had ordained, and I didn't ask why I should pray if God already knew the end. I believe in the providence of God, and I knew He was sovereign over life and death. I trusted that when I asked, He could deliver. Just as the psalmist said, "In my distress I called to the LORD, and He answered me" (Ps. 120:1 HCSB).

This is the truth about prayer. God doesn't want us to engage in philosophical inquiry, speculating about what He has already ordained or to ask why we should even bother praying since God already knew the outcome. All that struck me, in that desperate hour, was that God expected me, as His child, to bring my desperate prayers to Him. And as I prayed, I sensed how unworthy I was to ask anything of God. But I was praying in the name of Jesus, my Redeemer, who alone is worthy. In His name, I could boldly present my request to the Lord.

We're to pray to our Father as His distressed children, knowing, meanwhile, that He is in control and with the assurance that He will work everything for good. We'll never truly understand the dynamic of prayer, but we do know that God asks us to cry out to Him. We rest assured that He always accomplishes His purposes. Even though we'll never really comprehend it, we can agree with Charles Spurgeon who said, "Prayer is the slender nerve that moves the muscles of Omnipotence."[58]

QUESTIONS

about

BIBLICAL

CONCERNS AND

PRACTICES

Do we still need to keep the Sabbath since it is in the Ten Commandments or has that requirement been switched to Sunday?

There is a good bit of confusion about the fourth of the Ten Commandments, which reads, "Remember the sabbath day, to keep it holy. Six days you shall labor and do all your work, but the seventh day is a sabbath of the LORD your God; in it you shall not do any work" (Ex. 20:8–9). Some people think followers of Jesus are still obligated to keep the Sabbath on the seventh day just as Israel was commanded. Others think all the Sabbath laws have been transferred to Sunday. And still others think that, since this is the only one of the Ten Commandments not repeated in the New Testament, there is no need to take a day of rest—we're free to work seven days a week. So what *should* we think about the Sabbath? Let's examine what the Bible says about the Sabbath in the past, present, and future.

SABBATH IN THE PAST

Sabbath and the Law of Moses

The best place to start is by looking at what the Torah has to say about the Sabbath. First, at creation, God set an example for humanity by resting on the seventh day (Gen. 2:2–3). Why did God rest? After creating the world, it's not as if He was tired. God's omnipotence knows no fatigue and His omniscience doesn't run out of ideas. Rather, God ceased His creative activity to model for us what we need—to cease from our labors. Note that at creation there was no command or ordinance telling people to keep the Sabbath. It only says that God rested.

It was at Mount Sinai that God gave Israel a command to keep the Sabbath. The people of Israel, living as a theocracy under God, were to obey Him by keeping the Sabbath. The first time the Sabbath was commanded was when Israel left Egypt and Moses told the nation *not* to gather manna on the Sabbath but to rest that day (Ex. 16:22–30). Then, God included this command in the Ten Commandments given on Mount Sinai (Ex. 20:8–11). Later, as part of the covenant code in the Law, God declared the Sabbath to be the outward sign of the Mosaic covenant (Ex. 31:12–17), identifying it as "a sign between Me and you throughout your generations" (Exod. 31:13).

Sabbath in the Gospels

By the time of the earthly ministry of Jesus, as recorded in the Gospels, rabbinic tradition had developed a whole body of additional laws about the Sabbath, finding ways to make the Sabbath command more stringent in some ways and easier in other ways. The main point was that the religious leadership expected Israel not just to keep the Sabbath but to observe it according to the religious rules of Israel's leadership. That's the reason there was controversy between the Lord Jesus and the Jewish religious leadership about observing the Sabbath.

In one of these disputes, found in Mark 2:23–28, the Lord Jesus, as the Messiah of Israel, declares two perspectives on the proper observance of the Sabbath. First, He said, "The Sabbath was made for man, and not man for the Sabbath" (Mark 2:27). This meant that God never intended keeping a day of rest to become a burden for Israel but a benefit. So, according to the Messiah Jesus, it was permissible to find food and eat it on Sabbath, to do holy work on the Sabbath, and most importantly, to do good for others on the Sabbath, especially for Him to heal people on Sabbath. The Lord Jesus also declared that He, as the Messiah, was "Lord even of the Sabbath" (Mark 2:28). He was saying that, as Messiah, He created the Sabbath and therefore He alone, and not the religious leadership, could give the proper interpretation of how to keep Sabbath.

SABBATH IN THE PRESENT

Not Bound by Sabbath

The book of Acts records the birth of the church at Pentecost (Acts 2). With the conversion of the Roman centurion Cornelius (Acts 10), it became clear that the church, or the body of the Messiah, would be composed of Jews and Gentiles together. The epistles teach how the congregation of the Messiah (the church) is to view the Law of Moses, including the Sabbath. To begin, Ephesians 2:14–16 makes it clear that the Law of Moses was rendered inoperative by the death of the Messiah Jesus. Some versions use the word "abolish" but the word actually means "to render inoperative" (as translated by the International Standard Version). The Law still exists and can teach us much. But it is no longer the operating system for New Testament believers.

According to 2 Corinthians 3:7–18, the system that believers operate under today is the New Covenant, not the Old. Paul even says that the Ten Commandments, "in letters engraved on stones" (2 Cor. 3:7), had fading glory and was surpassed by the New Covenant (2 Cor. 3:7–11). Significantly, throughout the New Testament, it is possible to find nine of the ten commandments repeated. The only one left out was the Sabbath commandment, likely because it was an outward sign of the Mosaic law. By not repeating that command, it shows that New Testament followers of Jesus were no longer operating under the Mosaic Law but under the Messianic Law (also called the law of Christ or the New Covenant; Luke 22:20; 1 Cor. 9:21; Gal. 6:2).

In the New Testament era, legalists were pushing believers to observe the Sabbath as required under the Old Covenant. So Paul included this encouragement to believers in Colossians 2:16-17:

"Therefore, don't let anyone judge you in regard to food and drink or in the matter of a festival or a new moon or a Sabbath day. These are a shadow of what was to come; the substance is the Messiah" (HCSB).

So, even for us today, there ought to be no guilt trips about Sabbath-keeping that we put on ourselves or others. We have been given the true substance in the Messiah Jesus.

SUNDAY IS NOT A NEW SABBATH

Even if Sabbath observance isn't required, are we to keep Sunday as a required day of worship and rest? Some maintain that Sunday worship is required and treat the Old Testament Sabbath requirement as if it was transferred to Sunday in the New Testament. They cite three New Testament passages to make the case for Sunday worship and Sabbath-keeping, but a close examination of these Scriptures shows that none of them actually make these connections.

The first passage in Acts describes Paul's farewell meeting with the people of Troas and says, "On the first day of the week, when we were gathered together to break bread" (Acts 20:7). Although this group was meeting on the first day of the week, there is no mention of it being their regular worship time—they could have simply been meeting to say good-bye to Paul. Also, there is no clear command to worship on the first day. This argument fits with the nature of Acts, which is consistently more descriptive than prescriptive. The book of Acts records what happened but does not generally indicate what *must* happen. Also, Paul extended his words to midnight, showing that this was a night meeting. Since Luke usually used Jewish time, and the Jewish day was always reckoned as beginning in the evening (Gen. 1:5, 8, 13), this meeting likely took place on Saturday night, not Sunday morning.

Some cite 1 Corinthians 16:2 where Paul encourages the Corinthians to put aside money "on the first day of every week" for the offering he would collect when he came to Corinth. But this passage isn't talking about taking an offering during Sunday worship. In fact, it wasn't even referring to a public meeting. Paul uses the phrase *par heauto* (commonly translated "each of you") literally meaning "by himself, in his home." This refers to a private act of setting aside money in the person's own home. Paul was not requiring Sunday worship but was merely giving a sound budgeting principle: they were to set aside the money at the start of the week, rather than wait to the end when there would be no money left. By saving this way, the Corinthians would be able to give a substantial offering to Paul for the church in Jerusalem.

The final reference describes the Apostle John as being in the Spirit "on the Lord's day" (Rev. 1:10). The text never says what "the Lord's day" meant, but most likely it means that John received his vision on "a day filled with the Lord." Another possibility is that this phrase refers to "the day of the Lord," a cataclysmic period of time at the end of days just before the return of the Messiah Jesus. John may have been describing his experience in the book of Revelation, which transported him by vision to the future to see that period of time. Whatever it does mean, it clearly doesn't refer to Sunday.

Many believers teach that we ought to worship on Sunday because it remembers the resurrection of Jesus on the first day of the week. While this is indeed a great reason to worship on Sunday, it's not a requirement stipulated in Scripture. We can and should worship the resurrected Lord Jesus any day of the week.

A DAY FOR PHYSICAL REST
AND SPIRITUAL RENEWAL

As we evaluate these Scripture references, we should not dismiss any verse because it is found in the Torah. These passages are still God's Word and authoritative. But we do need to understand and interpret these Scriptures as Moses did. He described the Law as wisdom (Deut. 4:6–8). So we too should adopt the wisdom principle found in the Torah—namely, that we need one day a week for physical rest and spiritual renewal; we need a Sabbath rest. But even as we observe that Sabbath, we have a great deal of freedom as to which day of the week that might be. In Romans 14:5, Paul writes, "One person regards one day above another, another regards every day alike. Each person must be fully convinced in his own mind." So if we want our day of rest and renewal to be Saturday, that's fine. But so is Sunday, or Thursday, or whatever day.

We have New Covenant freedom to choose which day to rest our bodies and renew our spirits.

SABBATH IN THE FUTURE

The final biblical perspective about the Sabbath to consider concerns the future. Hebrews 4:9 teaches that "there remains a Sabbath rest for the people of God." This is a reference to the future millennial kingdom of King Jesus, when He will reign over the earth for a thousand years. The rabbis called this messianic kingdom "a day which is all Shabbat." So we too can look forward to the reign of the Messiah Jesus on earth, when this world will be set free from its corruption and futility and we'll be given the glorious freedom reserved for us as God's children (Rom. 8:18–25). And then, according to the book of Isaiah, we'll celebrate a Sabbath in that kingdom and in the new creation to follow, when "all mankind will come to bow down before" the Lord (Isa. 66:23).

FINAL THOUGHTS

Let's remember the most important principle of Sabbath for today. We need to trust, follow, and worship the Messiah Jesus, the Lord of the Sabbath. When we do, He will make every day a spiritual Sabbath rest in Him.

What is the significance of communion—does it grant us divine grace when we receive it or is it merely symbolic?

At the Last Supper, the Lord Jesus' final Passover celebration with His disciples, He broke some unleavened bread (matzoh) and commanded His followers to "Take, eat." Then He gave them a cup of wine and said, "Drink from it" (Matt. 26:26–27). Those commands are the reason followers of Jesus are to obey Him still today by observing the Lord's Supper or communion. Even so, the question remains, what is the specific meaning of this ceremony?

THE MEANING OF COMMUNION

Transubstantiation

The command to take communion has been understood in several different ways. First, some ancient church traditions have adopted a view called *transubstantiation*. This view maintains that when an ordained priest blesses the communion bread and wine, the elements are transformed into the actual flesh and blood of Jesus respectively, while keeping the appearance, taste, and odor of bread and wine.

The most problematic issue with transubstantiation is that it is most commonly taught as a re-sacrifice of the Lord Jesus. The Bible plainly states that the Lord's suffering and death was a "once for all" event (Heb. 10:10), never to be repeated. Hebrews 7:27 states that the Lord Jesus "does not need daily, like those high priests, to offer up sacrifices, first for His own sins and then for the sins of the people, because this He did once for all when He offered up Himself." Having suffered, died, and been raised from the dead, the Lord Jesus "always lives to make intercession for" those who have trusted in Him (v. 25). There is no need for the Messiah Jesus to be sacrificed over and over again in any kind of ceremonial way.

Consubstantiation

A second view, held by Lutherans and frequently called *consubstantiation*, is that while the elements of communion are not transformed into the physical body and blood of Jesus, the elements and the Lord's body and blood are both present concurrently. In essence, this view is saying that, when used in the Lord's Supper, the molecules of the bread and wine do not change. However, in addition to remaining as actual bread and wine, they also contain the Lord's body and blood. This seems to misunderstand the metaphorical nature of Jesus' words, to be discussed below.

Mystical Presence

There is a third view, held by Reformed churches, called the *mystical presence* view of communion. This view is based on taking Jesus' words about the unleavened bread ("This is My body . . .") and the cup ("This is My blood . . .") in a literal sense (Matt. 26:26–28). This tradition believes that the Messiah Jesus is mystically present in the elements of communion, meaning in a spiritual sense, but not a corporeal or physical one. This view believes that receiving these elements by faith is a sacrament, meaning a source of receiving divine grace. In a sense, this view sees the Lord's Supper as a way of receiving spiritual nourishment. Although the mystical presence interpretation is both responsible and respectable, it is better to take Jesus' words about the bread and the cup metaphorically.

Those who hold to the spiritual presence view believe it is taught in the Bread of Life discourse (John 6:41–58) when the Lord Jesus said "He who eats My flesh and drinks My blood has eternal life" (v. 54). But these words should not be taken literally nor are they related to communion. In the context, the Lord Jesus said, "He who *believes* has eternal life" (v. 47, italics added), indicating that eating His flesh and drinking His blood are merely metaphors for faith in the atoning work of Jesus. The text indicates that those who took these words literally, saying "How can this man give us His flesh to eat?" (v. 52), entirely misunderstood what the Lord Jesus meant.

The mystical presence view maintains that the Lord's Supper is a sacrament (or a means of receiving divine grace).

But the Scriptures teach that grace is received only by faith (Eph. 2:8–9) and that followers of Jesus experience union with the Messiah Jesus when they trust in Him. Paul frequently says that believers in Jesus are "in Christ" (e.g., Rom. 8:1; 2 Cor. 5:17), meaning that they are identified with and are in union with Him. Not only are we "in Him" but He is in us: "Christ in you, the hope of glory" (Col. 1:27). This is made possible by the indwelling work of the Holy Spirit from the moment someone trusts in Jesus (Rom. 8:9–10). Ultimately, Paul exhorted believers, "as you have received Christ Jesus the Lord, so walk in Him (Col. 2:6). This means that just as we received Jesus by faith, so we are to walk in faith in order to receive divine enablement.

Symbolic Commemoration

A fourth view, which has the most biblical support, teaches that the Lord's Supper is a *memorial and symbolic* meal. As for the memorial aspect, it is essential to recognize that the Lord Jesus inaugurated the Lord's table at a Passover meal. Therefore, it should be understood in a similar way. Scripture says that Passover was "to be a memorial for you [Israel], and you must celebrate it as a festival to the LORD" (Ex. 12:14 HCSB). Similarly, the Lord Jesus would tell His followers that when they celebrate communion, they do so "in remembrance of" Him (Luke 22:19; 1 Cor. 11:24). So the Lord's Supper was intended to memorialize our redemption from sin by remembering the body and blood of the Messiah Jesus.

With regard to the symbolic nature of the elements, we should recall once again that the Lord Jesus inaugurated communion at a Passover meal, called the *Seder* (order or service). By the New Testament era, Jewish people had developed all sorts of symbolic elements to be included in the Passover *Seder*, such as bitter herbs, representing the bitterness of slavery and a bowl of salt water representing the tears of slavery (Ex. 12:8; Num. 9:11). So, when the Lord Jesus said that the bread and wine were His body and blood, none of those present would have understood these words in a literal sense. As Jewish people, the disciples would have been familiar with the symbolic elements of Passover. Therefore, they would have recognized that the Lord Jesus was using a metaphor, meaning, "This bread is a *symbol* of My body and this cup is a *symbol* of My blood."

The Lord's Supper, celebrated as a symbolic memorial, remains a crucial outward celebration of the New Covenant. Since believers are commanded to observe this ceremony, some have called it an ordinance, a far better term than a sacrament.

THE IMPORTANCE OF COMMUNION

If the Lord's Table is only a symbolic memorial, some wonder if the specific elements are all that important. Would it be okay to observe communion with potato chips and soda pop? It must be remembered that these symbols have specific and important meaning. The Lord Jesus chose unleavened bread and the fruit of the vine to institute this ceremony because they represent His sacrifice. He used matzoh (unleavened bread eaten at Passover) for several reasons. First, matzoh was significant because leaven (yeast) in Scripture is frequently used as a symbol for sin. The Lord Jesus warned of the "leaven of the Pharisees" (hypocrisy) and "the leaven of the . . . Sadducees" (unbelief) (Matt. 16:6). Paul urged the Corinthians to clean out "the leaven of malice and wickedness" (1 Cor. 5:8). So, the unleavened bread represents the sinlessness of the Lord Jesus.

Second, ancient (and modern) matzoh was pierced in straight lines to keep it from rising. This symbolized that the Lord Jesus "was pierced through for our transgressions" and "by His scourging we are healed" (Isa. 53:5). Potato chips, fluffy loaves of bread, or even unleavened communion wafers miss the important symbolism of celebrating the Lord's supper with matzoh.

Additionally, the wine used during a Passover meal is a deep red and represents the blood of the Messiah Jesus that cleanses us from sin (Heb. 9:14). So soft drinks or even white wine or juice are inadequate in representing His blood. For the cup to communicate its symbol, we need to use red fruit of the vine, whether juice or wine.

The symbolic nature of the Lord's Supper doesn't minimize its importance any more than the God-ordained Passover celebration diminished God's deliverance of Israel from Egypt. We must observe it regularly because: (1) The Lord Jesus commanded that we observe it ("Do this in remembrance of me,"

Luke 22:19; 1 Cor. 11:24); (2) The Lord's Supper is a proclamation of our faith that the Lord Jesus died as our substitute,
that He will return, and implicitly that He is alive because the
resurrection is necessary for His return ("you proclaim the
Lord's death until He comes," 1 Cor. 11:26); and (3) The Lord's
Supper is a declaration of the fellowship of all believers because by it we share our unity in the Messiah Jesus ("Is not the
cup . . . a sharing in the blood of Christ? Is not the bread . . .
a sharing in the body of Christ? . . . we who are many are one
body;" 1 Cor. 10:16–17). The Lord's Supper remains a crucial
celebration—its value and importance is in no way diminished by viewing it as symbolic.

FINAL THOUGHTS

While some people call communion a sacrament (a grace-
giving practice) and others an ordinance (an observance
commanded by the Lord), I prefer to call it a New Covenant
ceremony. Ceremonies are designed to communicate a truth
by our actions. Every time we celebrate the Lord's Supper, we
are declaring that the Lord Jesus died for us, rose again, and is
returning as our King. Observing the Lord's Supper is a living
declaration of the good news that saved us from our sin.

What can we learn from the Bible about life in the womb and abortion?

48

Abortion has become so commonly accepted in today's culture that some followers of Jesus have begun
to question the Bible's position regarding life in the womb.
Some, who believe that life begins in the womb, wonder if it is
right to impose a biblical view on secular society. Still others
contend that the Bible does not teach that a pre-born baby
is truly alive. In addition, many live under guilt and pain for
having had an abortion. Since there are many aspects to this
important question, let's take them one at a time.

THE BIBLICAL CASE FOR LIFE IN THE WOMB

Biblically, we can deduce from a number of passages that
God considers a baby in the womb to be fully human and
fully alive. To begin, Scripture clearly states that God is the
designer of life in the womb. Psalm 139:13–16 says, "For You
formed my inward parts; You wove me in my mother's womb.
I will give thanks to You, for I am fearfully and wonderfully
made; wonderful are Your works, and my soul knows it very
well. My frame was not hidden from You, when I was made in
secret, and skillfully wrought in the depths of the earth; Your

eyes have seen my unformed substance; and in Your book were all written the days that were ordained for me, when as yet there was not one of them." These words clearly state that God forms, sees, and ordains the life of even an unborn baby. Not only that, God sets people apart for service to Him from the womb, as He did Jeremiah (Jer. 1:5) and Paul (Gal. 1:15). If they were not living persons while still in the womb, that would not be possible.

Moreover, it's possible for God to work spiritually even in an unborn baby's life. According to Luke's Gospel, John the Baptist was "filled with the Holy Spirit while yet in his mother's womb" (Luke 1:15). Luke goes on to say that the Spirit prompted John to leap while in his mother Elizabeth's womb when Mary, pregnant with the Messiah Jesus, visited (Luke 1:41). It's plain from Scripture that an unborn child is considered by God as a fully human living person, made in the image of God and therefore precious to God Himself.

PERSONAL FAITH VS. SECULAR POLICY

We need to remember that abortion is not a personal faith issue but a moral one. We can't very well say that I'm personally opposed to murder or rape because the Bible forbids it, but I don't want to impose my biblical values on others. That's because murder and rape are moral issues, not merely a matter of personal faith. And for all who say that abortion is a decision made between a woman and her doctor, we need to bear in mind that there's also a third person involved, the unborn baby. Who will speak on behalf of the child? Who will protect those who are unable to save themselves?

The Supreme Court ruling in *Roe v. Wade* has a shifting and shameful basis. The original ruling determined that abortion would be permitted based on medical viability out of the womb. So, if a premature baby could survive outside the womb, then it would be too late to abort that child. However, since 1973, that medical viability has changed. When *Roe v. Wade* was decided, the viability of a pre-born baby was only considered possible at 28 weeks of gestation. But now, through medical advances, a baby at only 20 weeks of gestation or even less can survive outside the womb. Before too long, a baby will likely be able to survive outside the womb at an even earlier time of gestation. This shifting of medical viability shows how mistaken the Supreme Court was in their original decision.

As believers, we need to keep in mind Proverbs 24:11–12, "Rescue those being taken off to death, and save those stumbling toward slaughter. If you say, 'But we didn't know about this,' won't He who weighs hearts consider it? Won't He who protects your life know? Won't He repay a person according to his work?" (HCSB). We must never tolerate abortion. Instead, we must use all of our rights as citizens and all legal means to protect the unborn.

ABORTION AND EXODUS 21:22

Some Bible believers maintain that Exodus 21:22 teaches that an unborn baby does not have the same rights as a fully living human person. The basis for this assertion is that the law of Moses seems to treat an unborn child as less than a fully living person. For example, in the 1977 version of the NASB, it says, "And if men struggle with each other and strike a woman with child so that she has a miscarriage, yet there is no further injury, he shall surely be fined as the woman's husband may demand of him; and he shall pay as the judges decide." Therefore, some argue in favor of abortion by saying that since there is no requirement of the death penalty for an assault and battery that causes a miscarriage, the Bible treats an unborn baby as less than a fully living person.

But this is based on a mistranslation. The Hebrew word translated "miscarriage" literally means "to go out." So if a man strikes a pregnant woman and the child comes out, in other words, she has a *premature* birth but the child lives, he still has to pay a penalty. This translation is reflected in virtually all contemporary English versions, including the updated NASB (which reads, "If men struggle with each other and strike a woman with child so that she gives birth prematurely . . ."). This corrected translation shows that God is even concerned for the rights of pre-born children. There is life in the womb.

GUILT AND ABORTION

Termination of a life, even before birth, is so serious, it makes some people think that this is the unpardonable sin, the one sin that God can't forgive. Jesus did indeed speak of a sin that was unforgiveable. He said: "People will be forgiven every sin and blasphemy, but the blasphemy against the Spirit will not be forgiven" (Matt. 12:31 HCSB). Clearly, the Lord was not speaking about abortion but the blasphemy of the Holy Spirit. According to the context, the blasphemy of the Spirit is declaring that the miracles of the incarnate Son of God to be works of Satan (Matt. 12:24–28). In essence, this is finally and fully rejecting Jesus as the Messiah and Redeemer of humanity.

Many years ago, a woman came to my congregation, plagued with guilt for an abortion she had undergone about 15 years earlier. She kept telling herself that what she had allowed was okay—it was just removing "unwanted tissue." But her conscience kept telling her otherwise. When she met with me and my wife, we were so grateful that we could tell her that God still loved her and that "God demonstrates His own love toward us, in that while we were yet sinners, Christ died for us" (Rom. 5:8). Furthermore, if she would only put her trust in Jesus' death on her behalf and His resurrection to new life, she would be forgiven forever. Paul wrote, "In Him we have redemption through His blood, the forgiveness of our trespasses, according to the riches of His grace which He lavished on us" (Eph. 1:7–8) and that "there is now no condemnation for those who are in Christ Jesus" (Rom. 8:1). This dear woman responded with joy and trusted in Jesus immediately upon hearing the good news. Amazingly, she has been free of guilt for all these many years.

FINAL THOUGHTS

But what about someone who is already a follower of Jesus and then has an abortion? The Scriptures teach that even that person can be restored to fellowship with God and experience true pardon. The apostle John wrote, "If we confess our sins, He is faithful and righteous to forgive us our sins and to cleanse us from all unrighteousness" (1 John 1:9). There is no sin greater than God's ability to forgive and restore, even abortion.

Is the spiritual life lived by the follower of Jesus alone or by God alone?

When I first became a follower of Jesus, we held a weekly Bible study in our home. The Bible study leader, a more experienced follower of Jesus, taught that the spiritual life called for believers to "Let go and let God." He maintained that people could only grow spiritually if they let God do 100% of the work in their spiritual development. Although he was trying to emphasize the work of the Holy Spirit, this thought led to a passivity on my part when it came to my spiritual growth. I believed that if I just "rested in Jesus" enough, it would lead to instant godliness in my life. Although I had this great desire to experience supernatural transformation, this approach only produced spiritual frustration within me. I found that I wasn't really growing in holiness at all.

After feeling discouraged for months, I decided to come up with a new game plan. The pendulum swung all the way in the opposite direction. I determined that spiritual growth would only occur if I never let go—I just needed to hang on and struggle for godliness. I believed my spiritual development would only happen if I did 100% of the work. Instead of emphasizing the Holy Spirit working in me, I focused on my own activity and effort. I began to strive for Jesus, not to rest in Him. Although I had a great desire to experience personal transformation, this approach only produced spiritual frustration in me because I wasn't really growing in holiness at all.

As time passed, I became convinced that Scripture teaches something different. Our spiritual growth is achieved by God working in us as well as our own effort. It is 100% God's work and 100% my work, recognizing that His 100% was worth far more than my own. Spiritual growth occurs as our new nature, under the control of the Holy Spirit, counteracts with our old nature. Only the mutual work of God and the believer will produce spiritual maturity. How does this work? Let's look at what the Bible teaches about spiritual growth.

100% GOD

To begin, spiritual growth involves the work of the Triune God. Paul prayed, "May the God of peace Himself sanctify you entirely" (1 Thess. 5:23). The word "sanctify" means "to set apart" and this passage indicates that God Himself will set us apart from sin and for His service. The Lord Jesus prayed that the Father would sanctify His followers "in the truth," (John 17:17), demonstrating that the Father is active in setting believers apart.

Not only is the Father active in the sanctification process, so is God the Son. In Ephesians 5:26–27, Paul reminds believers that the Lord Jesus gave Himself up for His congregation "so that He might sanctify her" and make her "holy and blameless." This indicates that the process of holiness begins with the substitutionary sacrifice of the Lord Jesus, giving us a positional holiness that becomes a practical reality as we grow.

The Holy Spirit is also active in the spiritual growth process. Paul reminds followers of Jesus that it is "by the Spirit" that we "are putting to death the deeds of the body" (Rom. 8:13). The Holy Spirit empowers believers to put to death, or separate themselves from, the behavior of their pre-faith lives. As we are controlled by the Holy Spirit (Eph. 5:18) and walk in the Spirit (Gal. 5:16), we will be transformed by the Holy Spirit (2 Cor. 3:18). Father, Son, and Holy Spirit all work together to produce spiritual growth in the life of the believer. But even though we now have positional holiness and the Holy Spirit at work on our behalf, we are also responsible to take action in the growth process.

100% HUMANITY

Although the sanctification process is under God's control, Paul also tells the Corinthians that God's people are to "cleanse ourselves from all defilement of flesh and spirit, perfecting holiness in the fear of God" (2 Cor. 7:1). To cleanse ourselves refers to our decision to separate from sinful behavior so that we may become complete or mature in holiness (the meaning of the word *epiteleo,* translated "perfecting"). Note that we are not passive agents in the sanctification process (letting go and letting God do all the work), but we participate with God by obeying God and living according to His standards.

The idea of our action in spiritual growth is supported by every imperative (command) in Scripture, calling us to obedience to God. If we were not involved, why would God bother to command us to obey Him? Also, the figures of speech used to describe believers describe taking strong action for ourselves in the growth process. For example, in 2 Timothy 2, believers are depicted as soldiers (v. 4), athletes (v. 5), farmers (v. 6), workmen (v. 15), and bond-servants (v. 24). Each of these figures are engaged in demanding work to do their jobs, indicating that believers are also to be engaged in strenuous effort. Additionally, we are commanded to adopt an active attitude in obedience to God. Paul says we are required to be "alert," to "stand firm," and to "be strong" (1 Cor. 16:13), none of which are passive attitudes.

One final aspect of a believer's activity in the growth process involves personal discipline. Paul commanded Timothy to "discipline yourself for the purpose of godliness" (1 Tim. 4:7). This exhortation is not limited to Paul's disciple Timothy but is required of all followers of Jesus who want to mature in the faith. For this reason, if we are to grow, we must engage in the practice of spiritual disciplines.

So what is a spiritual discipline? It is any practiced activity that enables us to obey God when our own efforts are inadequate. For example, I might want to obey God in the area of controlling my tongue, since unruly speech can cause so much damage (James 3:1–12). Still, try as I might, I keep spouting off in a way that causes damage. So, as a spiritual discipline,

I might practice silence in a setting where it is not required. Then, when I need to shut up, I will have practiced control of my tongue. So, for example, I might decide to practice silence for six months or even a year in a large monthly business meeting in my organization, never giving an opinion, especially if I'm not called upon. The Holy Spirit will use this practice of being silent, even when I have something to say, to strengthen me so I can keep quiet at those times when I absolutely should not speak.

Another example: If I need to develop patience (a fruit of the Holy Spirit, Gal. 5:22–23), I could develop a practice that teaches me to wait. Perhaps I might take a full year of grocery shopping as an opportunity always to choose the longest checkout line rather than the shortest. So when I need patience in another situation, the Holy Spirit will have taught me patience through this spiritual discipline of going to the longest line. When we discipline ourselves for godliness, we are developing a practice that enables us to do that which we can't do by mere effort alone.

100% GOD AND 100% HUMANITY

So, who lives the spiritual life? Clearly, it is 100% God's work and 100% ours. Amazingly, this truth is taught in a number of passages, side by side. For example, in 2 Peter 1:3–11, both ideas are taught. First, Peter speaks of God's provision for spiritual growth, including "His divine power" which "granted to us everything pertaining to life and godliness" (v. 3) and "His precious and magnificent promises" that enable us to "become partakers of the divine nature" (v. 4). Second, in light of God's provision, believers are to apply "all diligence" in developing godly virtues (vv. 5–7) and to increase these virtuous qualities (v. 8). We are to "be all the more diligent" and "practice these things" as well (v. 10). In this one simple paragraph, Peter presents the perfect balance between God's work and our work in spiritual growth.

Another passage that coordinates these thoughts are two verses that many people find problematic: "work out your salvation with fear and trembling; for it is God who is at work in you, both to will and to work for His good pleasure" (Phil. 2:12–13). Who is doing the work? Is it us or God? Notice that the first element to work out is our salvation. This does not mean we can bring about salvation by our own efforts but rather that it is a Jesus-follower's responsibility to engage in activity that stems from the salvation we already have. This same term was used to refer to tilling (or working) the soil in ancient Greek used outside of the Bible. It reflects the nurture of spiritual growth that should be evident in our lives because of the Lord saving us. This describes our 100% part of the equation. The second element is that, even as we cultivate spiritual growth, God is actively energizing our faithful obedience, which describes His 100% part. Once again, these two verses, when read together, show both God and us giving 100% in order to bring about our spiritual growth.

FINAL THOUGHTS

Growing in our walk with the Lord takes the balance of a tightrope walker. If we lean too far in one direction or the other, we're bound to slip. If we focus entirely on God's work in growing us, we can easily become passive and frustrated. If we lean too heavily on our own strength and effort, we can become legalistic and frustrated. Only by living with the balance of God's 100% of empowerment and enablement and our own 100% of diligence and discipline will we achieve mature, spiritual lives.

I know worry is a sin but I can't seem to stop. Is there some biblical advice about overcoming this problem?

Many people worry about worrying. We do this because we've heard the classic passage in Matthew 6:25–34, where Jesus told His followers not to worry. He told them this not once, but three times (vv. 25, 31, 34)! So, in addition to worrying about having our basic needs met, we now become anxious about disobeying the Lord Jesus and being in sin.

Let me encourage you to relax. Although Jesus does tell us not to worry, we should view His words as an encouragement and not as a prohibition. The Lord Jesus intended His words about worry to be a comfort to His followers, not to become a cause of guilt. We should not categorize worry as a sin. Instead, we need to recognize that the Lord's purpose in saying "do not worry" was to calm our hearts and minds, not to burden us under a pile of guilt.

This is similar to when my son would be studying for his final exams in high school. He would be stressed, and I would encourage him by saying, "Don't worry—you've studied. You've got this." It comes as no surprise that my words of comfort didn't make him instantly stop stressing. At the same time, I didn't think he was disobeying my fatherly direction by continuing to worry. No, I realized that I needed to keep encouraging and calming his heart when he continued to stress. That's how the Lord Jesus views us when we're anxious. His words of comfort are never intended to add to the many other worries that are troubling us. That said, Scripture gives us some helpful ways we can cope with worrying.

THE ALTERNATIVES TO WORRY

When I was a student at Dallas Seminary, the stress of school, work, and family really got to me. As a result, I went through a terrible time of anxiety. It seemed as if I was getting eaten up by worries. My wise wife encouraged me to put some study time into Philippians 4:6–9 and develop a plan to overcome anxiety. As I studied, I found the passage had three alternative actions to help me counteract worry and two promises for peace of mind. Here are the alternative behaviors we can adopt instead of giving in to worry.

Rather Than Worry, Pray

This first principle emphasizes prayer as an antidote to worry. Paul writes, "Be anxious for nothing, but in everything by prayer and supplication with thanksgiving let your requests be made known to God" (v. 6). These words highlight what most of us understand as prayer—asking God for something (evident in the words "prayer," "supplication," and "requests"). Yet, our requests should all be made with thanksgiving. Just as we're to pray about everything, we're to be thankful for everything that comes from God's good hand.

This verse led me to develop, for the first time in my life, an ordered and structured prayer notebook. I organized all my daily prayer lists, with some requests made every day and some different "asks" listed by different days. Regardless of the requests, I also wrote out all the specific items for which I was thanking God. Every day, my thanksgiving list grew longer and longer, and I never neglected to begin my prayer time by expressing my gratitude to God. This simple practice had a dramatic effect on my anxiety. I began to see all that God was doing in my life and to trust Him more. And when I found myself worrying, I would take a few minutes to pray with an emphasis on thanksgiving. But this was only the first step.

Rather Than Worry, Renew the Mind

A second antidote to worry is mind renewal. Paul's exhortation calls for worriers to dwell on "whatever is true, whatever is honorable, whatever is right, whatever is pure, whatever is lovely, whatever is of good repute, if there is any excellence and if anything worthy of praise" (v. 8). So many of our anxieties are based on fears and falsehoods. It's been said that 85 to 92 percent of our worries are illegitimate; they deal with events from the past that can't be changed or fears for the future that will not happen. I've been told that a thick fog covering seven city blocks with a depth of 100 feet, if put into liquid form, would fill less than an 8-ounce glass. Put in proper perspective, our worries, like the fog, seem much larger than their actual size.

That's why we need to focus our minds on that which is true, honorable, right, pure, lovely, of good repute, excellent, and praiseworthy. In my quest to overcome anxiety, I took several actions to change my thinking.

First, I memorized and meditated on Scripture. I found about 50 verses about God's presence and peace, wrote them on 3x5 cards, and memorized them. Every day I would review my verses, especially before going to sleep and immediately upon waking up. I carried the cards with me so I could review them periodically throughout the day. Then, I committed to memorizing long passages of Scripture that were especially meaningful concerning God's peace.

A second way I focused on true and excellent thoughts was to change my music-listening habits. I decided that I would listen to faith-oriented music exclusively, whether on the radio or my own collection. It's not as if my regular music was evil in some way, but while struggling with worry, I wanted to fill my mind with positive truth.

Yet a third decision I made was to be far more selective in my viewing habits. I used to think that I could brush off the vulgar language or ungodly behavior so common in media. Then I realized I could not, so I radically cut back on my viewing of any TV shows or movies that had negative content. At first, this left me with virtually nothing to watch, but I found I wasn't disappointed. I had much more time to add positive virtues into my mind. Changing thought patterns led to a tremendous downturn in worrying. But that's not all that changed.

Rather Than Worry, Live Obediently

Obeying God's Word as a lifestyle has a tremendous impact on overcoming worry. Paul told the Philippians that they were to remember what they learned, received, heard, and had seen in his life, and to "practice these things" (v. 9). Paul had taught them to live as he lived in obedience to God. I realized it was not enough for me to be satisfied with mere superficial obedience to God. I needed to take the Scriptures more seriously and live a godly life even when no one was looking or would ever know. This was a great challenge but it did help with worry.

The reason obedience is so crucial is found in Proverbs 28:1, "The wicked flee when no one is pursuing, but the righteous are bold as a lion." Disobedient behavior causes us to become anxious about potentially bad consequences. Obedience produces confidence and courage to face the future. God certainly wanted my total obedience in order to honor Him. But further, my fully committed obedience would also help me overcome worry.

THE PROMISES OF PEACE

In Philippians 4:6–9, Paul says that if we follow these antidotes to worry, we receive two promises from God that should encourage us. *First, the peace of God will guard us.* He writes that "the peace of God, which surpasses all comprehension, will guard your hearts and your minds in Christ Jesus" (Phil. 4:7).

The point is that God's peace is supernatural, granting us calm and comfort even when we have real worries. The word "guard" can be used to refer to a military guard providing security. When we engage the alternatives to worry, God becomes our personal guard, granting peace and security to us in a supernatural way.

The second promise is that *the God of peace will guide us.* That's why Paul says "the God of peace will be with you" (Phil. 4:9). Of course, we know that because we're united to Jesus the Messiah, God will never leave us or forsake us (Heb. 13:5). What Paul is saying is that God will be with us in the sense that, as we face uncertainty in the future, we know we have the Lord as our guide, directing our steps. That's why we can have peace as we walk with Him.

FINAL THOUGHTS

A friend of mine told me that worrying is like shoveling smoke—pretty useless. I have found worry to be like sitting in a rocking chair—we have lots of motion but we don't get anywhere. It's clear that worry is useless and debilitating. The Lord Jesus encourages us to overcome it. And Paul gave us some specific actions to use as alternatives to worry. If you find yourself battling worry, the path to peace is available. It will certainly take some effort to adopt these antidotes, but the peace they bring will be more than worth the effort.

FINAL, FINAL THOUGHTS

I want to end this book as I began, by encouraging you to keep studying the Bible every day. As you do, you will get to know the Lord better, love Him more, and grow in your walk with Him. When you read the Bible, you will certainly think of new questions and continue to seek answers.

Four days after I had put my faith in Yeshua (Jesus) the Messiah way back in high school, I attended my very first Bible study. The subject was 2 Timothy 2:15: "Be diligent to present yourself approved to God as a workman who does not need to be ashamed, accurately handling the word of truth." Studying that verse that Thursday night made me think about my Dad, who was a furniture and cabinet maker from Europe. He had no power tools except a table saw and a drill. Still, he produced the most exquisite furniture pieces. The end table in my living room and the library table in the midst of my books were both handcrafted by him more than 70 years ago. My dad was not boastful but when someone was considering engaging him to make furniture, he would unashamedly take them around our house, showing the furniture pieces and cabinets he had built. 2 Timothy 2:15 told me that I was to study God's Word diligently, handling it the same way my Dad crafted a piece of oak or mahogany.

That's why two short years later I enrolled as a Jewish Studies major at Moody Bible Institute. When I arrived on campus, I was surprised to discover that 2 Timothy 2:15 is MBI's theme verse. As a Moody student, I learned that growing to be a skillful student of the Scriptures takes diligence—devoted, energetic effort. Learning God's Word is not always easy but the results are well worth all of our time and effort. Even as I hope that this book answered at least some of your biblical questions, my greater desire is that it spurs you on to further study, eliciting more questions and even more answers discovered on your own. This kind of Bible study will transform our lives. As the Bible promises, "He who gives attention to the word will find good, and blessed is he who trusts in the LORD" (Prov. 16:20).

NOTES

Acknowledgments

1. C. S. Lewis, *Letters of C. S. Lewis to Arthur Greeves (1914-63)*. Edited by Walter Hooper (New York: Collier/Macmillan, 1986), 110.

Question 4

2. Claire Cloninger, "A Kiss for the Frog Prince," *When the Glass Slipper Doesn't Fit and the Silver Spoon is in Someone Else's Mouth,* Claire Cloninger and Karla Worley (Dallas: Word, 2003), 53–54.

Question 6

3. The destitute did not have to offer a blood sacrifice (Lev. 5:11) because their poverty kept them from even offering an inexpensive dove. Yet, they were still to sprinkle fine flour onto the animal sacrifice present on the altar of sacrifice, forming a bond between their grain offering and the blood sacrifice. In this way, the destitute could give a grain offering but still have it count as an animal sacrifice (Lev. 5:11–13).

Question 7

4. I am grateful to Stanley D. Toussaint, now present with the Lord Jesus, who was my pastor, ordained me into the ministry, and was my professor in an Acts course in seminary. He taught this explanation of Acts 2:38 to me and I have taught it to others ever since.

Question 8

5. David Berlinski, *The Devil's Delusion: Atheism and Its Scientific Pretensions* (Philadelphia: Basic Books, 2009), 73–76.
6. This quote, in some form or another, is all over the internet and in many books, always attributed to Charles Spurgeon, but I could not locate a primary source among Spurgeon's writings. Most likely that's because he didn't use it in a sermon but in answer to a personal question. Whoever said it, I agree with the sentiment.
7. Charles Spurgeon, as cited by J. I. Packer, *Evangelism and the Sovereignty of God* (Downers Grove, IL: InterVarsity Press, 1961), 35.

Question 11

8. Jesse Ball, "21 Overrated Books You Don't Have to Read Before You Die," *Gentleman's Quarterly*, April 19, 2018.

Question 13

9. Michael Rydelnik and Michael Vanlaningham, eds., *The Moody Bible Commentary* (Chicago: Moody Publishers, 2014).
10. Merrill F. Unger and R. K. Harrison, eds., *The New Unger's Bible Dictionary* (Chicago: Moody Publishers, 2006).

Question 16

11. John Woodmorappe, "How Could Noah Fit the Animals on the Ark and Care for Them," Answers in Genesis, October 15, 2013, https://answersin genesis.org/noahs-ark/how-could-noah-fit-the-animals-on-the-ark-and-care-for-them/.
12. Temple Grandin, *Livestock Trucking Guide* (Bowling Green, KY: National Institute for Animal Agriculture, revised September 2001), 5, https://www .stopliveexports.org/images/documents/Resources/Reports/Livestock_ Trucking_Guide.pdf.

Question 20

13. That is not to say all the people of Israel were automatically redeemed. Rather, God chose Israel as a nation to represent Him to the rest of the nations (Ex. 19:6). Individual Israelites still needed to exercise personal faith to enter a forgiven relationship with God (Gen. 15:6).
14. Public Domain.

Question 23

15. Ludwig Köhler et al., *The Hebrew and Aramaic Lexicon of the Old Testament* (Leiden; New York: E. J. Brill, 1994), 856.
16. The Hebrew root word is likely *'un*. F. Brown, S. R. Driver, and C. A. Briggs, *Hebrew and English Lexicon of the Old Testament* (London: Oxford, 1907), 731–32.
17. Walter C. Kaiser Jr., *Toward Old Testament Ethics* (Grand Rapids: Zondervan, 1983), 188.

Question 24

18. Meredith Kline, *Treaty of the Great King: The Covenant Structure of Deuteronomy* (Grand Rapids: Eerdmans, 1963), 111.

Question 25

19. Richard Dawkins, *The God Delusion* (Boston: Houghton Mifflin, 2006), 31.

20. The Amorites were one of the seven nations of Canaan. However, when used alone, as it is here, it is synonymous for all the Western Semitic nations of Canaan, or the Canaanites.
21. Walter C. Kaiser Jr., *Toward Old Testament Ethics* (Grand Rapids: Zondervan, 1983), 268.

Question 26

22. For a word study of the Hebrew word *almah* showing that it indicates virginity, see Michael Rydelnik, "The Virgin Birth in Prophecy" in *The Moody Handbook of Messianic Prophecy*, eds., Michael Rydelnik and Edwin Blum (Chicago: Moody Publishers, 2019), 820–21.

Question 27

23. Lewis Bayles Paton, "A Critical and Exegetical Commentary on the Book of Esther," *International Critical Commentary*, eds., S. R. Driver, A. Plummer, and C. A. Briggs (Edinburgh: T&T Clark, 1908), 96.
24. Arthur Waskow, *Seasons of Our Joy: A Modern Guide to the Jewish Holidays* (Boston: Beacon Press, 1990), 116–17.
25. These and other historical confirmations are discussed in Gleason L. Archer, *A Survey of Old Testament Introduction*, revised and expanded (Chicago: Moody Publishers, 2007), 396–98.
26. Ray Stedman, *For Such a Time as This: Secrets of Strategic Living from the Book of Esther* (Grand Rapids: Discovery House, 2013), 1–4.

Question 28

27. A. T. Robertson, *Word Pictures in the New Testament* (Nashville: Broadman, 1930), 2:294.

Question 29

28. For a far more thorough and in-depth discussion, see Michael Rydelnik and Edwin Blum, *The Moody Handbook of Messianic Prophecy* (Chicago: Moody Publishers, 2019).
29. Peter Stoner and Robert C. Newman, *Science Speaks* (Chicago: Moody Press, 1976), 106–12.

Question 30

30. John Lennox, *God's Undertaker: Has Science Buried God?* (Oxford, England: Lion, 2009), 10.
31. Josh McDowell, *A Ready Defense*, comp., Bill Wilson (San Bernardino, CA: Here's Life Publishers, 1990), 125.
32. A. T. Robertson, *Word Pictures in the New Testament, Vol. V* (Nashville: Broadman Press, 1932), 37.
33. Gilbert Highet, *The Art of Teaching* (London: Methuen & Co., 1951), 174.

34. John Charles Ryle, *Expository Thoughts on the Gospels: St. John*, vol. 1 (London: James Clarke & Co., 1957), 101.

Question 32

35. "How Deep the Father's Love," Stuart Townend Copyright © 1995 Thankyou Music (Adm. by CapitolCMGPublishing.com excl. UK & Europe, adm. by Integrity Music, part of the David C Cook family, songs@integritymusic.com). https://www.stuarttownend.co.uk/song/how-deep-the-fathers-love-for-us/.

36. Dietrich Bonhoeffer, *Life Together*, trans. John W. Doberstein (New York: Harper and Brothers, 1954), 46.

Question 34

37. Wayne Grudem, "He Did Not Descend Into Hell," *Journal of the Evangelical Theological Society* 34, no. 1 (March 1991), 104–05.

38. Ibid., 112.

Question 35

39. John Chrysostom, *Homilies Against the Jews*, Patrologia Graeca, vol. 48, ed. J. P. Migne (Paris: Garnier, 1857–66), 4.1; 6.1–4.

40. Michael Rydelnik, *They Called Me Christ Killer* (Grand Rapids: RBC Ministries, 2005), 5. Some other content in this chapter is adapted from *They Called Me Christ Killer.*

41. Augustine, *The Creed*, 3.10.

42. A. T. Robertson, *A Harmony of the Gospels* (New York: Harper and Row, 1950), 225.

Question 36

43. Johannes P. Louw and Eugene A. Nida, eds., *Greek-English Lexicon of the New Testament Based on Semantic Domains*, 2nd ed. (New York: United Bible Societies, 1989), 117.

44. Murray J. Harris, *Exegetical Guide to the Greek New Testament: Colossians and Philemon* (Nashville: B&H Publishers, 2010), 39.

45. Walter Bauer, *A Greek-English Lexicon of the New Testament and Other Early Christian Literature*, rev. and ed. Frederick W. Danker, 3rd ed. (Chicago: University of Chicago Press, 2000), 457.

Question 37

46. S. Lewis Johnson, "Paul and the Israel of God," In *Essays in Honor of J. Dwight Pentecost*, Stanley D. Toussaint and Charles H. Dyer, eds. (Chicago: Moody Publishers, 1986), 187.

Question 38

47. I am indebted to my friend and colleague Gerald Peterman for his excellent unpublished article, "Worshiping a Different God? Jews, Christians and the Paul of Acts 22–26." Evangelical Theological Society, 2008.

48. Walter Bauer, *A Greek-English Lexicon of the New Testament and Other Early Christian Literature*, rev. and ed. Frederick W. Danker, 3rd ed. (Chicago: University of Chicago Press, 2000), 427.

Question 39

49. Gleason L. Archer, *Encyclopedia of Bible Difficulties* (Grand Rapids: Zondervan, 1982), 344.

Question 40

50. The Greek word translated "caught up" (1 Thess. 4:17) is *harpazo*, and means "to snatch or take away." In the Latin translation of this verse, this verb was translated by the Latin word *rapturo*. This is why the event described in 1 Thessalonians 4:16–17 is frequently called "the rapture." Although there are a variety of views of when this will occur, my own is that the church will be snatched up before a future seven-year period of terrible tribulation on earth (this view is called the "pretribulational rapture").

51. Gerald Peterman, "Philippians," *Moody Bible Commentary*, eds., Michael Rydelnik and Michael Vanlaningham (Chicago: Moody Publishers, 2014), 1860.

Question 42

52. C. S. Lewis, *The Problem of Pain* (1940; repr., San Francisco: Harper, 2001), 91.

53. Dorothy Sayers, *The Greatest Drama Ever Staged: And the Triumph of Easter* (London: Hodder and Stoughton, 1938), 9.

Question 44

54. Ken Boa, *God, I Don't Understand: Answers to Difficult Questions of the Faith* (Wheaton, IL: Victor Books, 1979), 13.

55. Another example of *echad* referring to a compound unity is Numbers 13:23, which describes "a single cluster of grapes." It literally reads "a cluster of grapes of one" showing that there were many grapes but only one cluster.

56. Some people do cite 1 John 5:7 in the King James Version, yet this statement of the Trinity is not truly part of Scripture but a later scribal addition.

57. Boa, *God, I Don't Understand*, 35.

Question 45

58. Charles H. Spurgeon, "The Ravens' Cry," delivered January 14, 1866, Spurgeon's Sermons Volume 12: 1866, Christian Classics Ethereal Library, https://ccel.org/ccel/spurgeon/sermons12/sermons12.v.html.

ABOUT THE AUTHOR

D r. Michael Rydelnik is Professor of Jewish Studies and Bible at Moody Bible Institute and the host/Bible teacher on *Open Line with Dr. Michael Rydelnik*, answering Bible questions from listeners on over 225 stations nationwide across Moody Radio. The son of Holocaust survivors, he was raised in an observant Jewish home in Brooklyn, New York. As a high school student, Michael became a follower of Jesus the Messiah and began teaching the Bible almost immediately. Besides his work on *The Moody Bible Commentary* and *The Moody Handbook of Messianic Prophecy* as co-editor and contributor, Michael is also the author of several books and numerous articles. His doctoral research focused on the Messiah in the Hebrew Bible. Michael and his wife Eva live in Chicago, love hiking with their collie and boxer, and have two terrific adult sons, a delightful daughter-in-law, and the cutest two grandchildren in the world.